Creative Drama Resource Book for Grades K-3

Ruth Beall Heinig
Western Michigan University

Prentice-Hall, Englewood Cliffs, New Jersey 07632

Library of Congress Cataloging-in-Publication Data

Heinig, Ruth Beall
    Creative drama resource book for kindergarten through grade 3.

    Bibliography: p.
    1. Drama in education. I. Title.
PN3171.H333 1987   372.6′6   85–31241
ISBN 0-13-189325-4

Editorial/production supervision and
    interior design: Dee Amir Josephson
Cover Photo: Ellis Herwig
Manufacturing buyer: Harry P. Baisley

Printed in the United States of America

10 9 8 7 6 5 4 3 2 1

ISBN 0-13-189325-4   01

Prentice-Hall International (UK) Limited, *London*
Prentice-Hall of Australia Pty. Limited, *Sydney*
Prentice-Hall of Canada Inc., *Toronto*
Prentice-Hall Hispanoamericana, S.A., *Mexico*
Prentice-Hall of India Private Limited, *New Delhi*
Prentice-Hall of Japan, Inc., *Tokyo*
Prentice-Hall of Southeast Asia Pte. Ltd., *Singapore*
Editora Prentice-Hall do Brasil, Ltda., *Rio de Janeiro*
Whitehall Books Limited, *Wellington, New Zealand*

To all the teachers at Columbia Elementary School in Rochester, Indiana, during the years 1942 to 1950, who first opened the world of drama to me.

Contents

1

2

Using More Space   49

4

Narrative Pantomime With Children's Literature   63

5

6 Further Uses of Narrative Pantomime 83

7 Pantomimes For Guessing 100

Extended Drama Lesson Planning 202

12

Puppets, Shadow Plays, and Masks 227

13

Going To The Theatre 246

14

Preface

This resource guide has been written for you—the elementary teacher who wants to begin teaching theatre arts and creative drama in your classroom. I have assumed that most of you have had little or no previous drama training.

The material grows out of and expands upon my earlier text (*Creative Drama for the Classroom Teacher,* 2nd ed., by Ruth Beall Heinig and Lyda Stillwell. Englewood Cliffs, NJ: Prentice-Hall, 1981). Essentially the same format, principles, and philosophy in that text remain throughout this new one. However, much material has been revised and significantly expanded. New chapters on puppetry, masks, and theatre attendance have been added; story dramatization now covers two chapters; over twenty sample lesson plans have been included; all bibliographies have been increased and updated, and many new photos have been added.

I realize that for some of you the thought of teaching creative drama and theatre arts is overwhelming. But I know you are thoroughly capable of the task. As an elementary teacher, you are already highly skilled in knowing about children's educational and psychological needs. You already know how children think and what they like. And, just as this knowledge is vital in teaching other curricular areas, so, too, is it in teaching drama. So you need not be intimidated by any of this material. In fact, I hope it sounds as if it is "right down your alley."

I have tried to demystify drama by leading you through activities from the most simple to the more complex, slowly and gradually, using methods I have developed during my twenty five years' experience in elementary and college classrooms. As much as possible, I have tried to build skills for you, chapter by chapter. In addition, within many of the chapters, the activities begin with the simpler ones and progress toward those that are more advanced. The masks in the margins highlight specific drama activities for easy reference. Numbers in parentheses throughout the text refer to correspondingly numbered anthologies and children's novels listed in Chapter 15.

Chapter 1 gives you an overview, particularly of creative drama since that is the major theatre arts activity for elementary children. Chapter 2 explains many of the guidelines you will find useful before beginning any drama activities. Chapter 3 launches you with simple and often well-known games to begin on, as does Chapter 4, which also introduces some suggestions in expanding playing space. Both chapters present a sample lesson plan. Narrative pantomime, one of the most useful activities for beginners as well as those who are more advanced, is covered in Chapters 5 and 6. Extensive bibliographies of children's literature specifically selected for narrative pantomime work are included in both chapters. Two sample lesson plans are at the end of Chapter 6.

With Chapter 7 the focus moves to the many variations of pantomimes for guessing, while Chapter 8 explores the many variations of verbal activities. Both chapters present many games, ideas for incorporating curricular topics, as well as bibliographies of children's literature you can use. Chapter 9 gives special attention to creative work and ways to help children build their own plots and stories. Two sample lesson plans are included. Chapters 10 and 11 cover two methods for story dramatization that I call "circle stories" and "segmented stories" and include lesson plans for fifteen popular stories and books as well as an additional bibliography. Chapter 12 covers extended lesson planning, giving three sample extended lessons as well as a lesson plan reference chart. In Chapter 13 you will learn how to construct puppets and masks and how to use them in dramatization. Bibliographies of children's literature specifically suited to puppetry and masks are included. Chapter 14 addresses theatre attendance and theatre etiquette and includes a selected bibliography of theatre-related children's literature. A final bibliography of children's books and a glossary of terms completes the text.

I think it would be helpful for you to read through the material first in the order it is presented. After that, you need not feel bound to implement the book in lockstep fashion. Begin where you feel most comfortable and let that exploration lead you to your next attempts. Some may wish to begin with puppetry or story dramatization before trying material in the earlier chapters, for example. I believe I have given you more ideas than you can possibly use in a year's time so that you will have numerous choices and options. Feel free to experiment and to enjoy these activities with your students.

I wish to thank the following people for making this book possible: Coleman A. Jennings, Chairman, Drama Department, The University of Texas at Austin;

Kim Wheetley, Fine Arts Department, Texas Education Agency; the people at Prentice-Hall including Editor, Steve Dalphin and Production Editor, Dee Josephson; special friends Robin Nott, Renée Rossman, Elaine Sievers, Andy, Anna, Ben, Brian, Brianna, Melanie, Lee, Ravi, and Ryan; and most especially my dear husband, Ed, who helps me keep my sanity and humor even during the darkest days.

Introduction 1

WHAT IS CREATIVE DRAMA?

If you were to look in on several early elementary classrooms during a creative drama lesson, you might see a variety of activities. In one classroom, children might be exploring animal movements, imitating various animals and their characteristic actions while the teacher reads a poem; in another classroom they might be pantomiming a variety of occupations while classmates guess; and in a third classroom, children might be dramatizing a favorite story, making up the dialogue as they go along.

Creative drama is known by a variety of names. Some have called it "informal drama," "creative play acting," "developmental drama," "educational drama," and "improvisational drama," to name only a few of the other terms.

The American Association of Theatre for Youth, the largest national organization of child drama professionals in this country, prefers the term "creative drama" and defines it, in part, as

> an improvisational, nonexhibitional, process-centered form of drama in which participants are guided by a leader to imagine, enact, and reflect upon human experiences.[1]

[1] Jed H. Davis and Tom Behm, "Terminology of Drama/Theatre with and for Children: A Redefinition," *Children's Theatre Review,* 27, no. 1 (1978), 10–11.

The definition further explains:

> The creative drama process is dynamic. The leader guides the group to explore, develop, express and communicate ideas, concepts, and feelings through dramatic enactment. In creative drama the group improvises action and dialogue appropriate to the content it is exploring, using elements of drama to give form and meaning to the experience.[2]

WHAT ARE THE GOALS OF CREATIVE DRAMA?

In that same definition it is stated that participation in creative drama has the potential to aid children in such areas as language and communication abilities, problem-solving skills, and creativity. Participation in creative drama can also enhance self-concept, social awareness, empathy, and understanding of the art of theatre.[3]

Many of these goals overlap one another, but several deserve a closer look.

LANGUAGE AND COMMUNICATION

In the last twenty years, there has been an increasing emphasis on the importance of both verbal and nonverbal communication in the language arts curriculum. In the child's development, oral language naturally precedes written language. Therefore, it is reasoned, children need to develop their oral and nonverbal language skills, including abilities to focus attention and listen, in order to successfully undertake reading and writing tasks. One well-known language arts educator claims that "drama is nothing less than the 'basic skill' that is the foundation of all language development."[4] A past president of the National Council of Teachers of English emphasizes in numerous writings the importance of creative drama as a means to foster reading, the study of literature, oral language and vocabulary development, nonverbal communication, listening abilities, and creative writing.[5]

Creative drama offers a variety of communication experiences to children. The emphasis on self-expression helps them to form their self-concepts, expand their self-confidence, and increase their ability to communicate their thoughts and feelings both verbally and physically. Their increased abilities in self-expression lead to better interpersonal communication skills in informing and questioning, organizing

[2]*Ibid.,* p. 10.
[3]*Ibid.,* p. 10.
[4]Betty Jane Wagner, "Educational Drama and Language Development," in *Educational Drama for Today's Schools,* ed. R. Baird Shuman (Metuchen, N.J.: Scarecrow, 1978), p. 95.
[5]See especially John Warren Stewig, *Informal Drama in the Elementary Language Arts Program* (New York: Teachers College Press, 1983).

Rather than the production of an elaborately staged formal play for an audience, creative drama emphasizes process and the personal development of the players. (*The Prince and the Pauper*, Terre Haute, Indiana, circa 1905)

and sharing ideas, and in enjoying the companionship and group interaction processes with others.

In fact, children use oral communication in creative drama constantly as they respond to and discuss ideas, share personal observations, organize and plan their drama activities. Even in the characters they play, they will be communicating orally, working through the characters' dramatic situations and interacting with other characters. Enacting the dramatic scene or story itself encourages them to become more effective in their use of language.

When children improvise drama, they observe and participate in language spontaneously, the way situations are met in everyday life where we have no script to tell us what to say. They can experiment with various alternatives, learning first hand which alternative is most effective. And, they do not have to suffer any real life consequences for mistakes they may make. As a result, they are able to increase their communication options and to experience the self-confidence that comes as a result of rehearsing some of life's situations before meeting them.

POSITIVE SELF-CONCEPT

In order to grow into well-developed persons, children need to have faith in and to value themselves. Only when they feel secure in who they are can they be confident enough to explore and take risks.

It will be important in creative drama, as in all learning, for you to foster a climate in which children can grow to their maximum potential. Children who are afraid of themselves and of others around them cannot fulfill their maximum potential.

Creative-drama leaders have often noted that one of the most dramatic changes children experience in drama classes is the development of a more positive self-concept. Sometimes it is because they have played a role they have never experienced before—a powerful king, a hero, or a brave person. They see themselves in a new light, with a strength they never knew they had within them. Sometimes they discover talents they never had a chance to express before. Perhaps it is the offering of a new idea, or leadership in a group, or a creative suggestion they have made to a drama project. Thus, they find themselves further along the road to their own self-development.

Even when the goals of a particular creative drama lesson are educational (stressing curricular information) or aesthetic (encouraging imagination), the growth of the children is also being fostered in other ways. Many educators and specialists have found creative drama useful in helping to resolve reading problems, speech and language disorders, and socialization difficulties, to cite only a few examples.[6] It is this drawing out of the person that one educator refers to when he claims, "Just to be—really *be*—another person in an undistinguished play is to make one immeasurably free forever."[7]

---

[6]Ann M. Shaw and C.J. Stevens, eds., *Drama, Theatre, and the Handicapped* (Washington, D.C.: American Theatre Association, 1979). See particularly the review of literature and annotated bibliography by Linaya Leaf.
[7]Hughes Mearns, *Creative Power* (New York: Dover Publications, 1958), p. 96.

Drama can help develop a more positive self-concept.

CREATIVITY

Being creative, according to one writer, means continually evolving into one's own unique self, responding to life and its experiences to the fullest.[8] Because our educational system recognizes the importance of creativity and independent thinking in our society, it is generally a goal in almost all curricular areas.

Most researchers and writers on the subject of creativity believe that everyone has creative potential. In looking at people who are labeled particularly creative, characteristics such as fluency, flexibility, innovativeness, and curiosity emerge. They may even be constructively discontented, unpredictable, and a bit different. A spirit of playfulness is another frequently mentioned characteristic. In a complex society

[8]Clark E. Moustakas, *Creative Life* (New York: D. Van Nostrand, 1977). This theme is stressed throughout the book.

Everyone has the potential to be creative.

such as ours, one that is bursting with technology and sweeping changes constantly, it is the creative ones who will be able to tackle the problems and find the solutions necessary for us all. Their personal lives will also be richer because of the flexibility and risk-taking qualities they possess.

As a teacher you foster the inherent creative abilities in children when you provide the nurturing environment in which they can feel free to try and fail, to take risks and explore or when you encourage the spirit of curiosity, of playing with ideas, and of testing and rethinking. When you present problem-solving tasks, you also stimulate creative thinking.

Creative drama fosters creativity by encouraging spontaneity, imaginative thinking, brainstorming for solutions, and providing opportunities for visualizing possibilities. A reasonable "anything is possible" attitude on your part gives meaning to children's realization that there is always a place for their ideas and their contributions.

PROBLEM-SOLVING SKILLS

Drama can stimulate the development of problem-solving skills. When children are presented with problems, they are encouraged to imagine, to hypothesize, to test options, and perhaps even to redefine the problem.

Problem-solving is frequently apparent in the stories the children enact. What solutions will they suggest for helping a princess learn to cry? How will they pretend to be stupid in order to outwit a tyrant? How will they find a compromising solution in order to appease two groups holding differing viewpoints?

Children can experience group problem-solving in other drama activities as well. What machine will a group decide to create with their own bodies, and how will they demonstrate its working parts? How will they choose to stage their puppet play, and how will they handle the scenery and lighting? How will they decide in a group skit to demonstrate what a particular proverb means?

In all of these experiences children are encouraged to seek answers, push for new ideas, explore solutions, synthesize information, and exercise imagination. This is all a part of the problem-solving process which drama can stimulate.

EMPATHY AND SOCIAL AWARENESS

Empathy is the ability to see life from another person's perspective and to "feel with" that person. In drama, children have the opportunity to see the world from another point of view and to look at the inner attitudes of another. They can, as the Native American proverb encourages, "walk a mile in another's moccasins."

Drama can be a rehearsal of life itself. By reliving the experiences of others—the people from the pages of a history text, a reading book, or anyone else they find interesting and significant—children can identify and empathize with others. They can find out what it is like to play a different societal role—a community helper, a parent, a political leader—learning of their concerns and problems, finding appropriate solutions, and experiencing their difficulties as well as their successes.

Drama also provides experiences in social and group process. In many ways drama is a group art. Plays focus on social interaction; the theatre requires the talents and skills of numerous artists. So, too, as children engage in drama, they must plan together, enact their ideas together, organize and create the appropriate playing space, as well as experience the plays' social interaction. Often it is obvious to even the youngest child that effective socialization is required and that there are rewards for cooperative group behaviors. Truly, drama is an experience in cooperation.

AN UNDERSTANDING OF THE ART OF THEATRE

In creative drama, children learn about the theatre in a way best suited to their developing talents and skills. Rather than focusing on the memorization of scripts and the elaborate production of a play, children are encouraged to improvise dramatic materials. An emphasis is placed on discussing and internalizing information and then playing it out, using self-expression rather than prescribed materials.

At the same time, children are gaining insights into the important elements of theatre such as action, conflict, plot, mood, characterization, and spectacle. They will be exposed to plot structure and to the themes of stories. They will begin to understand characters, not only how they appear on the outside but also how they think and feel on the inside. They will be more attuned to the characters' motivations for their behaviors. Their own interpretation of the characters will give them experiences in expression through movement and voice.

Children will also have the opportunity to experience the aspects of theatrical staging and, in modified forms, all the related spectacle of setting, props, lights, costumes, music, and dance. In bringing all of the various art forms of the theatre together, students will learn the importance of working together to create a unified, artistic whole.

The study of theatre, along with the other arts, has been too frequently neglected in our children's education. A significant panel report, *Coming To Our Senses: The Significance of the Arts for American Education,* documents how we have been remiss as a nation in acknowledging and appreciating the arts as an integral part of our cultural heritage.[9] The arts have traditionally provided a way for nations and cultures to develop and communicate, as well as preserve, their identity.

The report further documents the many interrelationships of the arts to the traditional disciplines of learning. Because the arts also develop intellectual and social skills, they are, in a very real sense, as basic to the curriculum as the three R's. These relationships will be outlined in the next section.

CREATIVE DRAMA AS AN EDUCATIONAL MEDIUM

Drama in many ways has served as a method of teaching for centuries. The great dramas, both tragedy and comedy, though their primary purpose has been theatrical entertainment, have shown us our human faults and foibles. By showing us a slice of life, theatre give us the opportunity to study people's interaction with each other in a given dramatic situation. We identify with the characters as they deal with their problems and suffer or rejoice with them depending on the outcome.

Creative drama, while it can be considered as an art form by itself, is also a way of teaching. As we know in watching children at play, they naturally dramatize.

---

[9]David Rockefeller, Jr., Chairman, *Coming To Our Senses: The Significance of the Arts for American Education, A Panel Report* (New York: McGraw-Hill, 1977).

Most educators now realize that this dramatic play is a child's way of understanding life. In using creative drama in the classroom, you are actually capitalizing on something children already know how to do.

When children dramatize, they are using information in a more concrete and meaningful way. They experience the information kinesthetically, which deepens their understanding and their emotional involvement. They become an integral part of the ideas and concepts, internalizing information and increasing the likelihood of its being remembered. For some children this learning style is mandatory.

Creative drama activities can interrelate with language arts, science, social studies, mathematics, physical education, or the fine arts. In history, for example, students may enact the first Thanksgiving; in literature, they may enact and bring to life one of their favorite stories, such as *Charlotte's Web;* in music, they might dramatize a folk song such as ''Frog Went a Courtin' ''; or in science, they may enact the metamorphosis of a caterpillar into a butterfly.

Curricular topics can be previewed or extended through creative drama. Field trips can be enacted beforehand, to give children a sense of what they will be experiencing. After the trip, it can be replayed in creative drama, incorporating the newfound knowledge.

You will soon discover that you can check students' understanding of facts and concepts by playing them in creative drama. Do they understand, for example, the construction of simple machines as they enact pantomimes of them? Have they understood the character interactions in a piece of literature as they dramatize an important scene? You will be able to see where the correction of misunderstandings needs to be made. Often children are motivated to explore new or more detailed subject areas in order to play an activity with greater accuracy.

And, finally, though not unimportantly, creative drama is usually fun for all. Learning is made more enjoyable when it can be dramatized. Often children who have difficulty with other classroom tasks find success and a place for themselves in drama, a discovery that gives them a renewed interest in learning. Enjoyment and success together lead to self-confidence, a prime requisite for becoming a thinking, feeling, and creative person able to face life's challenges.

For some teachers creative drama may be a totally new experience. For others it may be an activity you have wanted to try but did not know how to begin. And for still others, creative drama may be something you have done throughout your teaching career.

This resource guide has been prepared with all of you in mind. It is hoped that there will be something for everyone to choose from. Begin where you feel most comfortable, but challenge yourself to move on to the new ideas as well. As an educator, you know the importance of trying new things, of experimentation and the right to fail and try again. You allow this of students. Be sure to allow yourself the right to try something new, to fail, and to try again, too. And enjoy yourself!

SELECTED BIBLIOGRAPHY

Bolton, Gavin, *Towards a Theory of Drama in Education.* New York: Longman, 1979. Using classroom examples to illustrate, a British drama educator presents his theories and outlines a drama approach which combines children's play and elements of theatre.

Cottrell, June, *Teaching with Creative Dramatics.* Skokie, Ill.: National Textbook Company, 1975. Presents a basic overview of creative drama with chapters on play, sensory awareness, pantomime, dialogue, drama in curriculum, and storytelling.

Heinig, Ruth Beall and Lyda Stillwell, *Creative Drama for the Classroom Teacher,* 2nd edition. Englewood Cliffs, N.J.: Prentice-Hall, Inc., 1981. The source of many of the techniques and activities contained in this resource guide.

McCaslin, Nellie, *Creative Drama in the Classroom,* 4th edition. New York: Longman, 1984. An introductory text presenting theory and practical application. Includes exercises in sensory awareness, pantomime, and improvisation. Story dramatization, puppetry, and formal production are also covered.

Shuman, R. Baird (ed.), *Educational Drama for Today's Schools.* Metuchen, N. J.: Scarecrow, 1978. Presents a variety of essays on some of the uses of drama by several authors and drama specialists. Extensive annotated bibliography.

Stewig, John Warren, *Informal Drama in the Language Arts Program.* New York: Teachers College Press, 1983. A well-known language-arts educator presents his rationale for the incorporation of creative drama into the language arts curriculum. Many language arts activities and references to children's literature are made throughout.

Wagner, Betty Jane, *Dorothy Heathcote: Drama as a Learning Medium.* Washington, D.C.: National Education Association, 1976. A detailed explanation of the techniques used in drama by a British educator, whose work has become familiar in this country in recent years.

Ward, Winifred, *Playmaking with Children.* New York: Appleton-Century-Crofts, 1957. The text that first introduced creative drama in this country. Discusses drama in elementary and junior high school. Emphasis is on story dramatization.

Way, Brian. *Development Through Drama.* Atlantic Highlands, N. J.: Humanities Press, 1967. Well-known British drama teacher presents his philosophy, focusing on development of the whole person. Practical exercises and activities in sensory awareness, imagination, speech, and improvisation.

The Drama Process 2

In creative drama the focus is more on the creative process of drama than on some finished product such as a well-mounted play. In this chapter we will look at some of the considerations important to that process and at your role in helping them happen.

Much of the information in this chapter will become obvious to you as you begin playing the activities, so you need not be overwhelmed. You will also find it applicable to other areas of your teaching, too, so you are probably already familiar with many of the ideas.

DRAMA GOALS AND GUIDELINES

In planning drama instruction, as with many other curricular areas, there are multiple goals that can be identified. Generally, in creative drama we emphasize:

1. drama goals (e.g. pantomime, improvisation)
2. personal development goals (e.g. creativity, group work)
3. additional curricular or other subject matter goals (e.g. career education, health and safety).

Each of these goals, by itself, can be a justifiable reason for undertaking a creative drama activity. So, at times you might focus mainly on one; often you will consider all three equally.

In addition to the major goals, you need to consider the level of difficulty in selecting appropriate activities. All the variables in the left-hand column *generally* precede their more advanced counterparts in the right-hand column.

EASIER	to more	**ADVANCED**
1. Desk area		Larger areas of space
2. Teacher direction		Creative or independent thinking
3. Pantomime		Verbal
4. Solo playing		Pair and group playing
5. Run-through playing		In-depth playing for greater involvement
6. Humorous or "light" material		Highly dramatic or "serious" material
7. Minimal informational content		High data content
8. Unison playing for one's own satisfaction		Playing to share/communicate with observers

This resource guide is designed to help you move from the easier activities to the more difficult. But it will still be helpful for you to consider the above variables for any given drama activity you choose to do with your class. (Further discussion of this point is covered in Chapter 12).

GUIDING CREATIVE DRAMA

CHILDREN'S PARTICIPATION

There is a natural tendency for many teachers to feel that children should participate immediately in all drama activities. Some may even feel that if children are not playing they are not benefitting from the activity or even having fun.

But children participate in drama in several ways. They may participate as observers, discussants, analyzers, or as players. Their participation varies according to their interest in the topic, their mood, their confidence, and their awareness of their own needs. They also need to know that their efforts will be accepted and encouraged rather than judged or perhaps be made fun of.

It is best to invite children to play and allow them to make their own decisions. Sometimes reticent children like to watch their classmates first. As they see you continue to give support they will gain the courage to participate freely. Resist the temptation even to cajole shy children into participation against their will. More often than not, when they see an activity being fun, within their capabilities, and guaranteeing their anonymity, they will enter in.

A good story that is well-told will capture attention.

But, there are also those children who are confident and secure
and who want to play all activities. Some may have difficulty watching their classmates or being able to wait for their turn. And some
may even need more reminding of rules and limitations in their ex-
uberance to be involved constantly.

When you have a classroom of eager participants, it becomes important to involve as many children in the activities as possible while
still maintaining order. Often you will have the children work in unison. An entire class can work individually, in pairs, or even in groups
in unison. This gives more children the opportunity to participate.
It also encourages the shy children since there is no undue attention
placed on anyone.

USE OF SPACE

Contrary to many other writers on creative drama, I do not encourage a beginning drama leader to use a lot of space. To me, most
classrooms are preferable to large, open rooms or gymnasiums. I
also prefer the desks, table, or carpeted areas to the more expansive,
less well-defined space. To me it is easier to concentrate on guiding
the activity itself when I do not have to worry about keeping thirty
active students organized in space.

There are also psychological advantages of using desk/table areas
or a circle arrangement on a carpeted floor. These are familiar spaces
for students that give a sense of security to the shy student and speak
of order for the overly active one.

In this guide we will begin with seat activities and move to the
use of more space gradually.

SELECTING MATERIALS

Be sure you like the material you are using and sense its importance. And, equally important, from what you know of your class, they should also find it appealing and worthwhile.

In my own experience, humorous material is easier to begin with than the more dramatic material. Humor relaxes most people and helps build group rapport. Children do not have to feel as much tension in playing humorous material because there is less concern about making a mistake. Dramatic material with a serious mood may take a little more work, as we shall discuss later in this chapter.

PRESENTING MATERIALS

Be prepared with all your materials, props, pictures, records, or whatever you use. Arrange them carefully so you will have exactly what you want when you want it.

Know the piece of literature you are using. Be able to read it well so that you can look up from time to time and check the children's reactions. If you are telling a story, be sure to go over it beforehand or have a brief outline on hand so you can tell it smoothly and accurately.

Create the appropriate mood with the material—is it eerie, exciting, serene, happy? Are you creating that mood with your voice and body? Are you asking your questions in a curious, stimulating manner? Are you aware of your vocal quality, pitch, timing, or loudness as you speak? Can your voice become soft when it describes a rabbit's fur, or be warm when speaking of a glowing fire, or moan like the wind, or boom like thunder? There is no need to overdramatize or sound phoney. Just be aware of the voice as a human musical instrument that has potential many of us never tap.

UNDERSTANDING MATERIAL

Children cannot play or enact material they do not understand. Are there pictures or visual aids that can assist? For some children the experiences may be totally new. What can you give them firsthand that will help them?

Are the words and events understandable to them and within their experience?

"In this poem, there are a lot of different words for the ways the animals move. Who can show us 'hop' and 'leap?' . . . Now what about the word 'stalk?' 'Lions stalk,' the poem says. Does anyone know what stalk means? Or, can you show us?"

"This is a story about maple sugaring. Who has seen maple sugar being made? Can you tell us how it's done?"

Perhaps an analogy is needed:

TEACHER: We've been reading about the desert, but some of us have never seen the desert before. Sometimes it gets very hot in the desert. What's the hottest weather you've ever experienced?

CHILD: It was sure hot in here the day the heat was turned too high and we almost suffocated.

CHILD: My grandpa says when it gets really hot you can fry an egg on the sidewalk.

CHILD: I had a temperature once that made me hot all over. My mom said she couldn't even touch me.

ANALYZING CHARACTERS

In drama, children will be playing many different characters. A character is any person, animal, or being in literature with distinguishing physical, mental, and attitudinal attributes. Children will need to develop their understanding of character in order for the playing to be meaningful.

Some characters are very simply drawn in the literature. They may even be stereotypes as "a wily fox," "a curious child," "a cruel king." Folk-tale characters are usually quite simple. There may be a young man or woman off on an adventure—"a clever, handsome fellow," or "a witty, comely lass." A villain may be "an old witch," or "an evil servant." Because of their simple characters, folk tales are the easiest stories to begin with and the reason so many are included in this resource guide.

Generally speaking, the more complex the literature, the more developed the characters. More discussion and more playing time is required for stories whose characters are not one-dimensional but unique. These characters usually appear in longer stories or book-length literature. It may take the author that length of time to show us the many facets of the character. By the time we reach the end of the book, we have the many sides of the character revealed. And, thus we can say more about the characters and can have many more discussions about them. Charlotte the spider in *Charlotte's Web* or Paddington Bear in the Michael Bond books are unique characters and ones we are not likely to forget.

In playing characters, however, we are also looking at how they are both similar to and different from us. Much of this information is revealed in the events that happen to them and how they feel about those events and how they react to them. Discussions are often necessary in order to examine characterization. And so is playing time. So, we discuss, play, discuss some more, and play some more, and eventually arrive at a better understanding of the literature.

The following discussion questions are examples of the sort of probing you will want to do to help your students.

"The 'Star-Bellied Sneetches' don't play with the Sneetches that don't have stars. Why do you suppose they don't? How do you think the 'plain-bellied' Sneetches feel about that?"

"*Salt Boy* was ashamed when his father said he must never rope his mother's sheep. Why was he ashamed? Why did he rope the sheep?"

"Why does *The Little Brute Family* have such grumpy and unpleasant days? What is the 'little lost feeling' that enters their lives?"

While these questions are probably no different from those you ask in a reading class discussion, they are doubly important in a drama lesson since the children will need to do this sort of exploring together in order both to understand and play the characters with meaning.

PLAYING THE MATERIAL

One of the most frequently asked questions from teachers is, "How do you keep the kids from acting silly in creative drama?" Most of the time, in my experience, children act silly because they either do not know what to do or because they are being asked to do something too difficult or something they have not been fully prepared for. Actually the silliness simply comes from embarrassment. Without understanding this, you might find yourself losing patience, and this will just add to, rather than solve, the problem.

HUMOROUS MATERIAL

As was stated earlier, beginning with simpler materials and with humorous materials should keep silliness at a minimum. If the characters are funny, there is less pressure on children to play the part in a formal or polished way. And, even if there is a bit of silliness with humorous material, it does not destroy the mood. You can all have a laugh together and then continue.

DRAMATIC MATERIAL

Yet, playing material rich in dramatic tension or conflict is often the most rewarding experience children can have. Once you have been successful with it, you will discover that it is worth the time and effort it may take to experience it. Sometimes it is also surprising to find that the children who are the typical class clowns often show another side of their abilities when challenged with more dramatic material and serious moods. Since you will want to move eventually to these materials, you will want to know how to handle them. Following are some suggestions.

1. Clarify the Nature of the Material and the Expectations You Have

Sometimes we think children will automatically understand that certain material is serious and highly dramatic and that they will respond appropriately. But often children simply will not know. Telling them at the outset can save later difficulties.

"We've been studying about the difficulty of surviving in an extremely cold climate. Today's story is about an Eskimo child who is alone on a hunt, becomes lost, and must fight for his life. We've never worked on a serious story like this before, so it will probably take a little more effort."

2. At First, Play Briefly

It is much easier for students to sustain a serious mood if they know they will not have to be involved for long periods of time. This fact can help them be less anxious and less embarrassed.

A brief playing will also help you become accustomed to creating a strong, dramatic mood. Your chances of success will be increased and that should give you and the children confidence to try such material further.

3. Create the Appropriate Mood

Your voice can do a great deal in conveying the mood of any material. The way you introduce it, discuss it, and the sidecoaching you do can make a great difference in conveying and sustaining the appropriate mood.

As in the theatre, the use of music, lights, and sound effects can also help create the mood for the children and can provide appropriate background for your voice as well. Pretending to be young

"You're looking in a crystal ball. . . ." Leader narrates, sidecoaches, and plays along to encourage involvement and concentration.

plants growing may be easier for you to narrate and sidecoach and the children to enact if you play a musical selection like Grieg's "Morning" from *Peer Gynt*. Or, an experience of visiting a bustling city might be encouraged by Herb Alpert's "Tijuana Taxi."

Just flicking the classroom lights off and on can help children envision lightning, the flashing of photographers' cameras, and the glittering lights of outer space. A darkened room can help create a cave, an underwater world, or a haunted house.

Sound effects, whether made by children's voices or by other means, can also build and sustain mood. Carefully made and orchestrated sounds of a jungle, drums beating ominously, or a storm arising at sea, can lend atmosphere for all.

4. Help Create a Good Working Climate by Limiting Distractions.
Separating children from each other can lessen distractions and aid concentration. Dimmed lights can, in addition to providing a mood, help children focus on their own work.

Another aid is having children close their eyes. (Obviously this works best when they are playing individually and in a limited space.) Not only does this help block out distractions, it helps the children focus on the images needed to visualize the experience.

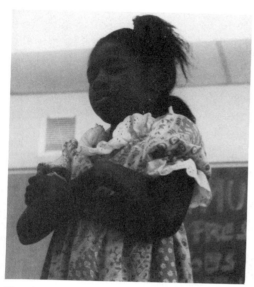

Keeping your eyes closed can help focus your thinking.

Ask children what aids and what distracts them. Even young children usually know what interferes with their concentration and will frequently list such things as: "having other kids too near me, especially touching me;" "my best friend making faces at me;" or "I don't like it if anyone watches me." This information can be helpful to you in making working conditions more favorable to individual children as well as to the whole class.

Distractions can keep a person from concentrating.

Talk with children after they have concentrated particularly well in a certain story or exercise. Having them reconstruct for you and for themselves the description of how they felt can be most revealing and useful.

"When I was being the bird with a broken wing, I remembered how hard it was for me to do anything with my right arm when it was broken and in a cast all last summer."

"When I was playing at being blind, I was trying to think of this lady who lives in my neighborhood. You wouldn't know she was blind unless you watched real close, so I tried to make myself look like her."

5. Select Volunteers for Initial Playings.
Although you want to let as many children as possible play an activity, it is often wise to select for first playings those few who can be the most easily involved. This is particularly useful when trying out new material and you cannot anticipate the class' response to it. The players can be a model for subsequent replayings. It is also easier to build on the mood set by the first players.

You might also ask for volunteers "who can really concentrate on the material and play it believably." Sometimes children who already have their hands raised for volunteering will think again about this requirement and sit out the first playing. This gives them the chance to self-select and avoid what they think they are not ready to handle. Using this technique, I have often been amazed at children's awareness of their own limitations and their willingness to approach a task with determined seriousness.

SIDE-COACHING

Side-coaching is a technique in creative drama in which the leader gives suggestions or comments from the sidelines to heighten and advance as well as control the playing. It is literally "talking the children through" an experience and is an indispensable aid to encouraging concentration and involvement. Side-coaching can also fill in awkward silences, giving security to those who are unsure and guidance to those who might need calming down.

You should always be prepared to side-coach, although you will probably never know exactly how much and what kind of side-coaching will be necessary until the playing begins. Side-coaching is a skill that will grow with experience and your own sensitivity to children's needs.

LEADER'S PARTICIPATION

In many drama activities your own participation will be helpful and sometimes even necessary. You may simply pantomime along with the children as you side-coach. You may take your own turn at a sequence game or play a role in a group narrative pantomime. You may even play a role in order to give children a character or situation to respond to.

By playing with the children, you are demonstrating a willingness to accept the challenge the activity presents. Your participation can also set the scene, create the mood, and highlight the dramatic tension. It can also be a lot of fun!

STRENGTHENING CONCENTRATION AND INVOLVEMENT

Even the beginning teacher knows when children are engrossed in their classroom work. You can see the furrowed brow of concentration, the oblivious attitude to disruptions, and the look of pleasure and satisfaction that acknowledges a job well done.

The same is true in drama. There are moments in drama, observable even to the novice, when the players/actors are truly concentrating and being involved in their activities and their art. They may be so absorbed and engrossed that they are unaware of anyone observing them. There is an attention to detail, the imagination at work creating believability, and a revitalization of energy with each repeated playing.

When children are not absorbed, there may be showing-off behaviors. In reality, these behaviors are the result of being embarrassed because others are watching or simply being too concerned about what others think. Being shy or insecure can also stand in the way of concentration and involvement. These are the children who may giggle with embarrassment, crowd against others in an attempt to hide or disappear in the masses, or hesitantly look at other classmates to see what they are doing.

All of the techniques discussed in this chapter will play a great role in helping you lead children to greater involvement in their playing over time. Sometimes you will be amazed at how easily it happens. Other times, you will be disappointed because you will not get the response you expected immediately. But when children once experience in-depth involvement in drama work, they will often not be satisfied

Involvement means believing what you are doing.

with superficial playing again. They may still need assistance in arriving at that goal. But with all working toward it, many more enriching experiences will be possible.

EVALUATION

When you and the children evaluate the playing together, there is increased possibility for further involvement in subsequent playings. When children are asked to say what they liked about their playing, they are verbally reinforcing themselves.

When you evaluate what the children have done, be sure to be as specific as possible. Saying "good," while it is nice to hear, does not really tell the children what you are referring to. If, however, you say, "Good ideas! I saw so many different animals," or "Good control. You stayed right with the music," then children understand your judgment better and also know what to repeat in further playings.

Believability is also important. "Good pantomiming; I could really see some zoo animals that time," or "Your robots were so believable, I almost wondered for a minute if my third graders had disappeared!" These comments place a premium on the look of reality, achieved only by controlled, imaginative thinking.

Without children's self-evaluation and the leader's evaluative guidance, drama work will probably only be superficial in the long run. Only when careful attention is given to all aspects of the playing will the best results occur.

REPLAYING

If a drama exercise or story is worth playing once, it is usually worth taking some time to replay it. Seldom is the best creative thinking and the deepest understanding forthcoming in a first playing, even if you and the children are experienced in drama work.

You may need to play an idea three times, even in one session. The first playing might be a run-through in order to get a total picture. A second playing gives the opportunity to add new ideas, to drop out less effective ones, and to do further refining and polishing. A third playing can become a final synthesis of ideas.

It is helpful to you and to the children to remember that the best work is not achieved immediately. Taking an experimental viewpoint is comforting to anxious children and will allay your own fears of not knowing what to expect. But, not only is it important to remember, it is important to *verbalize*—for your own sake as well as the children's.

"We've never done this before. Let's just try it and see what happens."

"I thought we did well for our first time with this story. What did you think was particularly good—and where might we make some changes for the next time?"

GROUP PROCESS

Working with children in creative drama is an experience in group management. Effective group work will depend on each unique individual in the classroom, including you. There must be a positive climate for all to work in for maximum growth. In a positive climate, the children and the teacher have a mutual trust and respect for each other. This climate is set mainly by leaders who show acceptance of themselves as well as their students.

ACCEPTANCE

Conveying acceptance is one of the most important factors in fostering a positive climate in the classroom.

Acceptance of Self

It is very difficult to accept another person if we have trouble accepting ourselves. To accept ourselves, we need to recognize our own

Creative drama is an experience in group management.

humanness, including our frailties as well as our strengths. If you expect perfection from yourself and from your students, you may have many frustrating experiences. If you are unaccepting, the result will be negativism.

When we are aware of our feelings, we can more easily express them in so-called "I-statements." For example, if you say, "I get really upset when I hear so much talking," rather than, "You're the noisiest bunch of kids I've ever had," you have expressed your own feelings and taken responsibility for them. The point is that the same amount of noise might not be interpreted the same by another teacher, so the feelings lie in you. The "You-statement" frequently places blame and negative judgment on the other person. "You-statements" cause guilt and resentment rather than the change of behavior you probably want. So, by learning to make "I-statements," you can get in touch with your own feelings and values and make them clear to others as well. You can also be more objective about your own needs, "Hey, this noise may not bother anyone else, but it's driving me crazy. Please hold it down."

Acceptance of Ideas
Acceptance is shown both nonverbally and verbally. A warm smile, an encouraging touch, a nodding head can indicate acceptance. Verbal statements can also indicate acceptance.

"Good idea."

"Um, I never thought about it that way before."

Acceptance of Feelings

Acceptance of feelings is important in creative drama because there will be so much discussion of character and dramatic situations based on daily living. Through creative drama you can help children understand what emotions are, how they are expressed, why people behave as they do, and how emotional responses differ. Since these topics are a part of other curricular areas such as social studies, literature, and health it is important to be aware of several considerations.

Although we think of feelings as good (happy, excited, loving) and bad (angry, lonely, unhappy) because of the effect they have on us, having a particular feeling is neither good nor bad by itself. It used to be thought (and some people still think) that we should be able to keep ourselves from having "bad" feelings. That is why many people will say, "Don't be unhappy," or "You shouldn't be afraid," or even "You must never hate anyone." But all feelings are normal and just *are*. We cannot keep ourselves from having them. It is what we do with our feelings that makes a difference.

When students talk about people and situations and emotions, they will often draw upon their own experiences. You need to be aware and accepting of these comments without showing judgments so that students will know they and the feelings they experience are normal.

CHILD: I'm afraid of the dark.

TEACHER: We're often afraid of what we can't see.

CHILD: The Star-Bellied Sneetches weren't nice to the ones without stars. I wouldn't want to be a Star-Bellied Sneetch.

TEACHER: You don't like the idea of being unkind to people.

Children readily identify with certain characters. Often these are the ones they choose to play, and through those characters they have the opportunity to release important feelings. They often feel safe under the guise of the character to express feelings they may not feel are allowed them otherwise.

Many creative drama leaders have noted shy children suddenly becoming assertive in a particular character role or an aggressive one becoming subdued. I remember distinctly the very feminine youngster who surprised her classmates and me by playing Tom Sawyer with great believability. I also remember the rather aggressive young boy who was a class clown but who asked to play a wish-granting sprite in a story we were dramatizing. I threw caution to the winds and allowed him to do it and was amazed to find a caring and kind personality emerge in the playing. Both these youngsters apparently felt safe in expressing their emotions through the characters they chose to play.

Acceptance of Mistakes

Accepting mistakes is often difficult for leaders and children who are perfectionists. Many people interpret mistakes as failure; and since failure must be rejected, so must the mistakes. But if I am afraid of making a mistake, then I will never try anything new and may restrict my own growth as a result.

If as a leader you can accept your own mistakes, children will soon learn that mistakes are tolerable. And, if you can do this verbally, you will demonstrate to the children and verify to yourself (That is equally important!) that neither you nor they will disintegrate if a mistake is made.

"Wow, I goofed that time! Let's try it again."

"You don't seem pleased with what you did. Would you like to try it again?"

Acceptance of Imitation

Sometimes in creative drama we are so concerned about encouraging creativity that we expect immediate and outstanding results. Often I have heard student teachers say, "Now be as creative as you can," or "Give me a creative answer," or even "I thought you'd be more creative than that."

But most ideas are rather ordinary at first until we have had a chance to experiment and probe deeper. And the amount of creativity we get from children is often in direct proportion to the creative planning we have done beforehand or the creative stimulation we have given while working with the children.

Frequently in creative drama activities children will imitate each other. How often have you praised one response from a child only to have the very next child say exactly the same thing? They want praise, too. Usually they really are not even aware that they are repeating what someone else has said. The desire to be accepted is so strong that they simply absorb the praised answer and assume it to be theirs.

To imitate is normal and natural. Indeed, imitation is the basic mode of learning. Yet some adults and children think of imitation as cheating and even say so.

"Janice is copying my idea!"

"Bob's cheating! He's doing what I'm doing!"

In response, you can communicate an acceptance of imitation in a way that protects the imitator and reassures the originator.

"Sometimes when people see an idea they like, they want to try it themselves. Bob must have liked your idea."

REJECTION

Rejecting Behavior

Even though you are an accepting person, you also have a responsibility to set limits on inappropriate behaviors. Sometimes ignoring a behavior will be sufficient to make it stop if it is a bid for attention. At other times, one must take action. A child needs to learn, for example, that even if he or she is allowed to be angry, that anger cannot be turned on others.

At the same time, it is helpful to reject the behavior without rejecting the person. Notice in the two statements below that the feeling is accepted, but the behavior is not.

"I know you're angry that I won't let you play this time. But you know the rules. You punched Joey and that means you sit this one out."

"I can tell you're all excited, but we can't start playing until you settle down."

Sometimes children's behaviors become disruptive to the rest of the class. When this happens, rules for participating should be reinforced as objectively as possible. When reprimanding individual children, it is also helpful to speak to them privately so they are able to "save face."

"Please sit down. When you feel that you can follow the rules to remain by yourself and not disturb others, you may rejoin the group."

"I'm sorry. I know you are disappointed. But I can't allow you to bother other people who are trying to do their work. Perhaps it will be easier for you to follow the rules tomorrow."

GROUP INVOLVEMENT

Creative drama encourages group interaction. Organization, cooperation, group problem solving, and decision making become an integral part of the group experience.

A group, even though composed of various individuals, also has its own personality—as if it were one huge person embodying separate individuals. Teachers note this phenomenon of group behavior when they say such things as: "My class this year is so silly all the time," or "My class would never like that story."

A group can also grow and change—just as individuals can. And, when a group is given the opportunity of working on its own, it can begin to have a life of its own. It may also take on a power that can be scary, especially if a leader feels his or her own control or influence is being usurped.

Some children have no trouble integrating themselves into a group. These are usually the children who are outgoing, friendly, and secure with themselves. Other children will have many difficulties. Some are fearful of a group and avoid interaction. Some demand constant attention from a group and have difficulties compromising and cooperating.

But the group is a microcosm of society, and the need to belong is strong. Often this need can be counted on to motivate children to integrate themselves with the group.

As much as possible, you will want to prevent cliques from forming. While there are times when you let the class form its own sub-

The need to belong to a group is strong.

groups for activities, you will also want to vary subgroups so that children learn to interact with all members. Counting off and placing 1's together, 2's together, and so forth is a common way to mix the group. Vary these methods of grouping, too. If children know you expect them to work together, they will begin to accept this procedure automatically. The procedure will prevent petty squabbling over who plays with whom. It also gets to the fun of the activity more quickly.

Some teachers find that it is helpful to establish ground rules with the group. Usually children can help formulate these rules with you. One class listed the following:

Because I like to have people listen to me, I will listen to others.

Because I wouldn't want anyone to say my ideas are stupid or dumb, I won't say that about anyone else's.

Because I don't want anyone to make fun of the way I feel, I won't make fun of anyone else's feelings.

I can enact my own ideas as long as I don't bother anyone else.

If I don't like an idea the group has, I don't have to play; but I shouldn't bother anyone.

Because I don't like being disturbed, I won't disturb others.

Because I want people to be a good audience for me, I will be a good audience for them.

Because I don't like being left out of a group, I will accept others into my group.

Throughout all experiences in creative drama, you will be helping children understand and empathize with others. You will want them to discover their common bond of humanness with others, whether those others are classmates, people in literature, or real life persons. This understanding and awareness is the essence of drama, which is, in fact, the study of life. And it is the basic goal of education in a society in which the quality of life will depend on the quality of human relationships.

RESOURCE MATERIALS FOR CHILDREN

The following materials are a selection of the many that are available, dealing with interactions. You will find them interesting just for children to read on their own or to use for reading and discussion with the entire class. Many will also provide material for creative drama lessons.

Aliki, *Feelings.* New York: Greenwillow, 1984. Brief stories and sketches of childhood feelings.

Berger, Terry, *I Have Feelings.* New York: Behavioral Publications, 1971. Situations and black and white photos covering seventeen different feelings, giving a brief story for each and followed by an explanation of each.

Buscaglia, Leo. *Because I Am Human.* Thorofare, N. J.: Charles B. Slack, Inc. 1972. (Distributed by Holt, Rinehart, and Winston.) Black and white photos illustrating text which describes all the things children can do because they are human—from rolling down a hill to chewing five sticks of bubblegum all at once. You can even do this one as a Narrative Pantomime (Chapter 5) or as a stimulus for Count Freeze Pantomimes (Chapter 7).

Chapman, Carol, *Herbie's Troubles.* New York: E. P. Dutton. 1981. Herbie does not want to go to school because of a bully. Upon advice from other children, Herbie is assertive, then shares, and then hits, but nothing works. Finally he ignores the bully, who then claims Herbie's no fun anymore and walks away with Herbie the winner.

Feelings, Tom, and Nikki Grimes, *Something On My Mind.* New York: Dial Press, 1978. Descriptions of many inner emotions that often are not expressed.

Schultz, Charles. *Love is . . . Walking Hand in Hand.* California: Determined Productions, 1983. Typical Peanuts. Lots of pantomime possibilities—in twos and threes.

Showers, Paul. *A Book of Scary Things.* Garden City, N. Y.: Doubleday, 1977. A child tells of all the things that can be scary—from spiders to monsters at night. This book is one good example of the many that can help get fears out in the open in a constructive way.

Tester, Sylvia, *Moods and Emotions.* Elgin, Ill.: David C. Cook, 1970. A booklet dicussing various ways to teach the subject of emotions in the classroom. Includes sixteen poster-size photos illustrating emotions.

Viorst, Judith. *Alexander and the Terrible, Horrible, No Good, Very Bad Day.* New York: Atheneum, 1972. Everything goes wrong for Alexander from the moment he wakes up till the end of the day. He thinks he will go off to Australia, until his mother tells him there are bad days there, too. Children will be glad to know they are not the only ones who have bad days. This story can be played as a solo narrative pantomime (Chapter 5).

TEACHER RESOURCE MATERIALS

Amidon, Edmund, and Elizabeth Hunter, *Improving Teaching.* New York: Holt, Rinehart & Winston, 1966. One of the first texts for making teachers aware of their specific verbal behaviors and the consequences of them.

Carroll, Anne Welch, *Personalizing Education in the Classroom.* Denver: Love Publishing Co., 1975. Although this book addresses itself to the special education teacher, the material is applicable to a wide variety of situations. Contains special chapters on communication in the classroom and on groups.

Cooper, Pamela J. *Speech Communication for the Classroom Teacher,* 2nd ed. Dubuque: Gorsuch Scarisbrick Publishers, 1984. Extensive look at several areas of communication including interpersonal, non-verbal, teacher influence, and communication barriers.

3 Getting Started

Everyone at one time or another has "done some drama," whether as a participant or as a leader. That is because many of the simple games and activities familiar to all teachers and children can come under the umbrella of creative drama. A finger play, an action song like "She'll Be Comin' 'Round the Mountain," or a game like "Simon Says" are good introductory activities to creative drama for various grade levels. Many games, in fact, have been used exclusively in the work of some drama educators.*

What is useful about these activities?

    a. They create relaxed, good feelings and promote security.

    b. They give students a good physical workout and develop muscular coordination.

    c. They promote group cohesiveness and focus on the importance of a unified effort in achieving a common goal.

    d. They help the students achieve some of the many skills that will be useful for all drama work.

---

*Most noted is Viola Spolin and her classic book *Improvisation for the Theatre*. Evanston: Northwestern University Press. 1963.

Forcing shy children to participate only increases
their reluctance.

    e. Many of the activities can be coordinated with experiences in other drama lessons
or with other curricular material.

    f. They can be used as a warm-up or cool-down for longer sessions.

Why are these activities also useful for the beginning teacher and beginning
group?

    a. They are easily organized.

    b. The rules and discipline are built into the activity or game.

ACTION/MOVEMENT/PANTOMIME

Drama is action or doing. For young children, movement is also their natural means
of exploring and discovering. Their constant activity integrates them physically with
everything they observe. Movement in drama continues this mode of learning.

You will want to help children express themselves freely and creatively through
movement, but you will want to work toward disciplined and thoughtful movement,
too. We will be working toward both these goals.

Pantomime is the expression of ideas and feelings through bodily action. It includes facial expressions, posture, gesture, and all body language used to purposely
convey a message. You will want to help children learn to interpret the actions of
others and express themselves more effectively through pantomime. In this section
we will begin work on the basics of pantomime.

Playing at the desk area provides control as well as security.

TEACHER DIRECTED DESK ACTIVITIES

As indicated earlier, the easiest kind of activity for you and your children to begin on will be those in which you direct or show the children what to do. They are easy to organize, keep the children in control, and use the desk area.

Following are a number of various kinds of activities you may want to try with younger children. Additional desk activities will appear in other chapters.

FINGER PLAYS

As a teacher of the young child, you probably already know a number of finger plays. A classic example is "The Eensy Weensy Spider." These games tell a simple, often dramatic, little story. Children love to act them out, demonstrating their skill in coordination and their ability to perform a "one person show." Some sources for finger plays are listed at the end of this section.

It is also easy to make up your own finger plays by adding actions to simple nursery rhymes such as "Hickory, Dickory, Dock." For example, you can act out a swinging pendulum for the clock, fingers running up the arm to show the mouse running up the clock, and holding up one finger for the clock striking one o'clock.

Finger plays are a good warm-up for more challenging activities.

ACTION SONGS

Action songs incorporate pantomime movement along with the lyrics. Traditional action songs include: "I'm a Little Teapot," "Did You Ever See a Lassie?" "Here We Go 'Round the Mulberry Bush" (or "This is the Way We Wash Our Clothes"), "If You're Happy and You Know It," "This Old Man," "Frog Went a Courtin'," and "I Know an Old Lady." Again, you can make up many of your own

An action song is a good warm-up.

actions to songs like Maurice Sendak's "Chicken Soup With Rice," which Carol King set to music. And, do not overlook many of the parodies such as Tom Glazer's "On Top of Spaghetti" (to the tune of "On Top of Old Smoky") or George Mendoza's *A Wart Snake in a Fig Tree* (New York: Dial Press, 1968), a bizarre version of "The Twelve Days of Christmas."

SINGLE ACTION POETRY

Some poetry suggests a single rhythmic movement such as running, hopping, or galloping. While you read the poem, the children simply perform the one action while seated at the desk or standing at the side of it. Actions are done "in place."
Try:

"A Farmer Went Trotting Upon His Grey Mare," Mother Goose (4*)
  Trotting can be done standing or sitting at the desk. The bumps and lumps can be acted out in various ways.

"The Grand Old Duke of York," Mother Goose (4)
  With this rhyme, you can march in place. Then, at the same time, stand for "up"; crouch for "down"; and half crouch for "half way up."

"Hoppity," by A. A. Milne (4)
  Poem about a little boy who hops everywhere he goes. You can even "hop" this one on seat bottoms at the desks. For variety, on the line beginning "If he stopped hopping," slow it down like a record player running out of electricity. Read lower and slower until you and the hoppers stop on "couldn't go anywhere." Then pick up the tempo again at "That's why he always goes. . . . " One class added "Pop!" at the very end!

"Jump—jump—jump," by Kate Greenaway (4)
  Children can jump three times on the first line of each stanza. Do this *in place.* Children hold crouched position while you read the next three lines. On last two lines they sit.

"Merry-Go-Round," by Dorothy Baruch (4)
  Children go up and down like one of the horses on a merry-go-round. As you read, the lines (and the horses) go faster and then slow down to a final halt. Fun to add music, perhaps "Carousel Waltz" from Rogers and Hammerstein's *Carousel.*

"The Swing," by Robert Louis Stevenson (4) (33)
  Swinging can be shown by leaning forward and backward in seated position or by taking four small steps forward and back for each two lines.

---

*Throughout the text, numbers in parentheses correspond to the numbered anthologies in the bibliography at the back of this book.

"Trot Along, Pony," by Marion Edey and Dorothy Grider (4)
Children can trot, clapping thighs in rhythm to this poem. The last line takes the pony home to supper, so you can finish off with feeding the pony and bedding him for the night. (The children can pretend they are feeding an imaginary pony—or, they can be the pony that *you* feed.)

"Rocking Chair," by John Travers Moore (10)
One can rock back and forth in this poem as the poet tells what fun it is to rock.

ACTION GAMES

Traditional games like **"Follow the Leader"** and **"Simon Says"** are also useful in drama. In each case, you specify the actions the group is to do. In the game "Simon Says," players are to perform the action only when the leader precedes the command with "Simon Says." There is no need to eliminate players, and, in fact, that would really be counterproductive to our goals. You can simply note, "Ah, a few were caught that time," and continue the game.

You can also vary the games and incorporate other curricular concepts. One teacher reviewed sizes and shapes with her class: "Simon Says: make yourself shaped like a box; walk in place taking giant steps; shape yourself like a piece of pie; become as small as a mouse," and so forth.

Another seat movement game might be called simply, **"Move to the Beat."** Beat a drum while children move in as many different ways as they wish—but only when the drum beats. Vary the beats to make it interesting, using different rhythms or halting suddenly so the students are encouraged to listen closely.

ACTION STORIES

Many of these activities, which incorporate actions with a story line, are well known in recreational circles. And many are taught by word of mouth. If you do not know "The Bear Hunt," perhaps you know "The Lion Hunt" or "The Brave Little Indian." Here is "The Bear Hunt" as I heard it many years ago:

THE BEAR HUNT*

LEADER SAYS: *(while tapping hands on thighs in rhythm)* Let's go on a bear hunt. *(Say rhythmically; children repeat all sentences and all action throughout the story.)* All right. Let's go. *(Tap hands for a few moments. Stop and sigh.)*

---

*Two picturebook versions also exist. See *I'm Going on a Bear Hunt* by S. S. Sivulich (New York: Dutton, 1973) and *Bear Hunt* by Kathleen Savage and Margaret Siewert (Englewood Cliffs, N. J.: Prentice-Hall, 1976).

LEADER CONTINUES: Oh, look. There's a bridge. Can't fly over it. Can't go under it. Have to go 'cross it. All right. Let's go. *(Tap hands on chest for a bridge sound. Stop and sigh.)*

LEADER CONTINUES: Oh, look. There's a swamp. Can't fly over it. Can't go under it. Have to go through it. All right. Let's go. *(disdainfully) ("Swim" with hands slowly, making sucking/slurping sounds with mouth. Stop and sigh.)*

LEADER CONTINUES: Oh, look. There's a tree, Can't fly over it. Can't go under it. Have to climb up it. All right. Let's go. *(Make climbing movements, thumb and forefinger of one hand alternately touching forefinger and thumb of opposite hand. Stop at "top" of tree. Sigh.)*

LEADER CONTINUES: Oh look. There's a cave. Can't fly over it. Can't go under it. Let's explore it. All right. Let's go. *(Climb down the tree as above; tap hands on thighs to indicate walking over to the cave)* Oooo, it's dark in here. *(Reach hand out to one side but keep eyes on the children.)* I feel something. *(Hand pretends to touch something.)* It feels furry. I feel an ear. *(Hand up a little and then move down the bear's face.)* I feel a nose. *(Gulp)* I feel a mouth. *(Whisper)* I think it's a bear. *(Look where your hand is.)* It **is** a bear! *(Now "run" out hurriedly; climb back up and down the tree; go back through the swamp; over the bridge; run a few more steps; stop and sigh—big sigh!)*

☺ SHORT ACTION STORIES AND POEMS FROM LITERATURE

Many poems and stories have a lot of action that children can pantomime while you read them. The following are some suggestions to get you started.

"The Adventures of Isabel," Ogden Nash. (4) Isabel meets a bear, a witch, and a doctor and handles each with dispatch.

Alligators All Around, Maurice Sendak. New York: Harper & Row, Pub., 1962. Something to do for each letter of the alphabet. You can make up your own lines, too.

"Boa Constrictor," Shel Silverstein. (30) The complaint of someone being eaten by a boa. You may know this one as a song, too. Ask children, "How can you pretend to make yourself disappear?" and see how many ideas they come up with!

"Busy," A. A. Milne. (4) A little boy pretends to be different people. In a repeated refrain, he turns "roundabout." Don't get dizzy!

"Cat," Mary Britton Miller. (4) A cat's movements are detailed. I read this one as it is written, but when the children act it out, I change the last two lines to read, "And sits on her rug with her nose in the air," so they end in a seated position.

"Hungry Mungry," Shel Silverstein. (53) A nonsense poem about a boy who eats everything, including himself.

"The Journey," Arnold Lobel. (28) A mouse goes off to visit his mother, using various forms of transportation.

"Jump or Jiggle," Evelyn Beyer. (4) Brief poem naming different animals and their way of moving.

"Mix a Pancake," Christina Rosetti. (4) Simple poem of mixing and stirring up batter.

ORIGINAL ACTION STORIES

You can make up similar action stories with familiar folk tales. For example, you can narrate a brief version of "The Three Billy Goats Gruff" with actions for each of the billy goats, the troll, and the bridge. Every time the words appear in the story, the children give the appropriate actions. All children can act out each word together. Or, for variety, specific words can be assigned to groups of children.

LITTLE BILLY GOAT GRUFF: "Trip-trap, trip-trap" *(Softly with fingers at side of head for horns. Can also take little steps in place.)*

MIDDLE SIZED AND BIG BILLY GOAT: *(Same as above but increase sound and size)*

TROLL: "Who's there?" *(Fierce faces and gestures)*

BRIDGE: "Creak, creak." *(Arch back and sway from side to side)*

NARRATOR: Once upon a time there were three billy goats named Gruff. There was **Little Billy Goat Gruff, Middle-Sized Billy Goat Gruff, and Big Billy Goat Gruff.** They wanted to go up on the hill for grass to make themselves fat. But on the way was a **Bridge.** And under it lived a **Troll.** The first to cross was the **Little Billy Goat Gruff.** The **Troll** said he'd gobble him up. But the **Little Billy Goat Gruff** said to wait for his brother. Next came **Middle-Sized Billy Goat Gruff** over the **Bridge.** The **Troll** said he'd gobble him up. But the **Middle-Sized Billy Goat Gruff** said to wait for his brother. Last came **Big Billy Goat Gruff** over the **Bridge.**

The **Troll** said he'd gobble him up. But **Big Billy Goat Gruff** butted him into the water. And **all the goats** *(Everyone together)* ate grass on the hill until they were fat. And the **Troll** still waits for them under the **Bridge.**

The End—Everyone takes a Bow!

For more ideas of simple activities, see the following sources:

Brown, Marc, *Finger Plays.* New York: E. P. Dutton, 1980. An illustrated collection of fourteen finger plays including "The Eensy Weensy Spider," and "There Was a Little Turtle."

Burroughs, Margaret T. *Did You Feed My Cow?* Chicago: Follett, 1969. A collection of street games, chants, and rhymes.

Carlson, Bernice. *Listen! And Help Tell the Story.* Nashville, Tenn.: Abingdon Press, 1965. Finger plays, action poems, and action stories for grades two and three.

Delamar, Gloria T. *Children's Counting Out Rhymes, Finger Plays, Jump-Rope and Bounce-Ball Chants and Other Rhythms.* Jefferson, N. C.: McFarland & Co., 1983. An excellent resource for numerous activites.

Steiner, Violette and Roberta Pond, *Finger Play Fun.* Columbus: Charles E. Merrill, 1970. Numerous fingerplays for the young child.

Tashjian, Virginia A. *Juba This & Juba That.* Boston: Little, Brown, 1969. A collection of chants, stories, and finger plays including "The Teapot," "Lion Hunt," and "Eensy Weensy Spider."

SIMPLE SENSORY AND EMOTION PANTOMIMES

Simple sensory and emotion pantomimes can also be acted out in limited space at the desks. These not only are fun to do, but they also encourage the children to remember past experiences, recall information, and form mental pictures. These skills are helpful for most learning tasks and can be sharpened by pantomime activities.

SENSORY PANTOMIMES

From our senses we learn about the world around us. We make observations, comparisons, discriminations, and form our concepts about the nature of things.

Sensory awareness is central to drama, as it is to all learning. Strengthening our sensory awareness and recall assists the imagination and is important to the actor as well as to the writer or any

To notice or see

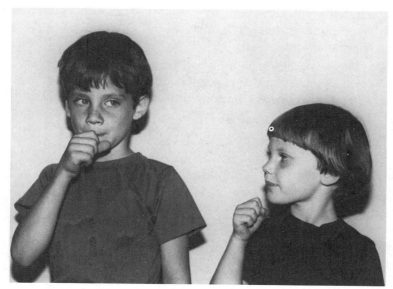

"Pretend to lick an ice-cream cone. . . . "

other artist. Since every story or other piece of literature has either direct or indirect reference to the senses, many sensory pantomimes can be developed from literature.

In sensory-awarenesss activities, you will need to do the following:

a. Describe details as well as encourage concentration. Often it is helpful to perform the real action and then perform the pantomimed action so that recall is clearer. For example, in pretending to read a book, you might actually do it first; then recall the experience through pantomime.

b. Pantomime along with the children in order to provide a model for them to imitate until their own skill and confidence develops.

Taste: Pretend to eat an ice cream cone. ("Take your first lick. Ummm, so cool, so delicious. It's your favorite flavor," and so forth.)
Eat a dill pickle or your favorite dessert. Take a spoonful of bitter medicine.

Touch: Pretend to pet a small, furry animal. ("Stroke it gently. Maybe it would like to have its ears scratched," and so forth.)

> Touch icy water.
> Rub hand across sandpaper.
> Feel sticky tar.

Hear: Listen to a clock chiming the hour of four o'clock.
You're asleep and the alarm awakens you.
You hear an insect buzzing and try to find it.

See: Pretend to read a book.
Thread a needle.
Watch a plane landing.

Smell: Smell your favorite cookies baking in the oven.
Smell a rose.
Take the lid off a garbage can.

Now try adding a little *conflict* to pantomimes. For example, while eating the ice cream cone, you could pretend it is a hot day and the ice cream is beginning to melt. How will the children hold the cone? ("Oh, there's a trickle of ice cream coming down on one side—better lick it quick," and so forth.) While reading the book, perhaps a puppy is bothering the reader to come and play.

Now you might try doing pantomimes with a little longer story line. For example, you could narrate a brief story of eating a picnic lunch, going on a hike, or any other experience that is strong in sensory stimulation. (See Chapter 6 for more ideas.)

ADDITIONAL SENSORY GAMES

You may decide that your class needs more help in sensory awareness. There are many traditional games that develop skills in sensory awareness. Many are useful for creative drama work as well as for other areas of the curriculum, such as science and language arts. Following are some examples you may wish to consider.

"I Spy"
This is an old favorite that is helpful for developing observation skills. Children take turns selecting an object in the room to be identified, saying "I spy something that is red." (You may use any identification like "round," or "brittle.") The rest of the children try to identify what the object is. Can be played in small groups.

"Scavenger Hunt"
Children are given a list of articles to collect within a given time limit. You might have them look for items in their desks: green pencil, paper clip, a picture of a scientist conducting an experiment, a poem about a dog, and so forth.

"Guess the Sound"

Different sounds (tearing a piece of paper, jangling keys, or running a finger along the teeth of a comb, for example) are made while children have their eyes closed. The one who guesses the sound correctly could be allowed to make the next sound.

"Touch Box"

Put a number of items children can identify by touch in a box. The items could include a fingernail file, a toy truck, a key chain, and so forth. Cut a hole in the box for a child to insert his or her hand.

EMOTION PANTOMIMES

In creative drama we will focus on emotions in numerous activities. Identifying, recalling, expressing, and being sensitive to emotions are important in understanding characters in literature. Understanding emotions and how they are expressed is also important to our own well-being. You might want to begin the study of emotions with the following game:

"Pass the Face"

One child starts out making a face (perhaps sad), and shows it to the next person. That person imitates the face and passes it on until it goes around the circle. A new person is chosen for the next face and the game repeats. As a variation, a person can receive one face and pass along a different one.

Other Possibilities

The following simple emotion pantomime can be other beginning activities for your class. Notice that presenting a situation or an activity (rather than just saying, "Pretend to be happy" or sad or angry)

a. gives children something to respond to, making the response more believable
b. helps sustain the mood and the playing a little longer

Examples:

Pretend to be watching a very *funny* television show.

Pretend you are all alone at night, reading a book, and you hear strange, *scary* sounds.

Pretend to be a *mean* witch stirring a magical potion in a cauldron.

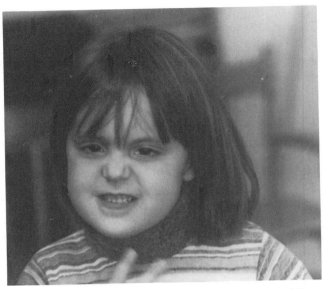

Be a mean witch mixing a brew in your cauldron.

These activities may also be lengthened even further by incorporating them into a story line or longer situation. For example, you can just add a conflict or another incident to the situation and change the emotion: "Pretend to be watching a very funny television show. Suddenly someone else switches channels and you're upset because you wanted to watch the other show. But as you start watching the new show, you see that it's your favorite sports show and they're right in the middle of an exciting moment. . . . " and so forth.

BRIEF STORY PANTOMIMES

Once you have tried several of the activities covered thus far, you might want to try your own hand at creating some brief story pantomimes. All you need are a few sentences of story line focusing on action. It is also helpful to include a variety of movements as well as levels and directions of movement—up and down, back and forth, left and right, bending over, turning around, going in reverse, and so forth. Changes of tempo and perhaps even slow motion and triple time are fun, too.

If you also add sensory and emotion details, the activities will be more interesting to play as well as being more dramatic.

"EXERCISING"

You can always do regular exercising, but let us be a character this time. In this first example it is fun for you, the teacher, to pretend to be Christopher Robin who cares about Pooh's health and well-being. ("Let's pretend you're Winnie the Pooh doing his stoutness exercies." As Christopher Robin: "Now, Pooh, put your hands on your hips. Good. Now, let's start out with head rolls.") Continue as you might for any exercise routine, working from the simpler to the more difficult or going from head to toe, noting that it is a bit strenuous for Pooh because of his protruding tummy. Maybe he even perspires a bit and you have to stop and pretend to dab him with a towel. Afterwards, you might let him eat a bit of honey as a reward and as a fun and quieting way to end.

Other exercising activities can also be done with robots, toys, or other interesting characters.

"PAINTING"

Have the children pretend they are skilled painters who are very confident. First, put on a painting shirt or smock, roll up the sleeves, and get out the jars of paint. Paint a picture of anything they like on the desk. Give it lots of color. Perhaps they might do some fingerpainting, too. Now the brush gets bigger and so does the painting. Have them stand at the side of the desk and paint a picture on a van; paint an elephant; a billboard; the landscape—the trees, flowers, sun, clouds in the sky, a rainbow, and so forth. Now the brush gets smaller, and the paint is nearly gone. Have them sit. Clean up the brush, cap the jars of paint, and wash up. Take off the painting shirt, fold, and put it away. Leroy Anderson's "Waltzing Cat," Strauss waltzes or other free-flowing music is good for this activity.

"PLAY BALL!"

Children pretend to be great athletes playing several sports. Have them play a little ping pong; hit the ball once, twice, three times; now they can stand at the side of the desk and serve a tennis ball (continue three times for each ball, encouraging different types of hits); pitch a curve ball; bat a baseball; serve a volleyball; spike it; dribble a basketball; shoot it; slam dunk it; hike a football; throw a pass; and so on. Now the crowd cheers them; they take a bow, sign an autograph, and sit down. "Sweet Georgia Brown," the Harlem Globetrotters theme song, is fun for this pantomime.

IMAGINATION GAMES

All artists, including actors, use imagination. But other fields of work, such as science, or other tasks, such as reading, require well-developed imaginations also. The following games can encourage the development of imagination.

"WHAT COULD IT BE?"

Use interesting, unusual objects which children are to imagine might be something else. An unusually shaped stone may become a good luck charm, a petrified animal, or a piece of furniture for a fairy's house. Odd kitchen utensils and tools are good to use for this game. Children may wish to bring in their own objects to share.

"PASS THE OBJECT"

Pass a wadded-up piece of paper and suggest that the object is "a small, frightened animal," "a flower," or some other object. The children are to pass the object on to the next person, handling and reacting to it in appropriate ways. The leader may change the object as interest wanes. Try this also without the prop and with the children naming the item. ("I'm giving you my cube of ice, but now it changes into a piece of sticky candy.")

"SCARF GAME"

Collect a number of scarves of varying sizes, shapes, designs, and colors. Children might have some to contribute also. The first player

What do you suppose this is? What could it be used for?

chooses a scarf and demonstrates a use for it—a tablecloth, shawl, tent, pocket handkerchief, puppet, and so forth. The colors, sizes, shapes, and textures of the various scarves should help children with their ideas.

QUIETING ACTIVITIES

A final category of desk activities is quieting activities. These are particularly useful if you are playing several activities in one session or when your drama period lasts for a half hour or longer.

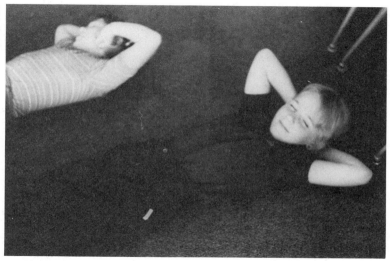

We are lulled to sleep while drifting along in a rowboat (quieting activity).

A creative drama period should come to a quieting end. Particularly if there has been a lot of movement activity, concentration, and hard work, it is essential to calm everyone down and not let them go to other schoolwork at a high pitch.

One technique is to read a very quieting selection, such as a poem. There are many suited to this purpose. Often the characters in the poems are relaxed or tired and the actions are subdued. Following are some suggestions:

"Keep a Poem in your Pocket," Beatrice Schenk de Regniers (33) A poem will sing to you at night when you are in bed.

"Lullaby," Robert Hillyer (34) We are in a rowboat, drifting along peacefully.

"Slowly," James Reeves. (52) Everything moves very slowly in this poem.

"Snow Toward Evening," Melville Crane (4) (34) A calm, peaceful snowy night described.

"Sunning," James S. Tippett. (4) An old dog sleeps lazily on a porch.

"Tired Tim," Walter de la Mare. (4) Poor Tim is just too tired to move.

"Who Has Seen the Wind?" Christina Rosetti (33) Leaves hang trembling and bow their heads when wind passes by.

It may be helpful to have children close their eyes as they enact the poem. You should also try to capture the quieting mood in your voice or perhaps use a quiet record for accompaniment. (Schumann's "Traumerei," Brahms' "Lullaby," or Humperdinck's "Evening Prayer" from *Hansel and Gretel*.)

You can also create a quieting activity by narrating a few sentences about a candle burning and slowly melting, a sun setting, or a marionette's strings being dropped slowly, one by one.

These activities should relax the children and calm them down. More importantly, they should help the children absorb the experiences that have been covered during the drama lesson.

Using More Space 4

Thus far, all the activities have not required much space. In this chapter we will introduce activities with more movement and more space demands. Hence, here are a few words on organizational procedures.

As was indicated earlier, use caution in choosing the space you work in. Many teachers have been led to believe that a lot of space is necessary for drama work. For me, nothing could be further from the truth.

Having a gymnasium to work in, for me, is usually a curse rather than a blessing. The space is so open that voices constantly echo and meaningful communication is extremely difficult. Furthermore, children associate a gym with active sports and the chance to blow off steam and energy. Their anticipation of doing that rather than experiencing a drama class is disconcerting and sometimes frustrating to them, which causes more problems for you. And, often large activity or all-purpose rooms create similar problems.

I believe very strongly in using the classroom and making use of the desk or table areas. If another kind of space is needed, the desks can be moved to the edges of the room. But, always make sure you really need more space and that changing the classroom arrangement is really desirable before you go ahead and do it.

ORDERLY, ORGANIZED PLAYING

Obeying rules and following directions are as important in drama work as in any other classroom work. In fact, they may even be more important, since drama work is so often a group activity.

Interestingly, adults working in groups actually behave very much like a classroom of children. Remember the last teachers' meeting you attended when the principal had trouble getting the group's attention? Or the last time you tried to get several guests seated for a dinner party? Frequently it is a phenomenon of group behavior and sheer numbers rather than age that causes difficulty in organization.

Although you are probably aware of them already, here are some hints to keep in mind:

1. Word directions explicitly and carefully. Children will usually do what is asked of them if it is clearly and firmly stated. Unfortunately, they usually cannot tell you when they do not understand, so they simply go ahead and do something—even if it leads to chaos. That is your clue that your directions were unclear, and you had better intervene before it is too late to rectify the situation.

2. Give directions while children are seated and you have their attention. Once any group gets up and begins moving, you will have difficulty getting their attention again without reseating them—and that is not easy for you or them. (It is a little like the old song, "How ya gonna keep 'em down on the farm, after they've seen Paree?").

3. If there is a problem, back up and start over. Do not try to muddle through something that just keeps getting more out of hand. You may need to repeat directions or even ask them what the problem is.

4. Do not sugarcoat directions.
   "Remember now, you're snowflakes and snowflakes don't talk." (If you are a kid with an imagination, your snowflake can talk. At least one child will think, or even say, "*Mine* does!")
   "Let's pretend you're like sticky gum, so don't touch anyone else or you may all stick together." (What an invitation that is for the curious minded! Think of it as a "Wet Paint" sign. How many people go ahead and touch the paint to see if the sign is really telling the truth!) It is best just to be straightforward with directions.

5. Use attention-getting devices. You probably have several of these already in your repertoire. Sound other than your voice and visual cues are often helpful for drama work. (Examples: audible cues like ringing a bell or beating a drum; visual cues like flicking lights or raising hand.)

6. Cultivate your nonverbal controls to minimize the need for constant scolding or verbal reminders:
   a. Wait with folded hands or a finger to the lips for a group to settle down before trying to talk above their chattering.
   b. Stand next to a hyperactive or talkative child for proximity control. (Close presence of an adult figure can speak authority.)

Attention-getting devices are useful.

7. Understand that problems will occur in spite of your best planning and intentions. Children often get excited as they get ready to participate in drama. Excitement leads to whispered talking. Sometimes you find yourself getting excited and rushing the children before they are ready. Or you may do too much discussing of an idea, and the children begin to get restless. For your own well-being, it is helpful to acknowledge the problem rather than blaming yourself or the children. For example, "Whoa! I think I've been rushing too fast and you're getting too excited. Let's slow down a bit" or "I can see we have a problem, but I'm not sure I know what it is. Let's come back, sit down, and talk about it."

Problems can occur, in spite of your best planning.

These hints, while they are not all inclusive, will help keep order and control so that everyone can focus on the drama activities rather than on discipline difficulties.

ACTIVITIES FOR SELF-CONTROL

The games and activities in this section will require more space, but they are also highly structured and encourage self-control and self-discipline. Children should learn that artistic discipline is necessary for an artist to perform at his or her best— just as a sound mind and body are important to the athlete. In fact, athletic training and artistic training have many similarities.

While children will enjoy playing the games, you will be looking for skill development in areas of concentration, disciplined coordination, and self control. The repeated playings of the exercises should result in increased skill. However, you should be aware that many similar exercises are practiced continuously by professionals, so the games can provide constant practice material at all ages and all levels of development.

Younger children can begin playing some of the activities, but exposure to the ideas is more important than extensive skill building. They should not be taxed beyond their abilities.

SOLO WORK IN SELF-CONTROL

 Parades

Young children love parades. They are fun, but they are also controlled and precise. Children can be assigned parts or may decide who they want to be. Begin marching in a circle with a few children, and then add on in ones, twos, threes, or more.

Parade ideas can come from music, literature, or other stimulus.

1. Music: "Parade of the Wooden Soldiers," Leon Jessel. Stiff, wooden movements. Good also for a parade of marionettes, robots, and windup or mechanical toys.

    "March of the Kitchen Utensils" *RCA Adventures in Listening* Album. Physical characterization of various cooking tools.

    "Baby Elephant Walk," Henry Mancini. Fun for an animal parade.

    "Circus Music" from *The Red Pony,* Aaron Copeland. Circus parade.

2. Literature: *And to Think that I Saw It on Mulberry Street,* Dr. Seuss. New York: Vanguard, 1937. Marco makes up a story about what he sees, after being asked daily, "What did you see today?"

    The Snow Parade, Barbara Brenner. New York: Crown, 1984. Andrew Barclay wants a parade, but his brother and sister say no.

Today's leader of the parade has a feather-duster baton and a cape.

He goes off by himself and is joined by a dog, duck, rabbit, pigeon, policeman on a horse, old man, boy with a sled, and girl on the sled and "hundreds more." And Andrew says, "Now this is what I call a parade!" (Try using Leroy Anderson's "Sleigh Ride" for accompaniment.)

The Wedding Procession of the Rag Doll and the Broom Handle and Who Was in It. Carl Sandburg. New York: Harcourt Brace Jovanovich, 1922. An unusual procession made up of many unlikely characters such as Spoon Lickers, Easy Ticklers, and Musical Soup Eaters. Fun for different movements. (Try Nacio Herb Brown's "Wedding of the Painted Doll" for this one.)

Caught in the Act

In this game children move in any way they wish while their feet are "glued" to the floor. A signal is given to freeze into position. Another signal is given and they may move about the room *in the position they were frozen in.* Another signal stops them, roots them to the spot, and the game repeats.

"Caught in the Act" being played in a classroom. Desks have been moved to the edges.

Freeze Game

This game establishes that space must be used with responsibility. Children may move quickly about the room in any way they wish (without bumping into each other), but on signal (for example, a ringing bell) they must freeze or stop. You may wish to specify a certain movement (hopping, skipping, and so forth). You may also ask them to freeze into a position or an expression (looking funny, becoming an animal, and so forth). Begin with only a few children at a time and gradually add on. The goal is eventually to have the entire class able to play the game, but this probably will not happen the first time.

Slow Motion Activities

Almost any activity can be played in slow motion. First children will need to learn the concept. Compare slow motion to moving underwater or through heavy syrup, to the television replays of sports events, or to astronauts working in anti-gravity atmosphere. Using slow music played at an even slower speed can help, as well as your side-coaching and encouragement to keep moving slowly. Children can be a balloon floating in space, an astronaut taking a moon walk, a sports personality playing a game. (Slow motion will be a technique used frequently in other activities.)

In-service teachers practice moving in slow motion.

Falling

Children love to fall. Tell them that *anyone* can fall, but it takes real skill to do it with control. (Be sure they do not fall on "unprotected" parts of their bodies like elbows, knees, and heads.) Ask them to think of different kinds of objects that fall and how they all differ (a leaf, a piece of string, a balloon losing air, and so forth). A demonstration of different objects falling is a good science lesson for younger children. Have children fall in slow motion. No one can reach the floor before you count (slowly) to 10. Have older children close their eyes so they focus only on their own work.

This activity is also useful for an overactive group if you move quickly. "Up again—this time fall like a leaf floating—1 . . . 10. Good. Now up again. Quickly this time like a shooting star in an arc on the count of 3—1, 2, 3, and down. Up again! This time a piece of string coiling—1 . . . 5. Up again."

Conducting an Orchestra I

Students are orchestra leaders and must keep with the beat of a particular recording. Use simpler, familiar tunes for younger children and more sophisticated rhythms for third grade.

Take a Walk

Organize the children in a circle. Pantomime walking through different substances—peanut butter, marshmallow creme, jello, or walking on a tightrope or curbing, keeping careful balance.

Carry the Object

Make a circle. Children pretend to carry a variety of objects like a heavy pail of water, a wriggling puppy, or a block of ice.

I Won't Laugh

Several students sit in front of the class. Volunteers, one (or more) at a time, do what they can (tell jokes, make faces) to get the others to laugh, but the volunteers cannot touch their classmates. The challenge is to increase the amount of time spent in keeping a straight face.

Noiseless Sounds

Children act out sounds as a lion roaring, dog barking, baby crying, or cheerleader cheering. But they can only use their bodies, not their voices. They might try this in slow motion, too. This is challenging, but fun.

Child tries to break up classmates in the game "I Won't Laugh."

PAIR AND GROUP WORK IN SELF-CONTROL

Often children need assistance in learning to work together. These activities require the children to work together in order to make the pantomimes believable. Since the games are fun to do, they usually make pair and group work appealing.

Mirroring

First you may have the class "mirror" you while you pretend to comb hair, brush teeth, wash face, and so forth. Do in slow motion to make it easier to stay together. Next, children mirror in pairs. One leads while the other mirrors. Switch parts. Consider a full-length mirror—exercising, dancing. Older children might like to try pairs mirroring pairs. For example, a sales person and someone buying new clothes look in a mirror at their images.

Sound Pantomime

One child pantomimes while another creates the appropriate sound effects. Sound effects should fit the pantomime. Try cutting down a tree, walking across a creaky floor, eating a piece of hard candy or celery, moving with the creaky joints of a robot.

Sound pantomime can be done in groups with third graders. For example, a group can be factory workers doing their jobs while each

"Mirror Game" demands close observation of partner's actions.

person has a counterpart who does the sound effects. It may be fun to start with one pair and add on until all are working; then gradually return to one pair.

Two Person/Group Jobs
Children act out pantomimes which require two people or a group. Carrying a ladder, moving a piece of furniture, sawing a tree with a cross-saw, or carrying a large pane of glass are possibilities. Children must coordinate their movements in order to make the objects believable.

Sculpturing
One person is the sculptor while the other is a piece of clay. The sculptor molds the clay into a statue, putting it in a certain position and perhaps even giving it a particular emotion. The clay must allow itself to be molded. With third graders, this can be done in groups using several statues in one scene.

Tug-of-War
Two teams stage an imaginary tug-of-war. Be sure everyone holds the rope so that it appears as one long rope and not a segmented one. You will need to side-coach this game, perhaps acting as an announcer. "Here we are at the playoffs. . . . Team A seems to be winning. (Team B must give in.) No, now Team B seems to have regained its fighting spirit. (Team A must give in.)" On your signal, the rope breaks and players fall in *slow motion* to the count of 10.

Conducting an Orchestra II
This time the children are in groups. One is the conductor while others play specific instruments to recorded music. March music is easiest to begin on. Then move to other rhythms and tempos.

SEQUENCING ACTIVITIES INTO LONGER LESSONS

Now that you have been introduced to a number of activities in the last two chapters, you may wish to sequence several of them into one lesson plan. Specific choices will depend on your determination of the group's needs and interests.

I find it useful to have a theme to tie activities together. It is most important to make the activities progress according to levels of difficulty. (Refer to the chart on

p. 12). With the activities and games covered thus far, you can select particularly from the following variables:

desk area activities	and move toward	those that use greater space
unison playing	and move toward	pairs and groups sharing their ideas
run-through playing	and move toward	concentrated playing, repeated playings, practice to improve

At this point, the other variables probably are not as distinct as they will be in later chapters.

Here are two examples to demonstrate. Note the flexibility of choice and how an activity can be adapted to fit a theme.

Adventures (theme)

1. "The Bear Hunt" (p. 37) (directed seat activity)
2. "The Adventures of Isabel," Ogden Nash (p. 38) or "The Journey," Arnold Lobel (p. 39). (pantomime at side of desk)
3. "Caught in the Act" (p. 53); or "Freeze Game," (p. 54) (more movement and use of space)
4. "Slow Motion Fall from Space" (pp. 54 and 55) (quieting activity)

Animals (theme)

1. "Trot Along, Pony" (p. 37), "Three Billy Goats Gruff" (p. 39), (directed seat activities)
2. "Exercising" (Pooh Bear) (p. 45), (more movement but still at desk area)
3. "Animal Parade" (p. 52), or "Freeze Game" (with animals) (p. 54) (more movement and use of space)
4. "Sunning" (p. 48), quieting activity

SAMPLE LESSON PLAN
Staging Fights (not recommended for lower than third grade)

Objectives

    a. Learn that theatrical fighting is a disciplined art.

    b. Learn how to "stage" fight scenes in stories in order to play them safely.

    c. Be challenged by the fact that anyone can shove and push people around; only the skillful and trained can make fake fighting look real.

Preparation and Materials

    1. **Space:** front of classroom for demonstrations; open to more space as lesson progresses

    2. **Supplies:** (optional) fight scenes from literature to practice with at the end of the lesson

    3. **Length of session:** approximately 30 minutes

Opening Discussion

Children are usually intrigued and impressed with the fact that the "realistic" fights they see on television, in the movies, and on stage are organized and artful pretense. Talk about this from your own personal knowledge and get them to share their information. Do they know about stunt people? Do they know how some of their favorite scenes on television were staged?

Activity

"Today we're going to learn, the way actors and stunt people do, how to hit without making actual physical contact with people. We'll learn to pretend how to receive and give hits in a convincing and believable way."

    A. First children work alone, imagining a partner. (You may wish to have a couple of students demonstrate this with the rest of the class first before letting everyone try.) They must practice and perfect their skill in stopping the blow at the precise moment before the contact. The point of contact they aim at may be imagined or may be a wall, their desk, or the palm of one hand.

        Try three hits at first. You call (count) the blows slowly, checking to see how they are doing.

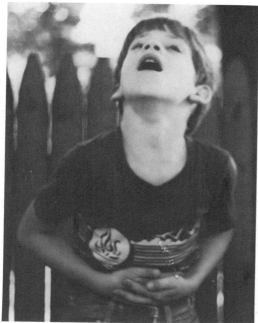

Pretending to hit; pretending to be hit. Learning
to master the pretense of fighting.

You might pretend you are the one receiving the punches and give appropriate verbal response: "One, (pause), Ugghh! Two, (pause), "Ooh, you got me there," and so forth.

B. Next the children pretend to receive the blow. Again the partner is imagined. As well as calling the blows, you might tell them where the punches will be—1, stomach; 2, chin; 3, left shoulder.

Now you might pretend to be the one giving the blows and say: "One, take that!; two, and that!, three, that'll teach ya, ya ornery varmint!"

C. Now they can work in pairs. (Again, you may wish to demonstrate with two children before letting everyone try it.) Again you count. Allow perhaps five punches this time. Count slowly, perhaps even freezing after each count to make sure all rules are being followed.

D. Speed up *only* when they exhibit appropriate skill and sensitivity to each other. If you see any problems at all, stop immediately!

E. When everyone has had a chance to try it out, you might want to let them "stage" a fight from literature.

Suggestions: Millions of Cats, Wanda Gag. New York: Coward, McCann, & Geoghegan, 1938. The cats all "bit and scratched and clawed each other" and finally ate each other up. How can they show this in pairs?

The Elephant's Child, Rudyard Kipling. New York: Walker, 1970. After Elephant's Child gets his trunk, he goes home and spanks all his relatives (various animals) the way they used to spank him. How can they show both spanking scenes in pairs? Before playing, you might want to discuss the different ways the various animals would spank.

Quieting Activity

(*At desk*) Have each child be a punching bag that slowly loses air and flattens out. You can count slowly to 10 at which time children must be seated.

Narrative Pantomime With Children's Literature

5

A number of years ago, while looking for an easy way to get teachers and children started in creative drama, we discovered that there were many stories and poems we could narrate while the children pantomimed them. We called both these materials and the technique of playing them "narrative pantomime.*

Narrative pantomime is easy for both you and the children to do. It also provides a way for children to experience excellent literature, trying on favorite characters and joining them in their adventures. Narrative pantomimes encourage children to focus on the literature, to listen carefully in order to know what to pantomime and when to do it. Narrative pantomimes also give them security and self-confidence to try more challenging drama work later. Another advantage of these materials, particularly the stories, is that they give children an introduction to dramatic structure. There is a plot with a conflict and a beginning, middle, and ending—the basic ingredients for drama.

Because children must follow the literature's directions in narrative pantomime, there is built-in organization. You are in control. You will quickly learn what literature works best and will soon find yourself being able to edit material easily and even to write some of your own materials. These materials will also help you in narrative description, useful in the technique of "side-coaching" in other activities.

*(See *Creative Drama for the Classroom Teacher* by Ruth Beall Heinig and Lyda Stillwell. Englewood Cliffs, N.J.: Prentice-Hall, 1974 and 1981).

Individual or solo playing lets students work by themselves and enjoy their own ideas.

Young children generally prefer those narrative pantomimes they can be involved in continuously—a story with one character, for example. So they will love being Harold in Crockett Johnson's *Harold and the Purple Crayon* and other sequels to that story. Or Peter in Ezra Jack Keats' *The Snowy Day*. Usually young children can also switch from one character to another easily and will enjoy being each of the animals in *Just Suppose* by May Garelick. Since each child is the "star" in his or her own little drama, solo narrative pantomime is a very satisfying experience for young children.

The entire class plays the character in *unison* while you narrate. This is particularly important in the beginning stages of drama. Playing in unison gives children a chance to experience their ideas for their own enjoyment without worrying about an audience evaluation. They can also rehearse and polish their ideas in case they decide later to share them with classmates. A final benefit of unison playing is that children do not have to wait to take turns.

As children become familiar with narrative pantomime, you will want to try both pair and group playing. We will talk about this in detail at the end of this section. First, look at the general considerations you will need to make in playing narrative pantomimes.

LESSON PLANNING FOR NARRATIVE PANTOMIME

SELECTING MATERIAL

Material used for narrative pantomime must have enough continuous action to keep children actively involved from beginning to end. The selections in the bibliography in this chapter are some of the

"Look at the world upside down. . . . "(*Kalamazoo Gazette*)

best we have found. But, since most authors and poets have not written their materials for narrative pantomime purposes, almost any selection can benefit from minor editing. Some material benefits from tightening the physical action, even to the extent of omitting a sentence or two, as long as the plot is not destroyed.

The most dramatic materials build to a climax and have a quieting ending. Many stories and poems even have the character in a settled position at the end, a welcome aid in getting the children back in their seats or in a stationary position after playing. In some cases, you will want to add this feature to stories. For example, even though I read the entire story *The Snowy Day* to the children, I end their playing of it with Peter going to bed and dreaming of tomorrow and another day of play in the deep, deep snow. This way the children are in their seats or on the carpet at the end. I find this works better than using the book's ending of Peter waking and going outdoors again.

Sometimes you will find that additional action is helpful, particularly in picture books where much of the story is told through the art work. Adding descriptive detail to action can also enrich the drama experiences. The line may read, "The farmer worked in the field all day long." You might add the words "cutting and stacking the hay" in order to give children an idea of what they might pantomime.

EDITING DIALOGUE

Some stories have brief lines of dialogue. If they are short, the children will enjoy repeating them. Longer lines can be dropped. Some dialogue is easily pantomimed (for example, "No," "I don't know," or "Here"). Generally, the mouthing of words is distracting, so if you see the children doing this as you narrate, it probably means there is too much dialogue and it should be cut (or, that children are ready to add dialogue, which we will discuss later in this chapter).

PRESENTING THE MATERIAL

There is no one way to present the material before enacting it. You might want to read the story first and discuss it to make sure the children understand it and know what they are to do. Other times you might want to read a story "cold" and have the children im-

When presenting a picture story from a small book, it may be helpful to have enlarged illustrations to show.

provise on the spot. In any event, you will always want to be sure the children know what they are to do, have ideas for doing it, understand how to use space, and can handle any physical action safely. Sometimes it is helpful to have competent children demonstrate to the others how to play difficult or problem situations.

CREATIVE INTERPRETATION OF MOVEMENT

There is no one way to interpret the action in narrative pantomimes. Doing a duck's walk can be performed upright or squatting, with wings shown by fingertips touching the shoulders or hands tucked under the armpits. Encourage children to find their own ways.

Some actions can be quite challenging. How does one pretend to be a bear riding a unicycle on a tightrope? All these ideas can be discussed prior to the playing, and perhaps be tried out and demonstrated before the entire selection is played.

LIMITING SPACE

As discussed earlier, it is most useful to keep the children working at their desks or in a designated place on the floor. In fact, the desks can become part of the drama by serving as a bed, a car, a table, or whatever the story calls for.

For pair and group playing, be sure the children understand the limits of their space. In some cases it may also be necessary to let only half the class play while the other half observes. (The observers might help with the sound effects, lights, or other technical aspects.)

NARRATING THE MATERIAL

Much of the artistic burden of narrative pantomime relies on the narrator's reading abilities. It is probably best not to let the children be the narrators, particularly at first. Later, when they become familiar with narrative pantomime, you may find superior readers volunteering to narrate and doing an excellent job. If you have several talented readers, you might want to let them all be narrators for one selection. Just divide the material at logical intervals.

You also need to know the story well enough so that you can keep an eye on the children's performance. If you have a soft voice, it may be necessary to allow only a few children at a time to play in order that your voice can be heard. Your timing and vocal intensity can also control the action and the noise level. If the children get a bit too noisy, just pause. As they quiet down in order to hear the next cue, you can speak in a softer voice. This should calm their playing down.

MUSIC

Some materials benefit from musical background, lending atmosphere, sustaining involvement, and encouraging ideas. (Some suggestions for music are made in the bibliograhies in this chapter.) At first, you may need to rehearse the narration with the music before trying it with the class.

EVALUATION

Both you and the children will be evaluating the playing throughout all drama work. Acknowledge the good work you see the children doing, although it is best not to praise one idea over another. Your acknowledgement can pertain both to the children's playing and their management of themselves:

> "You had so many interesting and different ways of being a cat. I saw some washing themselves; some were sitting on haunches; and I even think I heard some quiet purring."

> "I liked the way you were able to stay in your own space and not interfere with others' work."

Self evaluation is also important and can be encouraged by asking:

> "What's one thing you did that you liked the best?"

> "What do you think you might do differently the next time we play it?"

Some may like to share their ideas, both in telling about them as well as in demonstrating them.

REPLAYING

If children have enjoyed the material and their own expression of it, they may ask to repeat it. In repeated playings children can perfect their ideas with your encouragement. New goals may also be established.

> "This time you may want to try some new ideas."

> "I'll slow down this time in the part where you thought I read a little too fast."

NARRATIVE PANTOMIMES FOR SOLO PLAYING

The following stories and poems are arranged alphabetically according to titles. Numbers in parentheses refer to anthologies listed in the final bibliography. Suggested grade levels are listed in the left hand margin.

2 *The Adventures of Albert the Running Bear*, Barbara Isenberg and Susan Wolf. New York: Clarion, 1982. Albert, a zoo bear, gets too fat eating all the snacks people throw to him. When his food is restricted, he escapes and, after finding a jogging suit, winds up in a marathon race. Edit for solo playng. May want to shorten. Good health lesson.

K-1 *Beady Bear,* Don Freeman. New York: Viking, 1954. A stuffed toy bear thinks he should live in a cave. Edit so everyone can play the bear.

1-3 *Bearymore*, Don Freeman. New York: Viking, 1976. A circus bear must think of a new act even though it is time for him to hibernate for winter. Easy to edit so everyone can play Bearymore.

2-3 *"Could Be Worse!"* James Stevenson. New York: Morrow, 1977. Grandpa tells an incredibly tall tale about what happened to him one night. Everyone plays Grandpa when his adventure begins.

K-2 *Cowboy Small,* Lois Lenski. New York: Henry Z. Walck, 1949. A little cowboy ropes cattle, takes care of his horse, and plays a guitar, among other activities in his busy day.

3 *Fortunately*, Remy Charlip. New York: Parents', 1964. Good fortune and bad fortune go hand in hand in this adventure.

K-3 *Frances Face-Maker*, William Cole and Tomi Ungerer. New York: Collins, 1963. Frances does not like to go to bed at night. Daddy plays a game of face-making. Good seat activity.

1-3 *Giant John*, Arnold Lobel. New York: Harper Row, 1964. Everyone plays Giant John, who gets a job working for a very tiny king and queen in a very tiny castle. When fairies tempt him to dance, he accidentally destroys the castle. But he rebuilds it, and all is forgiven. All other characters can be imagined.

K-2 *Good Hunting, Little Indian*, Peggy Parish. Reading, MA: Addison-Wesley, 1962. A little Indian gets more than he bargained for in his hunting adventure.

3 *Great-Grandfather in the Honey Tree*, Sam and Zoa Swayne. New York: Viking, 1949. This is a very tall tale about a hunting adventure.

K-3 *Harold and the Purple Crayon*, Crockett Johnson. New York: Harper and Row, 1955. A little boy has many adventures with the help of a purple crayon to draw them.

1-3 *Harold's Circus*, Crockett Johnson, New York: Harper and Row, 1959. Harold creates a circus with his purple crayon and saves the day by getting the lion back into his cage.

1-3 *Harold's Fairy Tale*, Crockett Johnson. New York: Harper and Row, 1956. Harold has an adventure with a king and a castle.

1-3 *Harold's Trip to the Sky*, Crockett Johnson. New York: Harper and Row, 1957. Harold goes off on a rocket in this adventure.

1-3 *Harry the Dirty Dog*, Gene Zion. New York: Harper and Row, 1956. Harry will not take a bath and gets so dirty his family does not recognize him any more.

2-3 *Hildilid's Night*, Cheli Duran Ryan. New York: Macmillan, 1971. A woman tries everything she can think of to get rid of the night, until she becomes so exhausted she falls asleep just as day returns.

1-3 *If You Were an Eel, How Would You Feel?* Mina and Howard Simon. Chicago: Follett, 1963. Various animals described according to their characteristic actions. Children play all the animals solo.

1-2 *Indian Two Feet and His Horse*, Margaret Friskey. New York: Scholastic, 1964. A little Indian wishes for a horse and finally gets one.

2 *I Was a Second Grade Werewolf*, Daniel Pinkwater. New York: E.P. Dutton, 1983. A second grader's imagination turns him into a werewolf, but no one seems to notice. Edit for solo playing. Extra characters can be imagined.

2-3 *I Will Not Go to Market Today,* Harry Allard. New York: Dial, 1979. Day after day, Fenimore B. Buttercrunch attempts to go to market for strawberry jam. But there is always a problem: a dam breaks, a dinosaur is in his front yard, and he even breaks his leg and is laid up for six months. But he finally makes it!

2-3 *Just Suppose*, May Garelick. New York: Scholastic, 1969. Suppose you were a number of animals doing what they do. Opportunity to explore animal movement and habits.

K-1 *The Little Airplane*, Lois Lenski. New York: Henry Z. Walck, 1938. Pilot Small takes his airplane up for a ride. Basics of flying noted for the very young child.

K-1 *The Little Auto*, Lois Lenski. New York: Henry Z. Walck, 1934. Mr. Small has a little auto which he takes care of and drives around on errands. Young children will love beeping the horn and having a flat tire.

K-1 *The Little Sailboat*, Lois Lenski. New York: Henry Z. Walck, 1937. Captain Small has an adventure with his sailboat.

3 *The Man Who Didn't Wash His Dishes*, Phyllis Krasilovsky. Garden City, N.Y.: Doubleday, 1950. A lazy man's neglect poses problems in

housekeeping. Children's desks can be the man's easy chair, kitchen chair, and truck.

K-2 *Monday I Was an Alligator*, Susan Pearson. Philadelphia: Lippincott, 1979. A little girl pretends to be something different for each day of the week.

1-3 "On Our Way," Eve Merriam (7) In this poem children experiment with the walks of various animals.

3 *Salt Boy*, Mary Perrine. Boston: Houghton Mifflin, 1968. A young boy rescues a lamb in a storm and gets his wish: to learn to rope a horse. Edit for solo playing.

K-2 *The Snowy Day*, Ezra Jack Keats. New York: Viking, 1962. Young Peter plays in the snow and finds out that snowballs melt indoors. I end with Peter in bed at the desk, dreaming.

2-3 *The Story About Ping*, Marjorie Flack. New York: Viking, 1961. This is the adventure of a little duck on the Yangtze River in China.

3 *Theodore Turtle*, Ellen MacGregor. New York: McGraw-Hill, 1955. Forgetful Theodore first loses one of his rubber boots and then misplaces almost everything else he touches.

1-3 *What Will You Do Today, Little Russell?* Robert Wahl. New York: G. P. Putnam's, 1972. A little boy explores a farm.

1-2 *Whistle for Willie*, Ezra Jack Keats. New York: Viking, 1964. Peter finally learns how to whistle for his dog.

PAIR PLAYING WITH NARRATIVE PANTOMIME

Unless they are very little or socially immature, young children can also successfully play stories that have two characters, as long as each character has a fairly equal amount of action to perform. (Most children want equal stage time!) A good example of such a story is Margaret Wise Brown's *The Golden Egg Book*, which features a bunny and a duck.

But you will also quickly note that when a story has two or more characters, they frequently interact socially and even physically. For example, in Brown's book mentioned above, the bunny rolls the duck (who is still inside the unhatched egg) down a hill. Obviously you will want to make sure the children can perform such actions appropriately and safely before you let an entire class try this story. A preview demonstration with a pair of trustworthy and competent children will probably be required.

Second and third graders, as well as more mature first graders, will also be able to perform in paired playing for stories in which one character meets several other characters during an adventure. One child can play the major character while the second child plays each of the other characters that are met.

NARRATIVE PANTOMIME FOR PAIRED PLAYING

3 *Andy and the Lion*, James Daugherty. New York: Viking, 1966. A young boy reads about lions and imagines himself in an adventure similar to that of the fabled Androcles. You may prefer to begin with Part II.

2 *Beady Bear*, Don Freeman, New York: Viking, 1954. A stuffed toy bear thinks he should live in a cave. Thayer's part is important enough to make this story playable in pairs. Also listed for solo playing with just Beady.

3 "The Bear in the Pear Tree," Alice Geer Kelsey. (31) The Hodja meets a bear and hides from him in a pear tree. Note the subtle humor.

2–3 *Caps for Sale*, Esphyr Slobodkina. New York: Scholastic, 1947. Thieving monkeys take a peddler's caps. This version is easiest to use for narrative pantomime. It can be played in pairs, using one monkey to one peddler.

3 "The Crack in the Wall," George Mendoza. (11) A hermit loses his house to a crack in the wall that won't stop spreading. Pairs include the hermit and a crack that starts out "knife-thin, the length of the hermit's hand" and keeps reappearing on different walls until the whole place collapses. Plan carefully the hermit's examination of the crack. I let everyone fall at the end but in slow motion to a count of 3.

3 "Gertrude McFuzz," Dr. Seuss. (58) Gertrude finds that growing a big, beautiful tail may not be what she really wants after all. The same child who plays Lolla-Lee-Lou can also play Uncle Dake.

1–2 *Gilberto and the Wind*, Marie Hall Ets. New York: Viking, 1963. A young boy encounters all the things the Wind can do—and can't. You will want to discuss and perhaps try out some of the more abstract ideas in this one before playing the entire selection.

K–1 *The Golden Egg Book*, Margaret Wise Brown. New York: Simon & Schuster, 1947. A bunny and a newly-hatched duck discover each other. Plan the interaction carefully.

3 *Gone is Gone*, Wanda Gag. New York: Coward McCann, & Geoghegan, 1935. The old tale of the man who swaps chores with his wife only to discover her work is not as simple as he had thought. Another version is *"The Husband Who Was to Mind the House."* (4) You can combine the best features of both stories.

1–3 *The Gunniwolf*, Wilhelmina Harper. New York: E. P. Dutton, 1967. A little girl goes into the woods and meets the Gunniwolf, whom she charms with her "guten sweeten song." Children will probably want to say the phrases that repeat: the song "Kum kwa, khi wa," the running "pit pat," the Gunniwolf's question "Why for you move?" and the little girl's answer, "I no move." The running should be done in a small circle of space or may be done by tapping hands on thighs in rhythm.

3 *How the Grinch Stole Christmas!* Dr. Seuss. New York: Random House, 1957. This is the modern classic of a spiteful character who learns the true meaning of Christmas giving. While one child plays the Grinch, another child can be Max the dog and the Who child.

3 *How the Rhinoceros Got His Skin*, Rudyard Kipling. New York: Walker, 1974. A Parsee gets even with a rhinoceros who keeps stealing cakes. You may prefer to edit out the fact that the Parsee wears no clothes, even though this beautifully illustrated version by Leonard Weisgard is tastefully done. See also (24).

3 *Mrs. Gaddy and the Ghost*, Wilson Gage. New York: Greenwillow, 1979. Mrs. Gaddy lives in an old farmhouse with a ghost. When all efforts to get rid of him fail, she decides to move; but when she sees how dejected the ghost is, she decides to remain. Mrs. Gaddy talks to herself, but the dialogue can be kept in if the children just mime it.

1–2 *The Tale of Peter Rabbit*, Beatrix Potter. New York: Frederick Warne, 1901. The timeless story of a misbehaving bunny who finds adventure in Mr. McGregor's garden. Can also play solo, but most children will prefer to have Mr. McGregor on hand. The same child who plays Mr. McGregor can also play some of the other minor characters. You may want to simplify and shorten the text a bit for the playing, but children should hear the inimitable Beatrix Potter language the rest of the time.

2–3 *The Tale of Two Bad Mice*, Beatrix Potter. New York: Frederick Warne, 1932. Two mice find a doll house and create havoc when they discover the play food is not edible. Edit for just the two mice, Hunca-Munca and Tom Thumb.

3 "What Was I Scared Of?" Dr. Seuss. (37) A typical Seuss character is frightened of a pair of pants with nobody in them until it finds the pants are afraid of it!

GROUP STORIES INTO PLAYS

Often narrative pantomime stories will have several or even numerous characters. Second and third graders will want to enact these stories as a skit or informal play with each child having a part.

The size of the cast and the number of characters in the story will vary. Often the number of characters can either be increased or decreased easily.

Some of the characters in group stories have small parts, but if the characters are interesting, the children will want to include them. For example, in *The Story of Ferdinand*, the bull's mother appears only in one sentence in the opening. Even though her part is small, children may insist that she remain in the story rather than being eliminated. They may even want her to attend the bull fight and return home with Ferdinand at the end of the story.

By adding characters or by double casting (two children playing one part), an entire class can often play in one of these group stories. For example, there can be two or even three wives and husbands in *Brownies, Hush!* and any number of elves.

If you prefer to have a small "cast of characters," say, five, then several smaller parts in a story can be played by the same person. And unless it is confusing to the children, you might even try letting two small groups enact a story simultaneously. At first, it may seem a little like a two-ring circus, but it does give more children a chance to play. And the children who are left watching can see different interpretations of characters and lines.

With experienced third graders, it may even be possible to let them work out their portrayal on their own, giving each group a different story to enact. The working groups probably should not be larger than five, including the narrator, in order to keep the decision-making tasks simple. Children may draw lots to see who plays which part. An informal drama "festival," with each group sharing its performance with the rest of the class, can be the end result of this more elaborate procedure.

ADDING DIALOGUE

If a class enjoys a story and likes replaying it, they may begin to perfect it much as they might in rehearsing a play. This happens because these stories develop so easily into a play format.

Consider for a moment that if you were planning to put on a play, the first step you would take would be to select a script. And, what is a script but the dialogue or speeches of the characters? Actors must memorize the speeches (or script) and then add the action or stage directions so that the plot unfolds.

However, in the process we are using, we begin with the pantomimed action first, organizing and rehearsing it. Now, if desired, simple dialogue may be added to the pantomimed action. As the children work with the story, they often see opportunities for dialogue. All you may need to do is pause in the narration and allow the children to improvise a few words of simple dialogue. (In some cases and with some stories, the children may carry the story along so completely that narrating will be needed only sporadically. It may even be eliminated in time.)

SHARING

As the older children gain more confidence in themselves and in their work, they may ask to share it with an outside audience. However, sharing should always be the collective desire of the group rather than being imposed by you. And the audience must be a very supportive one—perhaps a few parents and friends or another classroom.

Children often have more success in sharing these narrated materials than they would with a scripted play. Fear of forgetting lines, usually the biggest worry in performing a play, can be eliminated since the dialogue is not essential to these stories. There is less pressure than with a scripted play since these plays go on as long as the narrating and pantomiming continue. Children who are not yet ready for simple dialogue can still participate in the playing, while those who are ready for a little improvising can add it.

AUDIENCE

When sharing drama with classmates, you have an excellent opportunity to emphasize what an audience is and how it shows its appreciation of theatrical events. An audience watches to learn and enjoy. It is polite and shows respect for the actors. Those children who form the audience from time to time should be as courteous to their classmates as they will want them to be when the roles are reversed.

ADDING TECHNICAL ASPECTS

Children will enjoy adding technical aspects to their plays, particularly if they are planning to share them with an audience. It is best to keep these additions simple and not clutter or overpower the most important part of a drama—the actors and the story.

Costumes can be simple pieces of material that are draped or tied around the child of any size. Cast-off-curtains, blankets, tableclothes, and fabric remnants do nicely. Hats and scarves are also useful.

Props should be made of simple materials. Many can still be pantomimed. Find ways to use objects creatively. For example, some third graders once played a version of "Jack and the Beanstalk" and for the beanstalk used a broom and a chair. Jack stood on the chair and held the broom high. Then, as he "climbed the beanstalk," he

A plastic bag, filled with a small amount of water and cooking oil, with added food coloring and aquatic ornaments, will give interesting visual effects when projected on a screen or sheet. Background scenery for *The Pond* by Carol and Donald Carrick.

went hand over hand along the broomstick. As the broom lowered to the floor, the illusion of climbing was effectively, yet simply, executed.

Scenery is usually never required. Children tend to get very literal about what is needed and should, instead, be encouraged to use their imaginations. Again, simplicity is the key.

Music and sound effects, if they aid the interpretation of the story, can also be added. Finally, some children will enjoy working on the technical aspects of the production more than performing in the story itself. Some may even show abilities in managing, designing, and executing these simple technical aspects. Encourage this and give as much attention to these technical artists as to the actors. You may even find some children exhibiting directing and other overall management skills. The theatre requires many artists to achieve the total picture. Who knows how many of these artists are waiting to be born in your own classroom?

NARRATIVE PANTOMIME FOR GROUP PLAYING

The following stories are arranged alphabetically according to titles. Suggested grade levels are listed in the left hand margin.

2–3 *The Bears Who Stayed Indoors*, Susanna Gretz. Chicago: Follett, 1970. Five bears and a dog named Fred spend a rainy day playing spaceship.

2–3 *Brownies—Hush!* Gladys L. Adshead. New York: Henry Z. Walck, 1938. This version of "The Elves and the Shoemaker" story has fourteen separate elves, but the story can be reworded so that all elves perform all the tasks.

1–3 *Chipmunk Stew*, Beth Weiner Woldin. New York: Frederick Warne, 1980. A fun story for three. Two chipmunks want to open a restaurant and hire a chipmunk chef, Pierre La Chippe. Dialogue can be mimed or easily edited out. Extra characters can be imagined or perhaps added in replayings.

2–3 *The Duchess Bakes a Cake*, Virginia Kahl. New York: Charles Scribner's, 1955. A bored Duchess tries her hand at baking and winds up on top of a huge cake. This is told in rhyme; dialogue can be pantomimed. Numerous characters. Some children can play more than one part, if desired.

2–3 *The Goblin Under the Stairs*, Mary Calhoun. New York: Morrow, 1967. A boy and his parents each have a special way of viewing the goblin who lives in their house. And the goblin lives up to each one's expectations. The narrator can also play the part of the neighbor.

K–2 *The Great Big Enormous Turnip*, Alexei Tolstoy. New York: Franklin Watts, 1968. Grandfather, grandmother, granddaughter, dog, cat, and mouse finally succeed in pulling up a turnip. One child (or more) can be the turnip. The text is simple and short. Encourage physical differences in the characters.

2–3 *Gregory*, Robert Bright. Garden City, N.Y.: Doubleday, 1969. Proud Gregory is fast, can jump high, and holler loud, but he has a problem listening. Use caution with the mule and bear riding. Encourage children to find ways to create the illusion of riding rather than simply sitting on one another's backs.

2–3 *Horton Hatches the Egg*, Dr. Seuss. New York: Random House, 1940, 1968. Horton, the Elephant who is "faithful 100 percent," hatches an egg for the lazy Maizie bird. It can also be done as a shadow play. See Chapter 13.

3 *Inspector Aardvark and the Perfect Cake*, Kathy Caple. New York: Windmill, 1980. Aardvark, with his two rat friends, searches for the perfect cake. Try it in threes. Although the rats do not have a lot of action, more can be added. Or, those who play the rats can also play the waiter, the police, and other minor characters.

1–3 *The King, the Mice, and the Cheese*, Nancy and Eric Gurney. New York: Random House, 1965. To get rid of mice, cats are brought into the palace. Dogs replace cats, followed by lions, elephants, and then a return to mice. There are numerous characters. Try slow motion for the chasing, with music or sound-effects background.

1–3 *Little Bear's Sunday Breakfast*, Janice. New York: Lothrop, 1958. The Three Bears story is told in reverse. Little Bear visits *her* house this time. You may want to edit the dialogue. Four characters are required.

K–2 *The Little Brute Family*, Russell Hoban. New York: Macmillan, 1966. Papa, Mama, Brother, Sister, and Baby Brute consistently have grumpy and unpleasant days until a little lost feeling enters their lives. A child can play the little lost feeling, or music can be played to represent it.

3 *Meal One*. Ivor Cutler. New York: Franklin Watts, 1971. Helbert and Mum, in Helbert's dream, plant a plum tree. It grows into the bed and down into the kitchen. Mum gets rid of it by setting the clock back an hour. Try it in groups of five: Helbert, Mum, and three to grow into the top of the tree and then to play the roots at the bottom.

1–2 *Papa Small*, Lois Lenski. New York: Henry Z. Walck, 1951. This is the story of the Small family, who all work together. Papa even hangs out clothes on the clothesline.

3 *Seven Skinny Goats*, Victor G. Ambrus. New York: Harcourt, Brace, Jovanovich, 1969. Jano, a young goat herder, does not realize his flute playing, which causes the goats and everyone else to dance, is not appreciated. Children will love the scenes of frenzied dancing. The control is that they must stop immediately whenever the music stops. And you (or a trusted designate) are in charge of the record player. You might let them all dance with one foot "glued" to the floor as in the game "Caught in the Act" in Chapter 4. Playing a recording of Sid Lawrence's "Swinging Shepherd Blues" at fast speed can also add to the fun.

3 *The Sneetches*, Dr. Suess. New York: Random House, 1961. Sneetches with stars on their bellies feel superior to those without. An enterprising salesperson, Sylvester McMonkey McBean, takes advantage of the situation. It is fun for children to become the machine. As many as ten children can play the various parts of the machine successfully if you plan with them their exact movements. (What part of the machine are they and what does that part do? See Chapter 9.) Because the story is Seuss and in rhyme, you will want to keep it just as it is, including the dialogue. Encourage the children to fill in appropriate

College students enact "The Sneetches" in garbage bag costumes.

mimed action during the speeches rather than mouthing the words. Seuss is easy to memorize for those who might want to add dialogue to the playing. The children may already be familiar with the story and the television production.

3 *The Story of Ferdinand*, Munro Leaf. New York: Viking, 1936. This classic story of Ferdinand, the bull who would rather smell flowers than fight in the bull ring, gives children the opportunity to learn about bullfighting customs. A parade of bulls, matadors, picadors, and others is always fun to add before the bullfighting scene. Use classical bullfighting music or Herb Alpert's "The Lonely Bull."

3 *Strega Nona*, Tomie dePaola. Englewood Cliffs, N.J.: Prentice-Hall, 1975. Strega Nona, or "Grandma Witch," has a magic pasta pot which Big Anthony misuses, and the town is flooded with pasta. There are numerous characters. Children also like to pretend to be the pasta pot, joining hands in a circle and jiggling to show the boiling. They might also like to become the spaghetti that boils up and over the pot and covers the town.

K–1 *Ten Bears in My Bed*, Stan Mack. New York: Pantheon, 1974. This is a counting story with each bear going out the window in a different way. Line up ten "bears" and let all the children sing out the "Roll over" lines. Even the littlest children can do this fun rhyme.

In-service teachers play dePaola's *Strega Nona*.

1–2 *The Three Bears*, Paul Galdone. New York: Seabury Press, 1972. This classic tale of a little girl who invites herself to the bears' house works nicely for a narrative pantomime. It can also be played solo with everyone being Goldilocks, but most children will want all four of the famous and familiar characters present.

3 *The Three Poor Tailors*, Victor G. Ambrus. New York: Harcourt Brace Jovanovich, 1965. Three tailors go off on the back of a goat to see the city and find fun, adventure, and trouble. It requires groups of four: three tailors, with a fourth to play soldier, innkeeper, and guards. It is more fun just to imagine the goat.

3 *The Way the Tiger Walked*, Doris J. Chaconas. New York: Simon & Schuster, 1970. Porcupine, zebra, and elephant try unsuccessfully to imitate the tiger's regal walk while monkeys watch the show. When the tiger imitates *their* walks, they return to their natural movements.

Three Poor Tailors (story by Victor Ambrus) ride off on a goat to seek adventure in the city.

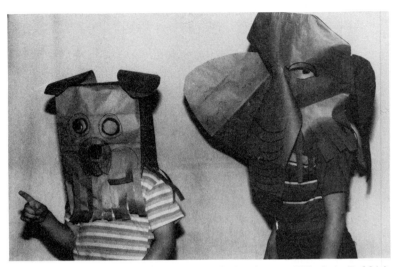

Rabbit tells Elephant about the monster in her house. (*Who's in Rabbit's House?* by Verna Aardema.)

It requires subtle humor and can be done simply or perfected into a finely tuned precision piece, perhaps with rhythm instruments for sound effects.

3 *Who's in Rabbit's House?* Verna Aardema. New York: Dial, 1977. In this African Masai tale, Caterpillar is in Rabbit's house and scares all the animals away. The pictures show the folk tale presented as a play performed by villagers wearing masks. Although there is dialogue, the narrator can still read while actors mime in masks. (Mask making suggestions in Chapter 13).

Further Uses of Narrative Pantomime 6

Once you have become familiar with narrative pantomime, you will quickly see that there are many other uses for it. You have probably already found a number of your own stories and poems suitable for narrative pantomime.

MATERIALS TO USE

NARRATIVE PANTOMIMES FROM LONGER BOOKS

Sometimes episodes from a single book can be easily adapted or spliced together for narrative pantomime. For example, Michael Bond's *Paddington* stories have many wonderful episodes useful for solo pantomime. This popular little bear is frequently undertaking an adventure such as wallpapering a room or cleaning out a chimney and, of course, running into all sorts of difficulties along the way.

NARRATIVE PANTOMIMES AND PUPPETS

Many of the narrative pantomimes in the previous chapter and this can be done very successfully with puppets. (See Chapter 13 for more information on puppetry.)

The narrative pantomimes can be used as a way to encourage

children to experiment with the various movements the puppets are capable of. Because the puppet's body has certain limitations of movement, much inventiveness will be required. But children will enjoy the discovery process and will get a basic anatomy lesson as well.

You will need to decide what kind of puppets you want to experiment with. Very simple stick puppets will not be able to move as much as a hand puppet, for example. Yet the simple puppets may be very effective with some stories. Very simple shadow puppets, for example, have been used successfully in telling Maurice Sendak's *Where The Wind Things Are* and *Horton Hatches the Egg* by Dr. Seuss.

NARRATIVE PANTOMIME WITH ADDITIONAL CURRICULAR SUBJECTS

Again, as you become familiar with narrative pantomime, you will quickly see that there are a great many excellent dramatic materials focusing on other areas of the curriculum such as social studies and science. Following is a list of excellent stories for younger children covering animal life cycles, career education, biography, and so forth. You can use these materials as they are, with editing in some cases, or as a stimulus for your own writing. Because they provide such rich experiences for children, you will not want to overlook any of them.

3 *All On a Mountain Day,* Aileen Fisher. New York: Thom. Nelson, 1956. This book has a chapter about each of the wild animals on a mountainside, from rabbit to bobcat.

2-3 *All Upon a Sidewalk,* Jean Craighead George. New York: Dutton, 1974. A yellow ant has an important mission to carry out in this exciting nature study.

2-3 *All Upon a Stone,* Jean Craighead George. New York: Thomas Y. Crowell, 1971. A mole cricket searches for and finds his fellow crickets. After a brief meeting he returns to his solitary life once again. It can be played solo. (Any of George's writings are superior science lessons and always dramatically written.)

2-3 *Amelia Bedelia,* Peggy Parrish. New York: Harper & Row, 1963. Amelia, a housekeeper, takes all her instructions literally. This popular character has been the subject of many adventures that are all good lessons in word usage. Usually it is easiest to let everyone play Amelia.

3 *And Then What Happened, Paul Revere?* Jean Fritz. New York: Coward McCann & Geoghegan, 1973. An accurate and amusing story of a national hero by one of the most popular history writers for children.

2 *Ants Have Pets,* Kathy Darling. New York: Garrard, 1977. This describes the life of Pogo, a farmer ant. It can be played in pairs to include the cricket ant.

2-3 *The Bakers,* Jan Adkins. New York: Charles Scribner's, 1975. This is a detailed description of bread making.

3 *The Barn,* John Schoenherr. Boston: Little, Brown, 1968. In an old barn, a skunk searches for food; yet to the mother owl, the skunk is food for her babies. It is suitable for solo playing.

1-3 *Bear Mouse,* Bernice Freschet. New York: Charles Scribner's, 1973. A meadow mouse hunts food for her young, escaping a hawk and a bobcat. It can be played solo.

2-3 *The Bears on Hemlock Mountain,* Alice Dalgliesh. New York: Charles Scribner's, 1952. Jonathan finds out that there are bears on Hemlock Mountain and discovers a unique way to hide from them. It is based on a Pennsylvania pioneer folk tale. Chapter 4 and part of Chapter 8 can be spliced and adapted easily for solo playing.

3 *Beaver Moon,* Miska Miles. Boston: Little, Brown, 1978. An old beaver is forced out of his lodge and searches for a new home.

3 *The Blind Colt,* Glen Rounds. New York: Holiday House, 1941. A blind colt must learn of the world, its joys, and its dangers. It presents a good lesson in adaptation to blindness.

K-2 *"Charlie Needs a Cloak,"* Tomie de Paola. Englewood Cliffs, N. J.: Prentice-Hall, 1973. This presents a simple narrative pantomime of the process of making a cloak, from sheep shearing to final sewing. There is not much dramatic tension unless it is played in pairs with the lamb who sometimes hinders and sometimes helps. Pictures show the lamb's antics, which are even more noticeable in the Weston Woods film of this story.

2-3 *Cosmo's Restaurant,* Harriet Langsam Sobol. New York: Macmillan, 1978. A young boy experiences a typical day at his family's Italian restaurant. Black and white photos add to the information.

3 *Coyote for a Day,* Roger Caras. New York: Windmill, 1977. A coyote searches for food and experiences several adventures in this story which begins, "Today you are a coyote . . . "

3 *C. W. Anderson's Complete Book of Horses and Horsemanship.* New York: Macmillan, 1963. There are many descriptive passages including a chapter on riding techniques.

K-3 *A Day in the Life of a Veterinarian,* William Jaspersohn. Boston: Little, Brown, 1978. This documents a vet's many duties with black and white photos.

K-2 *A Day of Winter,* Betty Miles. New York: Knopf, 1961. Numerous sensory experiences with snow are presented.

K-3 *Doctor in the Zoo,* Bruce Buchenholz. New York: Viking, 1974. It gives a fascinating account of the many duties of a zoo doctor and contains black and white photos.

2-3 *A Drop of Water,* Sam Rosenfeld. New York: Irving-on-Hudson, 1970. A drop of water is followed through its many changes in the environment.

K-2 *Elephants of Africa,* Gladys Conklin. New York: Holiday House, 1972. The adventures of a little elephant within the herd are presented.

2-3 *Fireman Jim,* Roger Bester. New York: Crown, 1981. A day in the life of a firefighter in Manhattan is documented with text and photos.

3 *Fox and the Fire,* Miska Miles. Boston: Little, Brown, 1966. A young red fox searches for food and is interrupted by a barn fire.

K-3 *How a House Happens,* Jan Adkins. New York: Walker, 1972. This presents the steps in the process of building a house, complete with diagrams.

K-2 *How Animals Sleep,* Millicent Selsam. New York: Scholastic, 1962. Descriptions of the sleep habits of several animals are given.

2–3 *How to Dig a Hole to the Other Side of the World,* Faith McNulty. New York: Harper and Row, 1979. Instructions are detailed for taking an imaginary 8,000 mile journey, beginning with a shovel and a soft place to dig to a no-spaceship with super-cooling system, fireproof skin, and a drill on its nose.

2-3 *The Little Old Woman Who Used Her Head,* Hope Newell. New York: Thomas Nelson, 1935. A little old woman of modest means lives alone on a small farm. The many problems she has and the unconventional ways in which she solves them have delighted children for years. It is good for introducing problem solving, since they will readily see her errors in logic. There are sequels available.

3 *Lone Muskrat,* Glen Rounds. New York: Holiday House, 1953. An old muskrat survives a forest fire and makes a new home for himself. His preparations for winter and his encounters with an owl, eagle, and other dangers make a dramatic nature study.

3 *Lone Seal Pup,* Arthur Catherall. New York: Dutton, 1965. A seal pup loses his mother and must fend for himself.

3 *Lucky Chuck,* Beverly Cleary. New York: William Morrow, 1984. A picture-book illustration of teenaged Chuck who pumps gas and has

a motorcycle is presented. He goes out for a ride and frequent references are made to the motor vehicle code that Chuck follows. Then he forgets himself, has an accident, and gets a traffic ticket. The last picture shows Chuck wondering how much gas he will have to pump to pay the fine. It teaches a good safety lesson with humor along with the fun of pretending to ride a motorcycle.

2-3 *Maple Harvest: The Story of Maple Sugaring.* Elizabeth Gemming. New York: Coward McCann & Geoghegan, 1976. Detailed description of the steps in the process of maple sugaring is presented.

2-3 *The Moon of the Winter Bird,* Jean George. New York: Thomas Y. Crowell, 1970. This shows the dramatic experiences of a sparrow trying to survive in northern winter weather.

2-3 *Nobody's Cat,* Miska Miles. Boston: Atlantic-Little, Brown, 1969. The adventures of an alley cat in the city and his struggles are told in a dramatic way.

1-3 *Octopus,* Evelyn Shaw. New York: Harper & Row, 1971. An octopus needs to find a new place to live.

2-3 *The Old Bullfrog,* Bernice Freschet. New York: Charles Scribner's, 1968. On a hot summer day, an old bullfrog sits on a rock looking asleep. The hungry heron edges up, one leg at a time, but at the last minute the wise old bullfrog makes his escape. Although the bullfrog does not have a lot of action, he is obviously the center of the conflict. It can be played in pairs or even 3's—as there are several other animals. A third player can play the other animals or create sound effects for them.

3 *Ox Cart Man,* Donald Hall. New York: Viking, 1979. This depicts day-to-day farm life in 19th century New England. Although more focus is on the father, we see the duties of each member of the household, so it can be played in a group. There is no strong conflict, but it is a very satisfying experience to play.

1-3 *Pagoo,* Holling C. Holling. Boston: Houghton Mifflin, 1957. The growth and adventures of a hermit crab are presented. Many sections of this longer book are suitable for playing.

K-3 *Pete's House,* Harriet Langsam Sobol. New York: Macmillan, 1978. This gives the steps in building a house with black and white photos.

3 *The Philharmonic Gets Dressed,* Karla Kuskin. New York: Harper and Row, 1982. Over a hundred members of an orchestra, including the conductor, are shown getting dressed and ready for a performance in this picturebook. You can read each section and let the children choose the clothes they want to put on and the instruments they want to play. Several can be chosen as the conductor, whose part can be rewritten to be female. At the end, play a short symphonic piece and

let the orchestra be conducted. (See "Conducting an Orchestra" in Chapter 4).

3 *The Pine Tree,* George Maxim Ross. New York: Dutton, 1966. A pine tree struggles for survival in this story. It is a simple topic, but the story is beautifully written and highly dramatic.

3 *The Plymouth Thanksgiving,* Leonard Weisgard. Garden City, N.Y.: Doubleday, 1967. Simply presented are the details of the events leading up to the first Thanksgiving. Numerous characters for groups or the entire class to play are included.

K-1 *Policeman Small,* Lois Lenski. New York: Henry Walck, 1962. Policeman Small is a traffic policeman on a busy day. Tension is built through his many activities including a traffic accident.

3 *The Pond,* Carol and Donald Carrick. New York: Macmillan, 1970. This is a sensitive, poetic description of movements of water, insects, and all life near and in a pond. Try Debussy's "La Mer" as background music. Children can play all the parts solo or divide for group playing. It presents beautiful movement possibilities and would also be good for live-shadow or shadow-puppet play. (See Chapter 13).

3 *A Prairie Boy's Winter,* William Kurelek. Boston: Houghton Mifflin, 1973. This is a picture book with separate descriptions of the many rigors and pleasures of living on the Canadian prairie in the 1930's.

3 *A Prairie Boy's Summer,* William Kurelek. Boston: Houghton Mifflin, 1975. This sequel to the above book is equally enchanting.

3 *Rattlesnakes.* G. Earl Chace. New York: Dodd, Mead & Co., 1984. A prairie rattlesnake is followed through her life cycle. It contains good detail and black and white photos. The story may be excerpted from the section where the snake first makes her move into the world through the end of Chapter 3 after she eats her first meal.

2 *Red Legs,* Alice E. Goudey. New York: Charles Scribner's, 1966. This is the story of the most common grasshopper in the United States.

2-3 *Roadrunner,* Naomi John. New York: E. P. Dutton, 1980. The hurrying desert roadrunner, a comic figure, spends his day running, chasing, and racing with twists, circles, and sudden stops.

3 *Salt Boy,* Mary Perrine. Boston: Houghton Mifflin, 1968. A young boy rescues a lamb in a storm and gets his wish: to learn to rope a horse. Edit this for solo playing.

2-3 *Skunk for a Day,* Roger Caras. New York: Windmill & Dutton, 1976. This book begins, "Today you are a skunk," and then details a day's events. It is illustrated with black and white drawings.

2-3 *Stores,* Alvin Schwartz. New York: Macmillan, 1970. This book presents much data on the day-to-day operations of forty different stores in one community. Short sections describe the work of each storekeeper or worker and numerous black and white photos illustrate the material.

2-3 *Sugaring Time,* Kathryn Lasky. New York: Macmillan, 1983. Through words and pictures we follow a family in Vermont during the maple sugaring season.

3 *Tarantula, the Giant Spider,* Gladys Conklin. New York: Holiday House, 1972. This explains that tarantulas are useful creatures that need not be feared.

K-3 *Three Days on a River in a Red Canoe,* Vera B. Williams. New York: Greenwillow, 1981. A young boy tells of his camping adventure with his mother, aunt, and cousin. With very little editing this can be played in groups of four with second and third graders. Some rewriting is needed for solo or paired playing.

2-3 *Time of Wonder,* Robert McCloskey. New York: Viking, 1957. This is a sensitive description of a summer's experiences in Maine. Detailed information on many aspects of summer life in this part of the country, including a storm, is given.

K-2 *The Very Hungry Caterpillar,* Eric Carle. New York: Collins Publishers, 1969. A voracious caterpillar prepares for eventual change into a but-

Mother and children huddle together during the storm.

terfly. This very simple nature lesson will delight even the youngest child.

3 *Vulpes, the Red Fox,* John and Jean George. New York: Dutton, 1948, The descriptive and sensitive story of the life cycle of a fox is presented. Many episodes are usable.

2-3 *The Web in the Grass,* Bernice Freschet. New York: Charles Scribner's, 1972. This colorful picture book tells the story of a little spider's dangerous and friendless life.

1-3 *What Can She Be? A Police Officer,* Gloria and Esther Goldreich. New York: Lothrop, Lee & Shephard, 1975. It tells of the day's work of law enforcement officers. (Other books in the What Can She Be? series include such occupations as farmer, geologist, and film producer.) Black and white photos illustrate.

3 *The White Palace,* Mary O'Neill. New York: Thomas Y. Crowell, 1966. This is a beautifully illustrated story of a salmon's life.

K-3 *Window into an Egg,* Geraldine Lux Flanagan. Reading, MA: Addison-Wesley, 1969. This is the detailed account, with black and white photos, of the development of a chicken egg which has had a ''window'' cut into it. Use the end section entitled, ''Hello Chick.''

1-3 *Who Needs Holes?* Sam and Beryl Epstein. New York: Hawthorn, 1970. A simple book illustrates some basic science concepts.

3 *The Wounded Wolf,* Jean Craighead George. New York: Harper and Row, 1978. Roko, a wounded wolf in the Alaskan wilderness, is saved from death by Kiglo, the wolf pack leader. It is based on fascinating research of wolves' behaviors. Solo playing probably is best.

1-3 *Your First Airplane Trip,* Laura Ross. New York: Morrow, 1981. This is a useful description of what an airplane trip is like. There is little conflict except for a bit of bumpiness in the ride, but it is a very satisfying experience to play.

WRITING YOUR OWN MATERIAL

As you work with narrative pantomime, it will become rather obvious what works well and what does not. Soon you will feel comfortable trying your own ideas, focusing on the experiences you want your students to enact. Eventually you will be able to narrate short passages ''off the top of your head,'' which is similar to the technique of side-coaching (encouraging or talking children through drama experiences). Remember the following tips:

1. Keep the action continuous and moving along from one event to another.

"Don't forget to put suntan lotion on your nose." Getting ready to go to the beach.

"At the fair you eat some salt water taffy—and it gets stuck in your teeth. . . . "

2. Keep the action as immediate as possible. Time lapses and repeated shifts from place to place can lessen the dramatic impact.

3. In side-coaching particularly, the sense of immediacy can be aided with the use of present tense and "you" (either stated or implied) in the wording. "Now, (you implied) zip up your jacket and put on your backpack. . . . "

4. Be aware of the beginning, middle, and end of any selection. Build to a climax and follow it with a satisfying and quieted resolution.

5. As you narrate or side-coach your material, add or delete details of action as they are needed by the children. Sensory and emotional description is often helpful to add. Some children will be very imaginative and will act out many ideas while others will need ideas described. Watching the children as they play will be the best way to know how much assistance your students need. You will have to find a happy medium between the most and the least imaginative child in your class.

The following short episodes are presented to stimulate your own thinking and get you started.

SAMPLE LESSON PLAN
A Plane Ride
Original Narrative Pantomime

(*Note:* This is an example of paired playing with action divided between the two players. The leader narrates and also plays a role of control-tower operator.)

Objectives

a. Give students an experience in paired pantomime in a dramatic storyline.

b. Learn about a form of transportation and details of flying a small biplane used by famous flyers.

Preparation and Materials

a. Space: Desk area

b. Equipment: (optional) record player and record

c. Music: (optional) "Those Magnificent Men in Their Flying Machines" playing softly in background

d. Visual aids: pictures of biplanes; flyers such as Amelia Earhart or Charles Lindbergh. See also: *The Glorious Flight: Across the Channel with Louis Bleriot, July 25, 1909* by Alice and Martin Provenson (New York: Viking, 1983).

e. Session length: 30 to 40 minutes

Motivation

Ask if children have ever taken a plane ride. Have they ever been in a small plane—not a jet or a large propeller operated plane—like a Stearman biplane? (Show pictures of plane and perhaps some famous flyers like Amelia Earhart or Charles Lindbergh.) Discuss some of the differences in the smaller planes and modern jets of today (only two seats, open cockpit, and so forth).

Preparation for Playing

"We're going to pretend to be flying a Stearman biplane. We'll do this in pairs at your desks; one of you will be the pilot and one the student learning to fly. We'll play twice so you will each have the chance to play both parts. (*Pair students and let them decide who is playing which part first.*) Now in this plane, the pilot sits behind the passenger-student. Pilot, take your place. The biplane will need to have its propeller twirled to help the pilot start the engine. Student, this would be good for you to learn, so you stand at the side of the plane by the propeller and be ready to do that."

Playing

(*Begin narration*) "You're going to take a ride across some low mountains and land on the other side. We're expecting some bad weather through the mountains, so there could be a little difficulty. The landing will also be difficult, because the mountains surround the landing field. Pilot, fasten your seat belt and shoulder harness. Make sure they're on tight. You'll have to take your signal from the control tower, so put on your earphones. You need to make contact with the control tower and make sure everything is all set for takeoff. You'll get your signal from me.

(*Leader holds hand to mouth to make a muffled sound as if speaking over the radio transmitter.*) "Biplane NC 211, cleared for takeoff.

"Pilot, adjust your engine controls. Student, rotate the prop several revolutions to redistribute the oil in the cylinders. Now, spin the prop to start the engine. Whoops, the engine just coughs and sputters (*sound effects from you*). Guess this old plane will need several spins to get started. You'll have to try again. There! The old engine throbs to life. Pilot, apply the brakes. Student, pull out the wheel chocks. Now, hurry and climb aboard. Be sure to fasten your seatbelt and harness, too.

"Student, listen carefully. In front of you is a stick that controls the plane's direction. It is connected to the pilot's control stick. By placing your hands lightly—I repeat, lightly—around it, you will be able to follow the pilot's sensitive control. In this way, you can get the 'feel' of the plane.

"Both of you be sure your goggles are in place. Now, pilot, let up on the brake and taxi down the end of the runway. You'll have to zigzag the plane so you can see beyond its nose. That's it, lean a little to the right, now to the left, right, left. Good.

"You're almost at the end of the runway now, so quickly pull the stick toward you. Remember, student, when the stick is forward, it makes the plane go down and when the stick is pulled toward you, the plane goes up. Now the plane is rising off the ground. Up you go! Check your compass to make sure you're going north toward the mountains. Look down below you. The airport is small and far away.

"You're going through the mountains now. You're starting to breathe a bit more rapidly because of the thin air up here. Oh, oh, It looks like you're going into a storm. Be sure to bank the plane so the wings don't tip too much one way. They should be kept level with the body of the plane. It's starting to rain hard now. Reach up to the top of your control panel and press the blue button on the right to start the windshield wipers.

"If you look over to the left you'll see a flash of lightning. Careful, don't look too long. Keep your eyes on the altimeter to be sure you stay well above the mountains.

"Keep watching for the mountain tops so you can be sure to pass over them. Careful! There's a peak right in your course. Quickly, bank the plane or you'll hit it. Whew! That was a close call.

"It looks as if you're passing through the storm safely. You're almost on the other side of the mountains now, and the landing field is coming up on the right. Pick up your radios and let's make contact with the control tower and let them know you're coming in for a landing.

(*Leader as control tower.*) "Flight NC211. Cleared for approach to landing. Approach from the southeast.

"Now check your seat belts and prepare to circle the landing field until you can come in for a safe landing.

"Let's bring the plane down easy. You have to go slow because the fog is thick and you might miss the field. There it is! You're right on course. Stand by for a landing. Check the air-pressure meter next to the lever control. Now get ready to pull back the brake lever when you touch ground. You're almost there. Bump, you're down. Ah, that was a good landing. Pull back on the brake lever and let's bring it to a stop. A perfect three-point landing! Congratulations!

"Pilot and student, shake hands and show thumbs up!''

SAMPLE LESSON PLAN
An American Colonial
Child's Morning
Original Narrative Pantomime

Objectives

a. Experience a paired narrative pantomime based on early American Colonial lifestyle.

b. Become more familiar with the tasks experienced by both boys and girls their age during Colonial times.

c. Become more familiar with vocabulary words such as: porringer, well-sweep, settle, churn, johnny cake, hasty pudding, tankard, and so forth.

Preparation and Materials

a. Space: Children can play at their desks or in a small area of space (*Note:* Even though this is a paired narrative, boys can play Thomas' part and girls can play Jenny's part without needing to interact. Other characters are just imagined.)

b. Equipment: (Optional) pictures of colonial homes and the items discussed in the pantomime to help children visualize the experience

c. Session Length: Approximately 30 minutes, assuming a brief discussion of information and one playing

Playing

(Narration begins.) "It is an early spring morning in your colonial home. You're awake, but you lie still for just a few moments, Jenny under the warmth of your quilt in your feather bed and Thomas in the turn-down bed with your brother in the corner of the kitchen. You're both called once again, and you hop up quickly and get dressed.

"Mother tells Thomas and his brother to go without shoes and stockings today in order to save the shoes. Thomas wriggles his toes on the chilly floor and shivers a little, but he is glad not to have to bother with shoes. Thomas dresses quickly in his pants and shirt and Jenny in a coarse dress.

"You both pour water in a basin to wash your face and hands. The well water is cold, so you wash quickly, then rub your face briskly with a rough linen towel from a roller on the door. Now it's time for breakfast.

"The grownups will sit on settles, but you will each take your

"The well water is cold, so you wash your face
quickly."

porringer from the dresser and stand quietly behind the settle.
Breakfast this morning is corn meal mush, or hasty pudding, a
large, thin johnny cake browned in a skillet, and a tankard of milk
that has been cooled in the cellarway. You are grateful for such
good food and a cow that gives you milk to drink because you
know this is a luxury many people do not have.

"After prayer, you eat quickly, as there is much work to do.
Father will work in the fields with the older sons. For Thomas and
Jenny, there is plenty to do in the kitchen. Jenny helps Mother
clear the table, folding the cloth and the napkins which will be
used again. Thomas is to take down the dried apples hanging from
strings on the kitchen rafters. Jenny takes them outdoors to the
well to wash them.

"Now Thomas begins churning the butter. The churn has been
left near the hearth so that the cream is warm enough. Thomas
churns the dasher up and down and wonders whether there will
be any time for play today. It will take a long time to make the
butter and there are many other chores to do today, so Thomas
knows he will have to just churn and be patient.

"Jenny returns from the well with the washed apples so that
Mother can make a pie of them. While Mother makes the crust,
Jenny is told to sew on some quilt pieces. She takes her sewing
basket to the dooryard in order to see better, because the sewing
must be in very tiny stitches. She settles herself in the doorway

and takes out the quilt pieces, needle, and thread. She threads her needle, making a very small knot in the end of the thread. Jenny is eager to work on the squares as she knows they will eventually make a quilt for her older sister who is to be married in the spring. The pattern is called 'Job's Troubles,' and has many hexagonal blocks of material. Jenny hums a little tune softly to herself and works diligently, pausing every now and then to watch the sun slowly rising higher in the Eastern sky. The sun helps to warm the chilly air of this early spring day.

"Mother tells Thomas he can stop churning now, as the butter must have 'come.' She will gather the butter while he is to go to the well to get a pail of fresh water. Thomas runs to the well outside the house, glad to be free of the butter churning. The wellsweep creaks in the spring breeze. Thomas pulls on the vertical pole to lower the wooden bucket into the water. Because the horizontal pole is weighted, it does not take much pull to operate. Thomas watches the bucket fill and then lifts the pole to bring the bucket up again. It's hard to carry a full bucket of water back into

A narrative pantomime of "The House that Jack Built," with simple cardboard scenery and paper masks, is shared with an audience outdoors.

the house, but Thomas carries it carefully and shifts it from one hand to the other as he makes his way, stopping once to set it down before going on.

"Thomas breathes a sigh of relief as he arrives in the kitchen. But then he suddenly stumbles and the bucket hits against the open butter churn. The churn, half full of buttermilk, crashes to the floor. Because the floor slopes toward the door, the buttermilk runs out toward the doorway where Jenny is sitting. She jumps out of the way just in time. Jenny and Thomas rush to help set the churn upright in order to save as much buttermilk as possible. Then they help mop up the spilled buttermilk with old cloths Mother gives them. It's a shame to lose good buttermilk. Jenny and Thomas can tell Mother is unhappy for the moment.

"Now it is nearly lunch time and father and the older boys will be coming in from the fields where they have been working all morning. Thomas and Jenny help set out the cold boiled salmon, and dried apple pie, johnny cake and milk. They both sit near the doorway to watch the workers come in from the fields, glad to have a moment's rest before lunch and the afternoon's chores."

7 Pantomimes For Guessing

When children play the narrative pantomimes in the preceding chapters, they focus on self-expression and the playing of ideas and stories for their own satisfaction. In this section, the emphasis will be on developing pantomime skills further, conveying and translating specific nonverbal ideas and messages.

Acting out pantomimes for someone to guess is an age-old game as well as an art form. The childhood game of "Statues" can be played endlessly as players enjoy being "swung" into frozen position for "It" to guess. You can make use of such games, capitalizing on their entertaining features, as well as encouraging the development of pantomime skills. You can also use numerous other curriculum topics for the pantomime games.

GUIDING PANTOMIME PLAYING

Because pantomime for guessing requires an audience/performer situation, try to avoid having only one child at a time pantomiming in front of the rest of the class. This places too much pressure on the performer, who may become shy and inhibited or develop show-off behaviors. Also, if the other children have to wait their turn too long, they can become bored. Therefore, all of the following games are designed to have as many children involved as possible while still focusing on skill development.

To guess a pantomime, you have to watch closely for clues.

You will be encouraging the pantomimers to communicate ideas nonverbally as clearly as possible and motivating the guessers to develop skills of observation, analysis, and synthesis in translating the messages. Challenges and learning experiences are thus equally shared by both pantomimers and audience guessers.

Pantomime, like all nonverbal communication, is ambiguous. This is its fascination. We speculate on it, guess, and test our accuracy constantly. You will need to aid the children in realizing that it may take a little time to figure out what a pantomimer is doing. And, a pantomime may look like several things at the same time.

As the children pantomime, you should identify, through verbal feedback, the various clues the children are giving:

"You must really have a lot of experience giving your dog a bath. I could almost see a real bottle of shampoo and the water splashing on you!"

Sidecoach and speculate out loud on the thinking process in making a guess, perhaps even giving a possible idea or two. Note how this can help the players as well as the guessers.

"I wonder what Sandy and Chris might be carrying? It must be something that's too big for one person to carry. I wonder if it's heavy?"

Discuss how pantomime is not always clear and how one thing might be mistaken for another.

TEACHER: John, how did you know that Marcos was looking into a mirror on the wall and not a picture hanging there?

JOHN: Because he was smoothing down his hair when he was looking.

Limit the guessing whenever possible. This challenges the performers and the guessers to do their best work. Little ones may even forget what their own pantomime was if the guessing goes on too long!

Shy children may seem disappointed to think they have been unsuccessful if their pantomimes are not guessed immediately. Sometimes they will even say you have guessed the right answer—even if you have not. With them you might say, "That's a hard one! You have us stumped. You'll have to tell us what it was," to point out the ambiguity of pantomimes.

Outgoing children often are disappointed, angry, or think they have been unsuccessful if their pantomimes *are* guessed immediately. Often they want to confuse an audience so they can keep on pantomiming. They may say the guess is wrong—or not quite accurate enough. For these children you might say, "You did that very well. We guessed right away," to encourage giving good clues.

PANTOMIME GAMES

 HALF AND HALF

One half the class acts out a pantomime for the other half to guess.

1. Divide the class into two groups.
2. Assign topics or let children take turns giving their ideas.
3. Ring bell or switch lights after perhaps 30 seconds to end the pantomime.
4. Individuals guess.

COUNT FREEZE

Several players pantomime simultaneously in front of the rest of the class, each performing his or her own idea on a given topic. Pantomimers may also work individually, in pairs, or even in threes.

1. Select topic.
2. Choose perhaps five to eight volunteers to pantomime.
3. Count to five or ten while audience watches (counting may be as slow or as fast as seems necessary) and then say "Freeze."
4. Audience guesses aloud only after players are frozen.

Eating different foods in a "Count Freeze" pantomime.

5. Players may be seated as they are guessed.

6. Repeat until all who wish have had a chance to play.

Tip: Challenge audience to guess as many of the pantomimes as possible. "Who thinks they can guess all five sports you saw?" Otherwise, children may just watch one friend and ignore the other pantomimers.

PANTOMIME SPELLING

Words are spelled out by forming letters with body.

1. Play as "Count Freeze" above.

2. Number of players determined by number of letters in word spelled.

3. All letters acted out at same time. Audience can try guessing the word even if they are not sure of each letter.

PANTOMIME SPELLING II

Words are spelled out by children acting out other words beginning with the appropriate letters. For example, the word "cat" may be spelled out by pantomiming other animal words such as c—camel, a—alligator, and t—tiger. Or, the topic might be transportation; the word "car" could be spelled out by miming the eating of various foods as c—corn on the cob, a—apple, and r—ribs.

1. Play as "Count Freeze" above.

2. Number of players determined by number of letters in word to be spelled.

In-service teachers spell out T-A-M-P-A using occupations: T-truck driver, A-artist, M-magician, P-pianist, and A-acrobat.

3. All letters acted out at same time. Audience can try guessing the word even if they are not sure of each letter. (Like working a crossword puzzle.)

Option: Let guessers work in groups to solve the "puzzle" word.

ACTING OUT TITLES

Similar to charades, this pantomime has several children at a time acting out the titles of songs, stories, or books. For example, four children might pantomime "Little Red Riding Hood." The first person could indicate "little" by crouching, the second could point to something red, the third could pretend to ride a horse, the fourth could mime putting a hood up over the head.

1. Play as "Count Freeze" above.
2. Number of players determined by number of words in title.
3. Again, all words are acted out at same time.

Option: Let guessers work in groups to solve the "puzzle" title.

FROZEN PICTURES

Small groups plan a scene appropriate to a given topic and freeze themselves into position. Scenes might be from favorite stories such as Max taming the Wild Things in Maurice Sendak's *Where the Wild Things Are.* Or, the scenes might demonstrate the working of community helpers like fire fighters or police officers.

SEQUENCE GAMES

Pantomime actions on cards are acted out sequentially by players.

1. Prepare cards, using pictures or written instructions, in a particular sequence with cues for each previous pantomime.
2. Cards are distributed at random to individuals, pairs, or even three players per card.
3. Cards are played in sequence with player(s) correctly interpreting the cue to their pantomime. There is much suspense waiting for one's cue and the chance to play as well as to see the chain of events or story unfold. (Note: Laminated cards will last longer.)

Example: The first card reads:

*You begin

YOU: Pretend to get out of bed. Yawn and stretch. Sit.

Cue: After you see the hunter point the gun. . . .
You: Pretend to be an angry cougar. (Sequence Game)

The second player's card reads:

CUE: After someone gets out of bed and yawns,

YOU: Get dressed for school. Sit.

Other cards might tell players to wash face, make the bed, eat breakfast, brush teeth, and so forth.

Tips:

Cues may be written in red (stop and look) and the directions written in green (go ahead). For very young children, pictures may be used instead of, or in addition to, the printed directions.

You should have a master list of all the actions in sequence in order to monitor the playing.

Children might also like to try their hand at creating and making the cards for their own sequence games.

Topics which are particularly fun and work well are activities which follow a step-by-step procedure (e.g. how to make something) or have a storyline. You can even convert children's favorite stories to sequence games.

Actions can also be alphabetized, perhaps even omitting the cues. For example, "food" might be the topic. First might be the miming of eating "Apple," followed by "Banana," then "Cereal," and so forth. The alphabet itself can serve as the cue. See *The Marcel Marceau Alphabet Book* by George Mendoza (Garden City, N. Y.: Doubleday, 1970) for an excellent example of this.

ADD-ON PANTOMIMES

These are similar to the sequence games except that the children act out their own ideas to fit with the previous player's.

1. You select a topic or let children select their own.
2. First player begins an activity such as vacuuming.
3. The rest of the players assist the first by adding on the actions of dusting, washing windows, and so on to create the scene of *cleaning*.

Tips:

It is more fun and more dramatic not to guess out loud, but just quietly add on. An entire scene of activity then unfolds before the audience's eyes almost magically.

You may wish to have children raise their hands when they guess the initial activity. You can then check their answers privately with them as well as their ideas for adding to the scene. This precaution saves confusion in case some children may be guessing incorrectly. More than once "vacuuming" has been mistaken for "plowing a field!" After children become more familiar with the game and with pantomiming, they will probably want the challenge of plunging ahead without having you check first just to see what will happen.

VARIATION ADD-ON

An object is created by several people, each adding on his or her part. Example: The first child might become the wheel of a bicycle. Others add on the rest of the parts (seat, handlebars, basket, and so forth) one by one.

Tips:

Small groups may decide ahead of time what they wish to create.

Audience can guess at any time during the adding on or they may be asked to wait until the group has finished.

For the adventuresome, one child becomes the first part of an object while others add on as they wish and as they *guess* what the object is. Of course, there is more room for error with this method, but it is fun to see the varieties of interpretation.

BUILD A PLACE

Children create a room or location by pantomiming the various furnishings or objects needed.

1. Mark off a space on the floor. If the space is to be a room, mark the doors and entryways. Use chalkboard erasers or books to mark the four corners. For young children you may want to use masking tape. For building a room area, use two doorways so that several children at a time can play.
2. Players pantomime bringing one item at a time into the space and place it appropriately. If the space is a room, they must go through the doors and not the walls. They must also remember where each previous item is and not walk over or through it.
3. Guess each object after it is brought into the space.

Tips:

As children show skill in this game, add the challenge of requiring them to use a previous item in some way after they have pantomimed

In-service teachers bring imaginary objects into an imaginary room in the pantomime game "Build a Place."

their own addition to the room. For example, after bringing in a table to the Three Bears' House, they might try sitting in Papa Bear's chair that has already been brought in.

Even spaces that are not enclosed (as a room) can be created in this game. Children have enjoyed building playgrounds, parks, shopping malls, and so forth.

INTRA-GROUP PANTOMIMES (Third Grade)

Pantomimers enact ideas just for the audience members in their small group. The advantage of this method is that the audience is small and the pantomimes go quickly, reducing the focus on the person. Even the most reluctant child will find it difficult not to get caught up in this game.

1. Divide class into several groups of five or six persons.
2. In each group, two will guess what the others pantomime in a limited time period of perhaps two minutes.
3. Instructions might be: "Pantomime all the words you can think of that begin with the letter *s*."

4. The pantomimers do not confer with each other; each thinks of his or her own ideas and enacts as many of them as time permits.

5. The two guessers work as quickly as possible and write down the ideas. If an idea cannot be guessed quickly, either the pantomimers or the guessers may say, "Pass."

Tips:

Avoid counting up the number of words on each list afterward and introducing competition into the game. A better learning experience is to discuss the words that were "most unusual," "hardest to guess," or "most frequently used words." Combine the lists for other purposes and projects: a class display of brainstorming for ideas.

Caution the students to work quietly *so they do not give away their ideas to the other groups.* (This game can get a little noisy, and this reasoning works better than just telling them to keep quiet!)

Use topics that have numerous possibilities or answers. For example: rhyming words for *at,* household chores, ways we use water, words beginning with the consonant blend *st,* and so forth.

ADDITIONAL IDEAS FOR PANTOMIMES

The following additional topics for pantomime may be used with one or more of the methods discussed in the chapter.

Who Am I (Are We)? Act out community helpers, storybook or nursery rhyme characters, people in the news, television characters, and so on.

What Am I (Are We)? Pantomime animals, toys, machinery, and so forth.

What Am I (Are We) Doing? Act out verbs (running, skipping, jumping), or more complete ideas like making a cake, driving a car, or milking a cow.

What Am I (Are We) Seeing, Hearing, Testing, Smelling, Touching? Pantomimers react to various sensory stimuli: seeing a ghost, tasting unsweetened lemonade, listening to loud music, smelling a flower, or walking on hot sand with bare feet.

What's the Weather? Players act out clues for classmates to guess the seasons or the climate. They may act out seasonal sports or daily chores related to certain times of the year or they could act out wearing appropriate clothing for the climate (rainy, cold, hot, windy).

What Am I (Are We) Feeling? Act out various emotions. Older children might try to limit expression of emotion to just the face, or just the hands. (You can hold up a sheet to make just face or hands visible.) Emotions can also be combined with the "doing" pantomime by showing an action as well as how you feel about doing it (e.g. a household chore you do not like to do). For older children the pantomime may be extended to acting out a brief scene showing more than one emotion or a scene in which something happens to change the feeling. For example, "You are happily packing a picnic basket when you suddenly notice that it's raining. So now you can't go on the picnic and are disappointed."

Where Am I (Are We)? Pantomime being in various locations—at a zoo, on a farm or ranch, in a haunted house, in a hospital, and so forth.

Let's Get Ready To Go. Pretend to pack supplies for various adventures such as going on a fishing trip, preparing for a hike, loading a covered wagon, preparing for a space launch, and so forth.

Transportation. Players pretend to travel in various ways: on foot, bicycle, skates, bus, airplane, and so forth.

Dress Up. Pretend to be certain people dressing in their appropriate clothing for what they are or do: an astronaut, a baseball player, a ballet dancer, a traditional Indian, a Pilgrim, and so on.

Foods. Pretend to eat various distinctive foods: spaghetti, corn on the cob, ice cream cone, pizza, hot dog, and so on. Students can also do the four basic food groups (fruits and vegetables; bread and cereal; dairy products; meat, fish, and poultry.)

Health and Hygiene. Players demonstrate various good (or bad) habits such as brushing teeth, washing clothes, getting exercise.

Occupations. Act out various jobs—perhaps what they want to be when they grow up; jobs described in stories they read; jobs held by people they know or those they have seen on television, and so forth.

Tools. Demonstrate various tools people use to perform certain occupations or tasks: kitchen, carpentry, sewing, household, doctor's, teacher's, and so on. Third graders may be challenged by historical tools such as a blacksmith's bellow, a weaver's loom, or a Pioneer's butter churn.

Machines. Demonstrate simple tools such as levers, wedges, and pulleys, as well as more sophisticated machines such as electrical appliances or construction equipment. Third graders may want to use their bodies to become the machinery.

Sports. Enact favorite sports or favorite athletes. For older children you may want to categorize into team sports, Olympic events, winter sports, and so forth.

Animals. Different groups of animals might be enacted: pets, zoo animals, circus animals, farm animals, and so on.

Musical instruments. Pantomime the instrument of choice.

Safety. Pantomime the *do's* and *don'ts* of various activities such as use of playground equipment, water sports, camping activities, household safety rules, or rules for dealing with natural disasters.

First Aid. Demonstrate proper way to treat a cut or scratch, insect bite, burn, or other minor accidents.

Festivals and Holidays. Act out various activities associated with holidays in the United States (Fourth of July, Thanksgiving, Memorial Day, and so on) or other celebrations children enjoy (Halloween, Valentine's Day, Christmas or Hanukkah, and so on.) Children may guess the custom and the holiday.

PANTOMIME SKITS AND STORIES

Some third graders may be ready to do some pantomime skits and short stories on their own in small groups. It will be easier for them to work with skits and materials they already know, such as familiar folk tales ("Three Billy Goats Gruff"), or a favorite story from a basal reader, or even a television show.

You may need to give guidance in choice of material, who plays which part, and other minor assistance. You may also have some simple costumes and props the children can use. Sometimes the story or skit will evolve from the costumes and props. For example, if children see a bowl and spoon, they will probably think of "Little Miss Muffet" or "The Three Bears." Or, a piece of red material may remind them of "Little Red Riding Hood."

You may need to allow time for groups to play at these stories. This is more easily handled if only one or two groups at a time are "rehearsing." Perhaps this can be done while you are working with the rest of the class on some other tasks; or it may be done during a recess time or lunch period. It is helpful to have a play corner which is somewhat secluded from the rest of the class so that playing can go on without disturbing others.

It is not always necessary for these stories to be shared with the rest of the class. Young children will need time to explore on their own before even desiring to present or share anything. But sometimes children will feel that they do want to share and will ask to do so. At such times, you can be fairly sure that their ideas, to them, have been worked out and they are ready to do their version of putting on a play.

As the children share their playing, the audience of classmates may become restless if they do not understand what the story is or what is happening. While they can be guided to focus on the more interesting aspects of the story, it is best not to subject them to extended periods of watching what they do not understand. On the other hand, you will also note that they sometimes understand their classmates' interpretation of a story better than we adults do, so be alert to that possibility as well.

Do not insist that children use only pantomime. Often in reenacting a familiar story, children will remember much of the verbal dialogue and want to repeat it. Furthermore do not expect a finished performance. This activity is suggested to provide those children who are ready for it the opportunity to share some ideas. Often what the children demonstrate is a loose plot and perhaps some episodes or parts of a story. But their satisfaction in doing so will make it worth everyone's effort.

Verbal Activities and Improvisation **8**

You will always be looking for ways to encourage children to express themselves through verbalizing, improvising dialogue, and interacting with others in drama activities. As you have probably already noticed, the children in your classroom vary in their readiness to verbalize. Some comfortably improvise dialogue at the drop of a hat while others are more reticent in self-expression.

You will want to have available to you a range of verbal activities to choose from which will correspond to the different skills your students exhibit. This chapter will give you many selections, ranging from the easier to the more difficult. Remember, however, that while the simple activities can be particularly useful for encouraging shy children to participate, they can also be creatively challenging to all children.

BEGINNING VERBAL ACTIVITIES

SOUND EFFECTS (Imitating Sounds)

Creating sound effects can be an excellent learning experience as well as great fun for all. The voice is a marvelous instrument of sound and can have an extremely wide range of possibilities when we take the time to explore it. Without saying a word at all, there can be great flexibility of communication.

Children will enjoy doing this sort of experimentation. And you will soon discover that there are so many places in the curriculum for this activity. While the children have fun they will also be learning facts, experimenting with the physics of sound, and creating settings and environments of the mind. Sound effects can also be highly dramatic by themselves or when coupled with other material.

Sound Effects from Literature

There are many excellent stories and poems in literature that children can experiment with. Some of the earliest sounds children imitate are those of the world around them—animals, transporation, weather, and so forth. Much of children's literature focuses on just such sounds.

The easiest way to begin these activities is simply to narrate the material (as you did before in narrative pantomime) and to pause for the children to make the sounds in the appropriate places. The list of literature at the end of this section covers a broad range of subjects for you to choose from. For example, the delightful books of Margaret Wise Brown tell stories about a little dog Muffin who, for different reasons in each book, must guess about all the sounds he hears. Many sounds are ordinary, but others are challenging and may require a bit of discussion. What would "butter melting" sound like? Or a grasshopper sneezing? Children are delighted by thinking of the possibilities and certainly have a greater appreciation of the story after working with it in this fashion.

Tips:

1. Some sounds are best made by one child or by just a few children while other sounds will require the entire class. Experiment to see what procedure will give the best effects.

2. Control the sounds by using an indicator for volume control. Some leaders use an arrow made of wood or cardboard or an oversized pencil. One teacher used a cutout picture of an ear on a stick and simply raised and lowered it to indicate on and off and intensity of volume.

3. It is probably best *not* to let children operate the volume control!

4. Do not try to do too much at a time. Children may get tired doing an entire book.

5. Try tape recording the stories after they have been rehearsed a few times so children can hear themselves. It will be easier for them to evaluate their work this way.

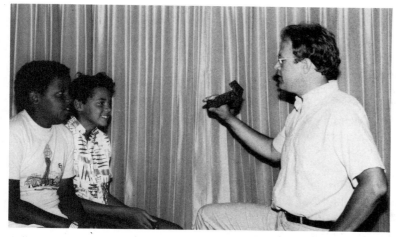

Follow the arrow to know when to make the sound and how loud it should be.

6. Try adding some musical sounds or other nonvocal sounds for variety. Rhythm band or Orff instruments have endless possibilities. Experiment also with objects in the classroom that make noise.

SUGGESTED LITERATURE

(*Note*: Numbers at the beginning of each entry indicate suggested grade levels. Numbers in parentheses refer to numbered anthologies listed in the bibliography at the end of this book.)

K–3 *Bam Zam Boom!* Eve Merriam. New York: Walker and Company, 1972. A poet graphically describes demolition day which brings the excavating and rebuilding of a city apartment house. The picturebook has black and white photos interspersed with colorful artwork.

1–3 "The Bed," Pura Belpre (49). The noise of an old-fashioned bed squeaking frightens the little boy and several animals under it in this Puerto Rican folk tale.

K–2 *Country Noisy Book*, Margaret Wise Brown. New York: Harper Row, 1940. There are farm and countryside animals for Muffin the dog to hear this time.

2–3 *Georgie and the Noisy Ghost*, Robert Bright. Garden City, N.Y.: Doubleday, 1971. Sound effects are important in the story of Captain Hooper's ghost getting a medal for bravery.

K–3 *Good-Night, Owl!*, Pat Hutchins. New York: Macmillan, 1972. Owl has trouble sleeping because of the sounds made by other animals in the tree. He gets his revenge when it is his turn to be awake.

1–3 *Klippity Klop,* Ed Emberley. Boston: Little, Brown, & Co., 1974. Prince Krispin and Dumpling go for a ride and meet a dragon in a cave. This is similar to "The Bear Hunt" in Chapter 3.

3 *The Little Woman Wanted Noise*, Val Teal. New York: Rand McNally, 1943. A woman moves from the city to the country and misses the city noises.

K–2 *Little Toot*, Hardie Gramatky. New York: G. P. Putnam's Sons, 1967. A little tugboat, who at first only wants to play, experiences accomplishment when he is able to help a stranded ocean liner.

K–1 *Mr. Brown Can Moo! Can You?* Dr. Seuss. New York: Random, 1970. Mr. Brown makes all kinds of sounds from a bee buzzing to a hippopotamus chewing gum and encourages readers to do the same.

K–2 *Mr. Grumpy's Outing*, John Burningham. New York: Holt, Rinehart and Winston, 1970. Children and animals join Mr. Grumpy in his boat. They all do what he says not to do and fall into the water. Children can add movement, too.

1–2 "Night Noises," Tony Johnston. (28) Mole and Troll learn that sounds in the night are not made by monsters. Young children will be able to identify with Mole's and Troll's fear and will be reassured themselves.

K–2 *The Noisy Book*, Margaret Wise Brown. New York: Harper and Row, Pub., 1939. Muffin, a little dog, gets a cinder in his eye and must guess at the many sounds he hears.

1–3 *Noisy Gander*, Miska Miles. New York: E. P. Dutton, 1978. A young gosling does not understand why his father honks at everything— until a fox enters the barnyard.

1–3 *Noisy Nancy and Nick*, Lou Ann Gaeddert. Garden City, N.Y.: Doubleday, 1970. Two children get in trouble for being too noisy.

K–1 *Oh What a Noise!* Uri Shulevitz. New York: Macmillan, 1971. A simple text and brightly-colored large pictures feature a little boy experimenting with different noises in order to delay bedtime.

2–3 *Plink Plink Plink*, Byrd Baylor. Boston: Houghton Mifflin, 1971. A young boy hears various sounds at night before he goes to sleep and imagines all the things they could be. For example, he imagines a "clump bump" to be a pirate clumping on a wooden leg, but it is branches hitting the door.

K–2 *Quiet Noisy Book*, Margaret Wise Brown. New York: Harper and Row, Publishers, 1950. Muffin, the dog, awakes very early and hears the very quiet and unusual sounds of a new day. This is a challenging listening lesson.

K–3 *Sounds All Around*, Jane Belk Moncure. Chicago: Childrens Press, 1982. This book presents all kinds of sounds from the ping of a toaster to fireworks and teaches some basic concepts about hearing sounds.

3 *Too Much Noise*, Ann McGovern. New York: Houghton-Mifflin, 1967. An old man tries to find the solution to too much noise in his house.

K–2 *Winter Noisy Book*, Margaret Wise Brown. New York: Harper and Row, Publishers, 1947. Muffin, the dog, hears the sounds of winter both indoors and out.

Original Sound Effects Materials

Once you have tried some of the above selections you will be ready to compose some of your own. You might even create a group story with the children or encourage them to write their own.

1. The stories can be based on a number of other materials being studied. For example, a story about the weather experienced during the seasons of the year or a story surrounding the events in a particular holiday. The stories might also center in a particular location such as a supermarket, a seaport, a zoo, or even school.

2. For speech improvement, some teachers of young children have focused stories on sounds many children have difficulty pronouncing such as ''s,'' ''sh,'' ''th,'' or ''r.'' The sounds can represent specific things such as the ''s'' indicating the hissing of a snake, ''sh'' might be waves on a shore, ''th'' could be air escaping from a balloon, and ''r'' the sound of a car motor. The sounds can be combined in a story about the adventures of a snake who travels by boat, balloon, and a car to seek his fortune.

3. Another variation of sound effects is to select favorite stories and assign certain sounds to each of the characters. Each time the character is mentioned in the story, the sound is made. Consider the characters' looks and personality in order to determine the most appropriate sounds. (Papa Bear's and Baby Bear's growls would be different, for example. Would Goldilocks' sound be a tinkling bell, a whistle, or perhaps a giggle?)

SEQUENCE GAMES

As in the pantomimes for guessing, we can create sequence games for verbal activities, too. In this case, the sequence game is really like performing a short, very simple, play script. For third graders, you will see opportunities to encourage appropriate interpretive

Interpretive reading skills are encouraged in verbal sequence games.

reading of the lines, pointing out how timing and vocal dynamics help.

Children will need to have time to work on sequence games. It will be helpful to treat the first reading as a run-through and a chance to get an overview of the material. Sometimes the first reading is very slow, and you may even wonder if the children are following what is happening. But usually children will ask to repeat the sequence games so they can switch cards and perfect their reading. After several playings, there is usually an automatic improvement in reading.

As with the pantomime sequence games, for verbal sequence games the cards are made up with a cue and a line to read. The cards are distributed at random. (*Note:* Again, it is a good idea to laminate your cards so they will last longer.)

The first card might say:

*You begin the game.

YOU: *Stand and say,* "Good morning, everyone. Welcome to the

Second Grade's Parade of Mother Goose Characters." *Bow and sit.*

Another player will have the card that reads:

CUE: "Good morning, everyone. Welcome to the Second Grade's Parade of Mother Goose Characters." *Bow and sit.*

YOU: *Stand and say,* "Brought to you by Henny Penny's Chicken Farm." *Sit.*

and so forth until a sequence of events or a story is told.

Sequence Games from Literature

There are a number of stories and poems which have interesting dialogue or statements in a series that provide excellent material for sequence games and can be used just as they are written. Alphabet and number books are also enjoyed by younger children as are simple riddle and joke books. Because of their built-in sequence, the alphabet, number, and riddle books may not require cues. Following are some suggestions:

(*Note*: Numbers at the beginning of each entry indicate suggested grade levels. Numbers in parentheses refer to numbered anthologies listed in the bibliography at the end of this book.)

3 *Alexander and the Terrible, Horrible, No Good, Very Bad Day*, Judith Viorst. New York: Atheneum, 1972. Everything goes wrong for Alex-

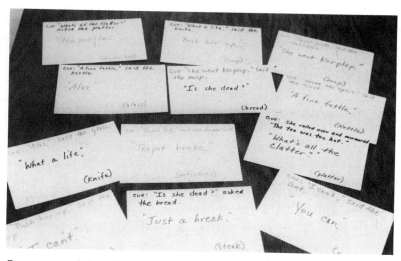

Sequence cards based on a poem or story make a game of reading aloud.

ander one day. He thinks he will go off to Australia until his mother tells him there are bad days there, too.

2–3 *Alfred's Alphabet Walk*, Victoria Chess. New York: Greenwillow, 1979. Alfred learns the alphabet by going on a walk and sees, among other things, "a herd of hungry hogs hurrying home."

2–3 *At Mary Bloom's*, Aliki Brandenberg. New York: Greenwillow, 1976. A little girl's mouse has babies and she wants to tell her neighbor, Mary Bloom all about it. But she worries about the series of events that may happen. Since these events are noises like baby crying and dog barking, you can add sound effects to this story, too.

3 *The Day Jimmy's Boa Ate the Wash.* Trinka Hakes Noble. New York: Dial Press, 1980. A chaotic class trip is told about through dialogue between mother and child.

3 *Don't Forget the Bacon*, Pat Hutchins. New York: Greenwillow, 1976. A grocery list—six farm eggs, a cake for tea, a pound of pears, and don't forget the bacon—turns into nonsense as a little girl struggles to remember each item. In the end she forgets the bacon!

2–3 *A Flea Story*, Leo Leonni. New York: Pantheon, 1977. Two fleas on a dog decide to go on an adventure. The book consists of the two fleas' dialogue with each other. Try this as a shadow play, too.

3 *Fortunately*, Remy Charlip. New York: Parents', 1964. For each unfortunate happening, a fortunate one follows.

3 *The Green Machine*, Polly Cameron. New York: Coward, McCann & Geoghegan, 1969. A reckless automobile creates havoc along country gardens. You may want to shorten this rather lengthy story.

3 *"I Can't," Said the Ant*, Polly Cameron. New York: Coward, McCann & Geoghegan, 1961. A broken teapot creates a problem for the various inhabitants of the kitchen to solve. This one is also rather lengthy and may need to be shortened.

1–2 *I Don't Want to Go to School*, Elizabeth Bram. New York: William Morrow, 1977. A little girl is reluctant to go for her first day of kindergarten.

2–3 *If You Give a Mouse a Cookie*, Laure Joffe Numeroff. New York: Harper and Row, Publishers, 1985. Once you give a mouse a cookie, he will want one thing after another until we are back to the beginning. You can add, "And you know what happens if you give a mouse a cookie," and play the game all over again.

3 *Jimmy's Boa Bounces Back*, Trinka Hakes Noble, New York: E. P. Dutton, 1984. This time the boa attends a garden party. This is a sequel to the above book about Jimmy's Boa. You can end with a frozen picture the way the book ends.

3 *Magic Letter Riddles*, Mike Thaler. New York: Scholastic, 1974. By adding and subtracting letters in words, you can find the answers to these riddles.

1–3 *My Mom Travels a Lot*, Caroline Feller Bauer. New York: Frederick Warne, 1981. This is a listing of the good and also the bad about having a mom who travels.

2–3 "One Inch Tall," Shel Silverstein (53). What is it like to be one inch tall? This poem is good for math concepts.

1–2 *One Was Johnny*, Maurice Sendak. New York: Harper and Row, Publishers, 1962. A forward and backward counting rhyme has some actions to add for extra fun.

3 *Pierre: A Cautionary Tale*, Maurice Sendak. New York: Harper Row, 1962. A little boy who always says "I don't care" decides to care when a lion eats him. Perhaps have one person play Pierre (with complete script if needed) to say the "I don't care" lines.

2–3 *The Popcorn Book*, Tomie dePaola. New York: Holiday, 1978. Children make popcorn while reading facts about it. Intersperse the popcorn maker's comments with the facts being read, just as the book does.

2–3 *Rain Makes Applesauce*, Julian Scheer. New York: Holiday House, 1964. A collection of absurd, but delightful, statements are fun to say in as many different ways as possible.

3 *The Sheriff of Rottenshot*, Jack Prelutsky. New York: Greenwillow, 1982. Almost all the poems in this collection are useful for sequence games and reading aloud.

3 "Sick," Shel Silverstein (53). Little Peggy Ann McKay complains of being too ill to go to school—until she discovers it's Saturday!

3 *Space Alphabet*, Irene Zacks. Englewood Cliffs, N.J.: Prentice-Hall, Inc., 1964. "A is for astronaut, a sailor among the stars."

3 *Squeeze a Sneeze*, Bill Morrison. Boston: Houghton Mifflin, 1977. This is a rhyming game of nonsense, such as "Can you tickle a pickle for a nickel?"

2–3 *What Do You Do, Dear?* Sesyle Joslin. Reading; MA: Addison-Wesley, 1961. This is a book of manners for unusual occasions. Pantomime is fun to add to this one.

2–3 *What Do You Say, Dear?* Sesyle Joslin. Reading, MA: Addison-Wesley, 1958. This is a book of manners for just the right thing to say in strange situations.

3 *Where in the World is Henry?* Lorna Balian. Nashville: Abingdon, 1972. In this question and answer game a mother and child cover an interesting geography lesson. ("Where is the city?" "The city is in the state," and so on).

2–3 *Where's My Cheese?* Stan Mack. New York: Random House, Inc., 1977. This is a story about a piece of cheese and is told in simple dialogue.

2–3 *Who, Said Sue, Said Whoo?* Ellen Raskin. New York: Atheneum, 1973. The moral of this story is "Words aren't everything!" Good sound effects exist in this one.

Original Sequence Games

After trying some of the above materials, you will soon find many of your own sources for sequence games. You may even be inspired to make up your own. Third and even some second graders might want to try their hand at this kind of game. For example, a simple riddle sequence game can be made up of quotes from favorite stories.

CARD 1: (You begin). "Little pig, little pig let me come in."

CARD 2: (Answer) The Big, Bad Wolf. "What a good boy am I."

CARD 3: (Answer) Little Jack Horner. "Who is the fairest of them all?"

BEGINNING IMPROVISATION

In creative drama, dialogue is usually played *improvisationally*. This means that it is created spontaneously, on the spot, as the children respond to the dramatic situations they are involved in. It is more natural than the memorization of "canned"

CUE: When someone says, "What time is it when the clock strikes 13?"

You stand and say, "Time to get the clock fixed!"

Joke books are easy to turn into sequence games.

speeches and is an excellent exercise in learning to "think on one's feet." The spontaneity of improvisation captures everyone's attention—even the players themselves. No one knows exactly what will be said, but what you do know is that it will evolve from a "real" person rather than from a printed script.

As you work toward the goal of encouraging improvisation of dialogue, you will need more challenging activities. We will begin first with the activities that do not require extensive response and build progressively to more extensive improvisation.

ONE LINERS

Often it is easiest to begin with one-liners since children need to say or create only one line of speech.

One Liners with Pictures

1. Keep a file of pictures of people or animals in interesting poses or situations, exhibiting unusual feelings. Pictures should be large enough for everyone to see easily. Large ads from magazines, calendar pictures, and posters work well for this activity.

2. Show pictures to the children and ask them what they think the person might be saying.

3. They pretend to be the person in the picture, saying the statement the way they think the person or animal might say it.

One Liners in Sequence

1. Many famous one liners already exist from television and from literature. Every child probably knows the one liner "Cookie!" from Sesame Street's Cookie Monster or "Let's get Mikey!" from the Life Cereal television commercial.

2. Children can generate a list of their favorites, perhaps placing them on cards, and read them as in the sequence games. It is particularly fun if the one liners seem to relate to each other. (Who's been sleeping in my bed?" "It is I, Big Billy Goat Gruff." "I'll huff and I'll puff and I'll blow your house down." "E. T. phone home.")

STORYTELLING

Storytelling is an excellent verbal activity to help children imagine and create plots. It also encourages the building of details and making of inferences.

Children may build group short stories using the round-robin technique, with each volunteer adding another line to the story.

When ideas flow freely and children are comfortable with storytelling, you may need to set limits on each one's contribution. Using an egg timer or a bell, make it into a game. A ball of knotted yarn is another intriguing way to conduct storytelling. As the "yarn is spun," the ball is unraveled. When the knot is reached, the ball is passed to another child.

Storytelling with Wordless Picture Books

1. One of the easiest ways to begin storytelling is to use wordless picture books which have no text but tell a story in pictures.
2. The children interpret what they see happening in the pictures, using their own words and sometimes even adding dialogue.

Not all wordless picture books tell a story, and not all pictures are big enough to show to an entire class, so careful choice will be important. Some of my favorite examples for young children are the following:

2–3 *The Bear and the Fly,* Paula Winter. New York: Crown, 1976. A bear family has difficulty getting rid of a pesky fly. Humorous violence occurs as the bears swat each other and the fly escapes.

1–3 *Changes, Changes,* Pat Hutchins. New York: Macmillan, 1971. A wooden man and woman create needed objects out of miscellaneous wood pieces to solve the many difficulties they run into. This is also available on film from Weston Woods.

1–2 *Clementina's Cactus*, Ezra Jack Keats. New York: Viking, 1982. A little girl waits patiently for a desert cactus to bloom and is finally rewarded.

1–2 *Deep in the Forest*, Brinton Turkle. New York: Dutton, 1976. Like Goldilocks, a curious bear cub visits a cabin in the woods and finds porridge, chairs, and beds to try. A must for all Three Bears lovers.

1–2 *Do You Want to Be My Friend?* Eric Carle. New York: Thomas Y. Crowell, 1971. A lonely mouse goes looking for a friend and finally discovers another mouse.

1–2 *Lily at the Table*, Linda Heller. New York: Macmillan, 1979. Lily has a problem with seven green beans, a chicken leg, and sliced potatoes—until she creates new uses for each of these and more in a fantasy world of food.

K–2 *Rolling Downhill*, Ruth Carroll. New York: Henry Z. Walck. A cat, who knocks over a sewing basket and becomes entangled in yarn with a dog, has quite an adventure with a series of other animals before getting out of her dilemma.

K–2 *What Whiskers Did*, Ruth Carroll. New York: Henry Z. Walck, 1965. A poodle puppy has an adventure chasing a rabbit down a hole.

2–3 *Who's Seen the Scissors?* Fernando Krahn. New York: E. P. Dutton, 1975. A tailor has scissors that fly away from him and set off on a cutting adventure through the town.

2–3 *The Wrong Side of the Bed*, Edward Ardizonne. Garden City, N.Y.: Doubleday, 1970. A young boy's day goes from bad to worse when he has problems with both family and older children.

Storytelling with Pictures

1. Large pictures of interesting people or animals involved in unusual situations can also stimulate storytelling.

2. Generally you will need to start out the story with a rousing or imaginative beginning to get the children interested. (Picture of a girl on horseback: "Once upon a time there was a girl who had a magical horse that could take her anywhere she wanted to go.")

3. You may also need to introduce conflict and help children bring the story to a close. *Variation*: Use several pictures with a related theme or setting. After beginning the story with one picture, add others to stimulate continued storytelling.

Storytelling in Character

Children will also enjoy telling stories, pretending to be another character. They may also want to try out character voices, gestures, and attitudes in their storytelling.

1. There are many literary sources that show storytellers in action. For example, in the story *Frederick*, by Leo Lionni (New York: Pantheon, 1967), the little poet mouse tells stories to help his friends and relatives forget their hunger. What sort of stories would a little mouse tell to entertain an audience of mice? And how might he sound, with his small, squeaking voice?

2. There is also Sam in *Sam, Bangs, and Moonshine* by Evelyn Ness (78) who tells moonshine, or unreal, stories. Students might try creating their own moonshine story.

3. There are also possibilities for storytelling in other areas of the curriculum. Some students of mine once were doing a lesson on cowboys in a second grade. When I entered the room, they were all gathered in one corner on a rug with the lights dimmed. They were pretending to be around the campfire at night, telling stories about their day's activities. Three children were given the role of "Chuck-

wagon Charlie,'' who periodically gave the listeners some ''bowls of stew'' to eat quietly while the storytellers entertained them.

More Storytelling Variations

1. ''What's Happening Here?'' Use interesting and colorful pictures with people or animals involved in unusual situations or even conflicts. These pictures may show us the middle of the story. But, how did the story begin? How will it end? (Children may even wish to tell the story from the point of view of one of the characters.)

2. ''What's the Word?'' When children show skill in storytelling, they enjoy greater challenges. Try telling stories using new vocabulary words, spelling words, foreign words, and so forth.

3. ''Math Manipulations.'' Tell stories using mathematical operations from simple counting (''*One* day, Big Bird decided to take a walk. *Two* monkeys decided to go along. Suddenly, *three* friends yelled, 'Help!')'' to other calculations, such as multiplication by 2. (Once there were *two* kings who lived in neighboring countries. They each had *four* daughters. The *eight* princesses were very good friends, but the kings were jealous of each other.)

4. ''Alphabet Story.'' Tell a story with each sentence beginning with a letter of the alphabet in sequence. (''*A*nthony wanted a bicycle. *B*ut, his mom said there wasn't money in the budget to buy one. '*C*an you think of a way to earn money?' she asked him.'')

5. ''What's that Sound?'' Tell a story suggested by a series of sounds (knock on the desk, blow a whistle, tear a piece of paper, and so on). What kind of story does that suggest? Or, start with one sound to begin the story and continue the story with each added sound.

6. ''Skeleton Stories.'' Make up stories using the skeletal framework of props, characters, or settings to stimulate ideas. Motivation will be enhanced if you have the props on hand along with pictures of the characters and settings. Examples:

Props: a miniature broom, a piece of jewelry, a decorative box
Characters: a witch, a king, a clown
Settings: haunted house, schoolyard, castle

Experiment with combining the categories, too. Endless possibilities exist for this one.

VERBAL GAMES

Games in which children pretend to be other characters set in verbal situations are useful for stimulating dialogue. These games are easy to organize and can involve the entire class. The goal of these games is to explore dialogue situations and to search for information and ideas. General procedures for verbal games are:

1. Groups of five to eight children take turns being panel members. The rest of the students are the audience/questioners.

2. You serve as the moderator/host. For young children, you may also need to do most of the questioning, especially in initial attempts, or have some questions written on cards for students to ask.

3. To encourage roleplaying, simple costumes may be employed, such as badges, paper bands for the head, or other special indications of status.

Experts

1. Panel members are declared to be experts on a subject; the rest of the class questions them. Kindergarteners might be Santa Claus's elves, answering questions on how they make certain toys; third graders might be the tooth fairy, explaining various ways to use the teeth collected from children.

Trinkets such as these can stimulate ideas for the Experts Game:
a. knitters of miniature leg warmers for birds
b. inventors of homes for insects
c. designers of hats for fairies
d. barbers who specialize in the troll trade

2. Whenever possible, try to give roles to everyone. While the panel is composed of elves, for example, the questioners could be parents. With the tooth fairy, the questioners could be dentists.

Juvenile Jury

1. As a variation of an old radio and television show, this game features a panel of children who give advice on particular problems.

2. The audience poses certain questions or situations, such as, "My little brother always wants to play with my toys and I don't want him to." Such problems can sometimes be more easily solved by peers than by adults trying to impose rules. Frequently, children repeat advice they have heard from adults, but it sounds more acceptable when a peer gives it.

3. Advisers will love wearing kindergarten graduation robes (disposable kind) for this activity.

Character Panel

For this game, panel members are characters from a variety of sources. For example, the panel might all be Goldilocks. The audience asks her whatever questions they wish. "Did you like being in the Bear's House?" "Did your mother spank you when you got home?" "What were you doing in the woods all by yourself?"

IMPROVISING DIALOGUE IN SCENES AND SKITS

Improvised dialogue is most dramatic and often most easily generated when tension or conflict is present. Have you ever noticed how talkative people become when there are two (or more) sides to an issue to debate or simply discuss? People seem to talk the most when there are problems to face. So, you will get more participation from the children if you choose topics where dramatic conflict and tension are present. They will also get caught up in the fun of the playing and be drawn into excellent problem-solving exercises as a result.

It is not always necessary to bring any discussion or debate to a final close. The airing of views is initially the most important goal. If you or the children do want to conclude—to settle upon some decision—you should probably set this goal at the beginning: "Try to find an answer to your problem." While not all children will be able to do it, problem-solving will be a challenge to those who can. Often a unique and unexpected compromise comes out of these discussions, and that can be a great source of satisfaction for everyone.

SOURCES FOR DIALOGUE MATERIALS

Literature is full of such dialogue situations. Some stories have crucial scenes focusing totally on verbal interaction. Remember the verbal guessing game between the Queen and Rumplestiltskin as she tries to find out his name? In fact, some pieces of literature are totally dialogue. For example, in a delightful story called *Not This Bear!* by Bernice Myers (New York: Four Winds, 1967), a little boy in a furry coat and hat has to convince a family of bears, who are sure he is one of their relatives, that he is not one of them.

Dialogue scenes can also be added to stories and incorporated with other areas of the curriculum. For example, scenes of buying and selling (social studies emphasis) can be added to *Caps for Sale* or *The Elves and the Shoemaker*. Characters in stories frequently have to ask for assistance or other favors, providing opportunity to learn appropriate skills in behavior. The Thanksgiving season prompted one group of second graders to be turkeys trying to talk hungry Pilgrims with muskets out of eating them for dinner!

Simple Debate (Method 1)

1. Divide the class in half and give each an opposite viewpoint to uphold. You can simply play this at the desks.
2. With this technique, everyone has a part to play and identify with even though they may not feel confident enough to voice their opinions. Let children switch sides after a while, so they have the opportunity to see both sides of an issue.
3. You play the role of discussion moderator/mediator.

Literature Example: In Watty Piper's story *The Little Engine that Could*, a stalled train cannot deliver the dolls and toys over the hill for Christmas. Other trains are asked for help, but they think they are too big and important to bother with toys.

Half the class can be the dolls and toys; the other half play the various bigger trains. The dolls and toys try to convince the big trains to help them. The big trains have to give their reasons for not wanting to be bothered.

You can play the engineer of the stalled train and call on those volunteers who have something to say. You may also pose questions to each side, if this assistance seems helpful. ("What will happen if the toys don't arrive on time? What sorts of jobs do the big trains have to do that are so important? Dolls and toys, has this ever happened to you before? Do the big trains know of anyone else who could help?'')

Social Studies Example: A similar kind of scene might be played between the pilgrims and the crew of the *Mayflower* based on Wilma Hays's book (63). The captain wants to help the Pilgrims get settled before leaving them to fend for themselves in a new country. But he is also worried about his crew. They are anxious to get home because it is December and the sailing will be difficult. Each day the crew members are becoming more hostile. Both the crew and the captain had wanted to be home for Christmas, but now it is impossible.

One half the class plays the Pilgrims; the other half plays the ship's crew.

You can play the captain and moderate the two sides of the argument, encouraging a discussion of the various reasons for going or for staying.

Simple Debate (Method II)

1. Select a situation that has two points of view. (You can use the above examples, but here is a new one: a moon creature meets an astronaut and wants to come back to Earth in the spaceship; the astronaut says "no.")

2. Brainstorm in a discussion with the children some of the different reasons the space creature would give for wanting to go to Earth. Then brainstorm some of the reasons the astronaut would give for not being able to take the moon creature.

3. Now pair the students and let them rehearse/try out the debate briefly—at their desks—all talking at the same time. (It will be a little noisy for a few moments, but you will survive.) Switch roles and repeat.

4. Let students share their ideas as follows:

    a. Select several volunteers for sharing. You might have five pairs in front of the class. (Do not forget that you can double cast and have more than one child in a role.)

    b. Give each pair a number. The pair may talk when you call out their number.

    c. Call numbers randomly and give each pair a few moments to share.

There are several advantages to this procedure for sharing. First of all, a number of children are allowed the opportunity to share, so they do not have to wait long to get a turn. Second, you are in control of the sharing. If some children have little to say, you simply call another number to relieve the pressure on them. Some children, if they cannot think of something to say, may begin to giggle with embarrassment or possibly start to fight. By being able to simply call another number, you can bail them out, too. (You can call their numbers again after they have had a little break to collect their thoughts.) This procedure also makes it easy to cut off those who would go on forever if you let them.

Creating and Playing Short Skits

Children, particularly third graders, may eventually want to create their own skits in small groups to show to the rest of the class. Usually, they will reenact stories that are fairly familiar to them, such as folk tales or shows they have seen on television. Some youngsters who have seen the·famous MGM *Wizard of Oz* film several times, for example, can reenact the scenes quite accurately and with great detail.

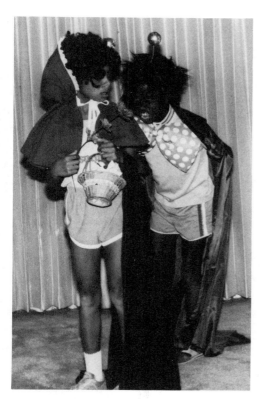

Little Red Riding Hood is met by a different sort of Wolf.

Often their skits will be short and rather episodic (without a completed ending). If they enjoy doing it and seem to get satisfaction from working together to create their stories, then you will probably want to encourage them to work toward an ending. You may need to press for this, particularly if their skits have strong conflict. If they have not thought of an ending, then arguments, shouting, or a physical fight may be all they can think of to do. And, sometimes they cannot even bring *that* to a close!

Once, after asking some children to be sure to plan an ending for their scene, I asked if they knew *why* I had requested it. One answer was, "So we'll all know when to quit." I think that says it pretty well, and I often share this with children to make my point.

In spite of this precaution, there still may be times when children reach a dead end. You then have several options.

a.   You may walk up to them privately and quietly ask, as a reminder, "Do you have an ending?"

b.   If an ending is not forthcoming, you may be able to narrate them out of the difficulty.

c.   You might even step into the scene as a mediator character and negotiate. For example: Some third grade children were playing the story of "Taper Tom" or "The Princess Who Couldn't Laugh" (40). They had divided into groups of contestants who were to attempt to make the Princess laugh. As in the story, the groups came to the palace, tried their hand at getting laughter from the Princess,

A "play-makers' corner," complete with some costume pieces and props, encourages skits and play making.

and were dismissed after being unsuccessful. One group, pretending to be a musical band, was reluctant to leave, arguing that they thought they were the best group and should be declared winners. When it was clear that there was no end to the argument, the leader narrated:

"And so, even though the band thought they were very good musicians, the Princess was not amused enough to laugh. The Princess was called to dinner by her parents, and the band left to play an evening concert in a neighboring kingdom."

The leader might also have stepped in as the King, Queen, or other higher authority and perhaps pretend to give a token gift to the musicians and then ceremoniously announce the next group of contestants.

Audience for Skits: As before, you may have to guide the audience's behavior. Some children are not unduly critical of each other and may, in fact, identify with and be sympathetic to classmates who falter.

But there are those who will become impatient. They think *they* would know what to say or do in the same situation, so they may call out instructions. "Maybelle, tell him you don't want to go!" "Psst, George, given him a shove!" Sometimes, just a quiet reminder will do. At other times you may need to explain that prompting from the audience interrupts the players' thinking and does more harm than good.

Evaluation: Children sometimes say they need more rehearsal time or that they do not like what they have planned. Obviously, they are aware that elements are lacking, and the best remedy may be to allow them to keep improvising together and working out the ideas rather than evaluating them.

If children have a great deal of confidence in their ability to create skits, you may decide to ask the audience of classmates to give their evaluation. Positive evaluation is paramount so you will need to word the discussion questions carefully. Your own positive feedback will be important, especially if some students insist on being overly critical of classmates.

Standard questions might be:

What did you like about the scene?

What moments were the most enjoyable for you? Why?

If you could do it over again, what would you want to change? Why? How successful do you think the ending was to your scene? Why? What dialogue was especially believable?

SKIT IDEAS

Familiar Stories

An easy beginning for group skits are reenactments of familiar material such as favorite fairy tales or television shows, television commercials, and other material students have seen numerous times. After brainstorming for topics as a class, children divide into groups to plan their dramas.

Silent Movies

Students can create skits from old silent movies or films shown with the sound turned off. Check the school media center for films and filmstrips of wordless picture books that may be used for this purpose.

Sunday Funnies

Select Sunday cartoon strips with enough action that the basic plot of the situation is understandable. Block out the dialogue and have students create the story in their own words.

Talking Pictures

Select pictures that show several people (or even animals or objects) in a problem situation. Students select the picture they want to work with and develop a skit around it.

Planning a group story with props takes cooperation.

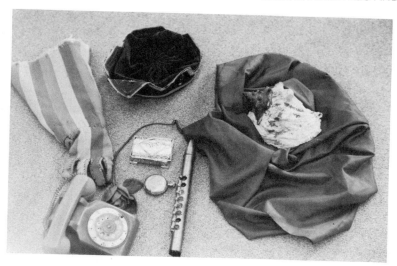

Props can stimulate story ideas.

Prop Stories

a. Keep a selection of props and some costume pieces.

b. Select three or four for each group to base a skit on.

c. After the stories are planned, students may add other props and
    costumes to the skits.

9

Encouraging Creative Work

Many children create easily and freely. Others will need encouragement and guidance from you in developing into creative thinkers. This chapter will help you find ways to encourage creative work. First we will look at some fairly simple creative activities and ways to guide their playing. In the second half of this chapter, we will show you a way to help children create their own stories for dramatizing.

WHAT IS A CREATIVE ACTIVITY?

In creative drama, whenever we ask children for their own thoughts and ideas about what to play or how to play it, we are encouraging creativity. The activity may range from acting out one's own idea in a brief pantomime to creating an original story.

EXAMPLES OF SIMPLE CREATIVE ACTIVITIES
FOR SOLO UNISON PLAYING

1. Exploratory Movement: "Squeeze into the smallest (or biggest, softest, or longest) thing you can be. What are you?"
2. Favorite Story: "Let's pretend that you are the Troll under the bridge in 'The Three Billy Goats Gruff.' The story doesn't tell us, but I wonder what the Troll does all day long. I'll let you decide. When the music starts, you pretend you're that Troll." (Play some-

Be as small as you can be. . . . What are you?

    thing like Grieg's "In the Hall of a Mountain King," from *Peer Gynt*.) (Children might pretend to fish, twiddle thumbs and wait for juicy billy goats to pass by, or file claws.)

3.   Study of Shapes: "This time, pretend you're using something that is in the shape of a circle—maybe you'll ride a bicycle, or eat a doughnut, or swing a lasso." (Idea based on Ed Emberley's *The Wing on a Flea,* Boston: Little, Brown, 1961).

4.   Interpretation of Musical Selection: "As I play Saint-Saëns' 'Danse Macabre,' you'll be the skeletons rising from your graves and dancing on this one night a year you have to be free."

5.   Exploratory Movement Based on an Intriguing Picture: "This picture shows a very different kind of person. The bottom half of this person's body is an egg beater. With one hand this person turns the egg beater crank. I thought it would be interesting for you to pretend to be this person doing something—maybe going shopping, perhaps at work, or whatever you'd like to try. You have to think how you're going to move your legs like an egg beater."

EXAMPLES OF SIMPLE CREATIVE ACTIVITIES FOR PAIR AND GROUP PLAYING

Similar activities may be created and played in pairs and groups.

1.   Based on Robert Louis Stevenson's poem, "My Shadow," (3)(4)(35): Decide between the *two of you* who will be the child in the poem and who will be the shadow. Think about all the things you do in your day from the time you get up in the morning to the time you go to bed at night. Think of how the shadow changes size during the day, too."

2. Being Robots: "After you divide into *groups,* you'll need to decide what sorts of job you (as robots) are doing—are you painting a house, or working in a restaurant? Then, once you've decided on the job, you'll need to plan all the things the robots do in that job."

GUIDING CREATIVE WORK

Before one can feel free to create, one must be in an accepting, nonjudgmental environment. Consider the following techniques you can use to help children feel as comfortable as possible in their work.

1. Brainstorm some ideas verbally before playing. ("What kinds of community helpers are there?") You can also brainstorm by playing. ("While I count to five, see if you can act out five different community helpers.")

2. Keep the playing brief at first and let as many children as you can manage play in unison (with little or no audience watching). This technique lets children work privately without the pressure of being judged by others.

3. If you need to check on what the children are doing, keep the ideas private. After the children play for a few moments, say "Freeze." Then you may go around and talk to a few quietly. (Your responses need only accept the idea. "Ah, that's interesting." "Oh." "Um, hum." "Really?" and so forth. No judgments of good or bad need be made.)

4. Sidecoaching.

   a. As children play, remind them of the different ideas they mentioned in discussion, note some the ideas you see being played, or suggest other possibilities for them to consider.

Leader listens appreciatively to child's pantomime idea.

    b. Use recorded music to stimulate children's thinking as well as to provide a background to fill in any awkward silences.

5. When the playing is ended, you can comment on what some of the ideas were without identifying the players. ("I saw some people sailing, some were flying an airplane, and some were even roller skating—many transportation ideas.") This technique shows acceptance of the children's ideas and lets the rest of the class know what the various ideas were.

6. As children become confident in creating, they will want to share their ideas with each other. Those who wish may do so, either by telling what they did or even by demonstrating. But be cautious of pushing anyone who is not yet ready. Remember the flower bud that cannot be forced to open before its time.

CONTROL TECHNIQUES IN CREATIVE WORK

Sometimes we are afraid to let children be creative in their playing because we feel they will get out of control. Providing a definite structure or framework for children's creativity can lessen our anxiety. Always be definite about when the children should start and stop their pantomiming. Following are some suggestions:

    a. You may simply say, "Begin—Freeze."

    b. You may count, saying for example, "Think of three things you can do as I count to 3—1, 2, 3."

    c. "When the record begins, you may move; when it stops, you freeze."

    d. For more extended playing, you may be more inventive and say: (mysteriously) "When the lights go off, that will be the signal that Halloween night is here. And all you little hobgoblins will come out from your hiding places (desks) to dance your own little dance (solo at the side of the desk) in the moonlight. But when the clock strikes five o'clock (hammer on a small gong), you must return to your hiding places again where no human eye can see you."

    e. Children's inventiveness and the length of playing time needed will vary with each individual. Therefore, just tell the children to sit down when they have finished their pantomime and wait quietly for others to finish. While this technique may seem unusual at first, you and the children will soon become accustomed to it and find it is helpful for many activities.

MECHANICAL MOVEMENT

Mechanical movement is another technique you can use for controlled, creative work. You can be the operator who manages the on and off switches.

Suggested Characters

Robots

Windup or mechanical toys

Marionettes

Mechanical circus or merry-go-round with Aaron Copland's "Circus Music" from *The Red Pony*

A Possible Story Outline: Last year's toys in Santa Claus' workshop help Santa finish making all the new toys. Their batteries run down and they slowly come to a stop. You might recharge them, one by one, so they can continue their work and return to the shelf before Santa awakens.

"SETTING PICTURES IN MOTION" OR "COMING TO LIFE"

For still another technique, children create a picture that is frozen but comes to life on cue. Each child is assigned a number. When you call out all the "1's," they move, "2's" add on to the "1's," and so on. You can even reverse this counting so the picture returns to its frozen position once again. For example, in Maurice Sendak's *Where the Wild Things Are,* the Wild Things have a "rumpus." Children can be frozen as their own version of a "wild thing." Assign several ones, twos, and threes. As you play music and count, the wild things with the appropriate numbers can move.

CREATING STORIES

Many children are capable of creating stories on their own that they can enact with little assistance from you. Others, however, may be dependent on you to give them ideas to work with and guidance through plot outline. In this section we will look at some of the ways you can help children create and play out simple plots of their own.

In the process of plot building, you will be giving the children a framework for developing a story that is meaningful and satisfying to them. The stories are action based and played out in pantomime. But you will also learn how to extend the story by adding verbal experiences after the pantomiming.

Steps in the Process of Creative Plot Building

1. Present an intriguing idea that can be played in pantomime to the children. The playing may be solo, in pairs, or (for third graders) in small groups.

In a creative story, children make up and act out their own plots.

2. Guide the children through a series of approximately five discussion questions to assist them in planning their own stories. The questions help them create a beginning, middle, and end to their stories as well as a conflict and a resolution.

3. Sidecoach the unison playing of the stories. (Sometimes half the class plays for the other half and then we switch.)

4. Followup discussion may be with you in character role or other verbal activities.

5. Replaying (optional).

Now let us look at each step a little closer.

CHOOSING AN IDEA

The topics for a creative story, whether fact or fiction, can come from any number of sources as you tap your own imagination.

Literature

"Harold has such interesting adventures with his magical purple crayon. Today let's pretend that you have a crayon like his and you're going to draw an adventure for yourself. . . . " (based on Crockett Johnson's *Harold and the Purple Crayon,* New York: Harper and Row, 1955. See pp. 147–150 for complete lesson plans.)

Social Studies

"Let's suppose that you are members of a conservation crew working with wildlife in Africa. It's your job to catch the wild animals and tag them so you can learn more about them. . . . '' (pair or group playing)

Science

"Now that we've learned about the honey bee, suppose you were one and you were on your way to gather pollen. . . . where would you fly to first?''

Music

"Listen to this music called, ''In the Hall of a Mountain King.'' This is where your adventure will take place as you search for the dwarves who will take you to the mountain treasure. What are some of the things you might find in this Hall of the Dwarf King?''

DISCUSSION

The questions follow general plot outline. Five well-worded, intriguing questions are usually sufficient to develop the story. (You can combine several short or related questions into one.)

Generally the *first* question introduces the idea, the *second* and *third* questions build the adventure, by the *fourth* question the conflict is introduced, and the *fifth* question brings the story to a close.

Through the questions you ask, children plan the details of who they are, what they are going to do, what problems they might have, how they will solve them, and how their story will end.

Hints in Wording the Questions

1. The questions must continually focus on *action* since the stories are going to be pantomimed.
2. Keep the questions following the chronological order of the story, moving it forward. Do not back up and change the direction of a story or ask questions that are not directly related to it.
3. Ask questions that are open-ended and encourage elaboration of ideas. If a question can be answered with just a ''yes'' or ''no,'' it will build minimal plot.
4. Ask intriguing questions that will draw the children into the idea. The characters should be significant and important. Sometimes you can make them experts in their adventure—''the world's smartest detective,'' for example. Use words like ''special,'' ''clever,'' and ''unusual.''
5. Adding tension to the story as it evolves will intensify the drama. Perhaps there is the pressure of time—a job must be finished by midnight or a magic spell will wear off, for example.

6. It is helpful to word the questions tentatively so the children can change their story as they hear more ideas discussed. "What *do you suppose* you'll do next?" for example, leaves the way open for flexibility.

7. Do not try to get answers from everyone on every question. Discussion should continue only as long as it is motivating the children and the ideas are flowing. Most children want to get to the playing as soon as possible.

As children gain skill in this kind of story building, they may not always need a lot of discussion time. You may be able to give the entire outline of your discussion questions and let them plan it all in one gulp. It is not unusual for some children to tell a complete story in answering the first question you pose. They may already be several steps ahead of you!

The importance of the class-wide discussion is for the evolving of numerous ideas, the cross-fertilizing of thinking, and the expanding and elaborating of creativity. Children may hear ideas that will mesh with theirs; or they may hear an idea they like better than their

A Borrower assists her "injured" partner in a creative story.

own. Discussions are most valuable when this kind of creative process is taking place.

Discussions are also helpful to you since they will let you know what ideas you can expect to see the children playing. And you will have a better idea of what questions and feedback to expect in the verbalizing later.

PLAYING / SIDE-COACHING

At first, young children may be able to create very brief stories of perhaps only a minute in length; gradually they may increase their playing time to three minutes and even longer.

Children will not all play for the same length of time. Therefore, it is best to have them sit down when they have finished their stories and quietly watch others.

Even though children are making up their own beginnings and endings for their stories, you should give signals for both. Your signals will add more to the playing if you make them as imaginative as possible.

"When you hear the clanging of pots, you'll know the cook's signaling you cowboys for the new day of driving cattle on the open range. You'll know the day is ending when you hear the soft strums of the guitar by the campfire."

When most of the children have ended their playing, you can narrate/sidecoach an ending for those still playing if it looks as if they need help. (Some can go on forever if you let them!) It is also wise to narrate/sidecoach an ending if you see the playing deteriorating at any time.

Side-coaching Hints

1. As before, music will play an important part in encouraging the children's ideas and providing a background for their dramas.

2. Since children have created their own stories to play, they may not need more than just a few reminders of the stages of their plot—the beginning, the action, the problems they may be encountering, and the solutions they may have. Many will be too engrossed in their playing to pay much attention to sidecoaching.

3. Sidecoaching is usually needed more for individual playing than for pair and group playing. When children work with each other in these stories, they rely more on their classmates than on you for assistance.

4. In your side-coaching you can also lend to the drama by playing a character role. In the following example children are creating stories about race-car driving. They are in groups that include the drivers and their pit crews. You enhance the believability of the experience by playing the role of the official announcer of the race:

    "It's a great day for the races, all you fans out there! The cars are lined up for the beginning of this day-long race. The excitement here is high—the atmosphere is tense. The engines are roaring, and the race is about to begin. At the wave of the flag, each team is on its own. Good luck!. And they're off! What will be the outcome of this race is anybody's guess. . . . "

5. Usually it is best to word the side-coaching tentatively since the children's ideas are all different and you do not really know all the details of each story. Also, the children are not moving through the various stages of their stories at the same speed.

    "It *seems as if some* people have already left on their mission. . . . "

    "I *wonder if anyone* has run into a problem yet. . . . "

    "You're all such clever detectives, I'm sure you'll all be able to *find the clues you need* to solve the case. . . . "

6. Do not interject any new idea in the side-coaching. If you call out ideas such as, "Look out for that shark!" or "Suddenly you discover gold!" you will only confuse the playing. Such side-coaching is appropriate to narrative pantomime but would be interruptions in these original stories.

DISCUSSION / DIALOGUE FOLLOWUP WITH LEADER IN CHARACTER ROLE

When the playing has ended, many children will want to tell you what happened in their stories, elaborating on the ideas they mentioned originally. There may be times when you will ask them to write their stories, draw a picture, or just discuss what happened.

However, you will not want to miss the opportunity to extend the story/plot idea through character dialogue. If you play a character role, you have the chance to explore so many more ideas and concepts with the children.

Ideally you want to extend the story and build on the children's creativeness. Often it is helpful to use props, pictures, costume, or anything else that will stimulate ideas. Opinions, evaluations, descriptions, or other categories of verbalization can also be explored. You may even introduce new problems to be solved.

DIALOGUE WITH VERBAL CHILDREN

Generally it is best to ask questions of the group as a whole and then call on volunteers. If children are highly verbal, you need to move quickly from one child to another.

Sometimes highly verbal children will want to join you as questioner. You might then give them a general role as "my assistants," "my colleagues," and so forth.

If children have played their dramas in small groups, they may see even more opportunities to create dialogue. And, if the majority of the class is highly verbal, you will want to utilize other verbal activities such as Panel of Experts (p. 127) or even Verbal Skits discussed in Chapter 8.

DIALOGUE WITH RETICENT CHILDREN

If the creative story has been intriguing and the questions captivating, often even the shyest child will want to become involved. However, it is a good idea to be prepared with simple questions that can be answered "yes" or "no" for children who find it difficult to speak up in a classroom. Even nodding or shaking the head in answer to a question can be a big undertaking for some youngsters.

As another precaution, it is helpful for you to have an "out"— a reason you can give in case a child appears ready to speak and then freezes up at the last moment. For example, as a "newspaper reporter" you might say to an "inventor," "I can understand your not wanting to talk to me; this invention of yours could be top secret stuff."

REPLAYING (Optional)

Once the children have tried an idea they like, they may ask to play it again. They may have new ideas. Some may want to include ideas they have heard from others. Or, they may want to work with a partner or a group after playing solo.

You can take the opportunity to have them evaluate by asking what they might like to change or what they particularly like about their previous playing.

SAMPLE LESSON PLAN
"Harold and the Purple Crayon"
Objectives

a. Experience a creative movement and creative verbal experience based on literature.

b. Create a story with a beginning, middle, and end, including conflict and resolution.

c. Have opportunity to imaginatively draw and pantomime an adventure of own choosing.

d. Have opportunity to respond to character questioning related to the experience.

Preparation and Materials

a. Space Solo playing can be done at desk, if you wish. More space can be used if you clear the center area and put desks around the edge of room. Pair (or group) playing will require the larger space.

b. Supplies

1. Record player and recording. I like to use Henry Mancini's "Baby Elephant Walk" because it is lively and rather whimsical—like Harold's pictures. But almost any "adventuresome" music will do.

2. (optional) Copy of Crockett Johnson's *Harold and the Purple Crayon* (Harper and Row, 1955) or other Harold books.

3. Several large-sized pictures, perhaps of an animal, an unusual form of transportation, or a group of interesting-looking people, and so forth to use for dialogue interaction at the end.

4. (optional) Toy telephone for dialogue interaction at the end.

c. Length of Session (Variable)

1. Recommendation: It will work best if the children are already familiar with the stories and if they have also done a narrative pantomime of one of them. (See pp. 69–70) So you might want to do the narrative pantomime one day and the creative story on another day.

2. On the second day, discussion planning for creating original stories takes about 10 to 15 minutes.

3. Playing takes about 3 to 5 minutes. Double this if you split class in half for two playings.

4. Discussion with you in character role is nice to do for about 10 minutes, but can be as long or as short as you wish.

Warmup and Motivation

Recall the books (perhaps showing them again) and the class' previous narrative pantomime adventures. Talk about the variety of adventures there are, and of how clever and resourceful Harold is in drawing his adventures as well as in getting out of his difficulties.

Discussion Questions

"Now that we've done a narrative pantomime of *Harold and the Purple Crayon,* and have read some of the other stories about Harold, I thought it might be fun for each of you to create your own magical adventure. Let's suppose you have a crayon like Harold's that will draw anything you want."

a. "What special place would you like to go on your adventure?" (Children's answers might include to visit Grandma in Arizona; to the moon; to Disneyland.)

b. "Harold has all kinds of ways to travel in his adventures. How will you get to this place you want to visit? Do you need to take any special supplies with you?" (Take a bus; I need a space suit; I need money for the rides in Disneyland.)

c. "What are some of the things you'd like to see and do in this special place?" (Grandma always takes me to the zoo; I'm going to look for moon people; I'm going to ride all the rides at least once and eat lots of junk food.)

d. "Harold's trips are not without some problems." (Remind them of some.) "What kinds of problems might happen to you on this adventure?" (Once Grandma got a flat tire on her car; I might lose contact with the space shuttle; I could get stuck in one of the rides.)

e. "But Harold is always very clever, and with his magical crayon he usually figures a way out of any problems and gets back home safely. How do you think you could solve your problems and how will you return home in time for supper?" (We could draw a tow truck and get it fixed; I can draw a new radio transmitter; If I was way up high, like on the Matterhorn ride, I could draw a crane that could lift me down.)

Directions for Playing

"As we did when we played the narrative pantomime, we'll start out like Harold does, trying to get to sleep at night. Our desks will be our beds. Then we'll decide that an adventure will help make us sleepy. After you play your adventure, you'll come back home to bed. You might even bring back a souvenir of your adventure."

Side-coaching

(Start record player.) "You're in bed but it's so hard to get to sleep. You toss and turn. Fluff up the pillow. Nothing seems to work. Ah, you think, maybe a purple crayon adventure will help. So you go off on your journey." (Now you might pretend to be Harold's mother or father.) "Oh, Harold's not in bed tonight. I wonder if he's off on one of his adventures again? I'll look out the window and see if I can see him. . . . Umm, looks like a bus just turned the corner there, I wonder if Harold was on it? . . . I hope he has everything he needs . . . Guess he can always draw something with the crayon . . . Well, I hope he's having a good time tonight . . . I do worry about him . . . He sometimes runs into difficulty . . . Wonder if he's had any problems yet? The sky looks a little funny tonight . . . Well, Harold's always is clever enough to get himself out of problems . . . I hope he doesn't stay out too long . . . He does have school tomorrow . . . Oh, oh, I think I hear something . . . Maybe he's on his way back . . . "(now as yourself) "It looks as if most of you have finished . . . Better get back pretty soon . . . Someone may be worrying about you . . . Good, everyone's home again . . . Put your crayon in a safe place . . . Hop in bed . . . Good night." (Fade out record.)

Follow-Up Discussion with Leader in Character Role

"Suppose I'm your mother or father and I've been worried about where you've been. I find you in bed and want to talk with you about where you've been and also ask some questions."

a. (softly) "Harold, wake up." (Go to a child who is pretending to wake up and seems ready to talk.) "Oh, good. I was so worried about you. Where did you go this time?"

b. "What souvenir did you bring back?" (Almost any "souvenir" can have some problem you can discuss. If animals are brought back, you can talk about what to feed them and how to care for them. Maybe the house is getting full of all of Harold's souvenirs and you have to decide what to do with them.)

c. "Harold, this is very difficult to say, but I think maybe we ought to get rid of the purple crayon. I know you enjoy it and these adventures, but what would happen if someday you ran into a problem you couldn't solve?"

d. "Oh, there's the phone. (You can pretend or use toy telephone.) "Hello? Yes, this is Harold's house. The police? You found something of Harold's out in the street and you want to talk to him? Just a minute, please." (Whoever wants to can "talk" to the police on the phone. You can stand by and add comments and ask questions the way one might with real phone calls. Other phone calls might come from someone who stopped by to visit and was disappointed that Harold was not home, or from a store asking about Harold's order for more purple crayons, or from someone Harold might have met on a previous adventure.)

e. "Harold, I was looking through your photo album and came across these photos. I know they came from some of your adventures, but I don't remember which ones. What about this one?" (Show class a picture.) "Who are these people?" (or "Where did you meet this animal?" "What's this funny looking thing?" "How did you get out of this awful situation?")

Quieting Activity

"Oh, gosh, look at the time! Tomorrow is a school day and you need to get to sleep. I'll turn out the light. Shut your eyes. Goodnight." (as yourself) "And Harold snuggles down into bed, draws up the covers, and slowly drifts off to sleep as the bedroom door closes." (Pause for a few moments to let children settle down or play some quieting music.)

SAMPLE LESSON PLAN
"The Borrowers"
Objectives

a. Experience a creative movement and creative verbal experience based on literature.

b. Create a story with a beginning, middle, and end.

c. Deal with concept of size relationships: small borrowers in normal-sized home.

d. Imagine problems that could be encountered and create appropriate solutions for those problems.

e. Have opportunities to respond to character questioning related to experience.

Preparation and Materials

a. Space Use the area in center of room with desks around edge of room.

b. Supplies

1. Small objects such as: small metal pillbox, fancy beaded ball-point pen, small decorative mirror. One prop for final discussion: small pair of child's plastic craft scissors, for example.
2. Record player
3. Copy of Mary Norton's book *The Borrowers* (60)
4. "Arabian Dance" from Tchaikovsky's *Nutcracker Suite*
5. Pictures from the text (enlarged, if possible)
6. Length of session: 45 minutes (approximately)

Warmup

Recall the book or simply tell the children briefly about the tiny people who live under the floorboards of a person's house. When the people in the house are asleep at night, the little people search for and "borrow" small objects from the house to furnish their own miniature home.

Motivation

Show illustrations so children can see objects such as postage stamps, thimbles, and pins being used in the Borrower's house in unique ways.

Discussion Questions

a. "Suppose you were a Borrower, and you needed to redecorate your home. Look at these objects and tell me what you think you might be able to use them for." (Children's answers might include such ideas as the pillbox for a baby bed, the pen could be a decorative column for the porch, and the mirror might make a skating rink for the children.)

b. "Suppose that tonight's the night for the borrowing trip. You're going to get these objects—or perhaps something else. What equipment will you need to take with you on your trip?" (string and safety pins to hook various objects with and to use to climb up the drapes; a wagon from a doll house to carry things in; cotton to stuff in the dog's ears so he won't hear us)

c. "What other things will you be looking for tonight?" (I need a new picture for the wall; my rug is worn out, and I want to get a handkerchief for a new one; I want a swimming pool, and there's a pretty soup bowl that would be perfect.)

d. "Borrowing is a dangerous business. Homily, you know, always worries about her husband, Pod, when he goes on one of these missions. And Arrietty had to wait a long time before she was old enough to go with him. What's so dangerous about borrowing, and what particular problems do you think you might run into?" (Household pets could hurt you; if you got near a bathtub filled with water and fell in, you might drown; if anyone sees you, you'll have to move out and go to another house because they'll be after you for sure.)

e. "How will you be able to avoid these problems and get home safely with all your new furnishings?" (I have a map of the house and all the danger points marked; I'm just gathering the stuff tonight and will make another trip tomorrow to carry it back; I always wear very dark clothes so it's harder to see me.)

Directions for Playing

"I can see you have all your ideas worked out, so we'll get ready for the mission. I'll dim the lights so it will be more like nighttime. Now, you have all your gear ready, so you'll just be resting and waiting for the household to go to bed. When you hear the clock strike one o'clock, you'll know you can be sure everyone's asleep. Remember that you must be as silent as possible or you might wake someone up, and you know what that will mean. You know the household awakens at five o'clock, so when you hear the clock strike five, you'd better scurry back home. When you have reached back home, just sit down quietly in your playing space and wait for others to finish."

"Now, we need to do this in two shifts—so Shift One will work from one o'clock until three o'clock; Shift Two will work from three o'clock until five o'clock." (Designate who is in which shift.)

Side-coaching

(Start record player.) "It's very quiet now and almost one o'clock. . . . Everyone's gone to bed . . . (Strike a metal object for clock.) . . . It's time . . . Quietly you begin your adventure . . . I believe some people are checking their equipment for one last time. Some have already started out . . . I hope you'll be able to see well enough . . . It's so dark this time of night . . . There are so many dangers out there, too—oh, oh, I think someone may have had some difficulty. All we can do is hope they'll be okay. Borrowers are used to living by the skin of their teeth, so I guess they'll do all right. Ah, it looks as if some have been successful and have all the things they came for . . . good . . . Some appear to be heading home . . . (Over half of the children are now seated.) Oh, dear, it seems to be very close to three o'clock and time for the Second Shift to take over . . . I hope everyone is nearly finished or they'll run out of time . . . (Strike "clock" three times.) Three o'clock and everyone who's left needs to scurry home. And it's been such an exhausting night, you all fall exhausted into bed." (Fade out the record.)

"Now while the First Shift rests, the Second Shift will begin their work." (Repeat playing as above.)

(Turn up lights) "Well, that was an exciting adventure. Let's hear about what happened to you. What was the scariest part for you?" (Discuss)

Leader in Character Role

"Now, let's suppose I'm a Borrower from another house and I've come to visit you. I've never been borrowing before, and my parents sent me here to talk to you so I could learn. They told me you're the most famous Borrowers, and you know all the ins and outs of this business. Will you help me with some questions?"

a. "How did you get to be so good at borrowing?"
b. "What was the closest call you ever had in borrowing?"
c. "Can you tell or show me what you're most proud of having borrowed? What's the nicest or best thing you have?"
d. "What's the most important thing I should know about borrowing? Do you have any secret tricks you could tell me about?"

    e. ''My parents told me you're planning to have a garage sale soon. What things are you planning to get rid of? Why?''

    f. ''I found this on your doorstep.'' (Show the scissors.) ''I wasn't sure if you lost it or if you have it out there for a reason. What is it used for?''

''Thanks for talking to me. I have to go home now. I know you've had a very busy night, so I'll let you get a little sleep. 'Bye.''

Quieting Activity

(As Leader) ''And, so the Borrowers put away their things, fluff up their pillows on their beds, lay down their heads, and quietly go to sleep.'' (Play restful music like ''Aquarium'' from Saint Saëns' *Carnival of the Animals.*)

Story Dramatization: Circle Stories **10**

The term *story dramatization* refers to the process of creating an informal play improvisationally from a story under the leader's guidance. Generally the procedure includes:

a. sharing a story or other piece of literature with a group of children,
b. planning the characters, scenes, and events,
c. playing,
d. evaluating, and
e. replaying.

After much interchanging of roles and experimenting with ideas, the story/play is "set" much like a rehearsed play.

The process, however, has been the improvisational method. No script is memorized. No one child is cast in or "owns" any one role. And the play is the result of the group's work, facilitated by the leader.

Within this general framework, there can still be many ways to dramatize any given story. We will take several approaches, giving you many lesson plan samples to select from, and eventually you will decide for yourself what methods you want to use.

SOME PRELIMINARY CONSIDERATIONS

SELECTING THE STORY

First, you will need to select a story of good, literary quality. (Many sample lessons are included for you with additional bibliography at the end of chapter 11 for those who are ready to make their own lesson plans.) The story should also be one that appeals to you as well as to the children.

There should be plenty of interesting *action* in the story that can be played without elaborate staging. The *dialogue* should be interesting, but not so difficult that the children become frustrated in their attempts to improvise from it.

The characters should be believable. There should also be enough characters (or the possibility of adding characters) so that a significant number of children, if not the entire class, can be involved in the playing.

PRESENTING THE STORY

You may wish to read the story or tell it in your own words. Picture books are usually shared visually with the children. There may even be times when you will want to use filmed versions or audio recordings of a story.

Simple folk tales should be shared orally, if possible, since they were originally told rather than read or recorded. Besides, oral telling allows you to maintain eye contact with the audience, helping you judge how the children are reacting to it.

PRESENTING THE DIALOGUE

Presenting the dialogue in the story is important. Children listen to the dialogue and repeat much of it in their playing.

Sometimes it is helpful to add dialogue to a story that is too simply told. For example, a line might say, ''The little boy asked the fox for advice.'' You can help the children visualize and enact this encounter if you say, instead, ''The little boy asked, ''Mr. Fox, what should I do?' ''

Simplify dialogue that is too complicated. Otherwise, children might be frustrated trying to remember it. Even if you encourage them to ''tell it in your own words,'' they may feel compelled to recreate the original wording and experience failure in the attempt.

CASTING THE STORY

Because you will be playing the story several times, and because you will want each playing to build on the previous one, you will want to establish a solid beginning. The following suggestions should help.

a. Cast the most competent children for the first playing in order to establish an appropriate model for the rest of the class to build on. Shy or slower children can benefit from seeing the story enacted by others before they undertake it themselves.

b. Double and even triple casting (two or three children playing one character) will also be useful. It will allow more children to play the story and will provide the security needed for improvising freely. "What one can't think of to say, the other one usually can."

c. You may need to assist with the main role, particularly in first playings, even with some of the most competent children. By using the technique of double and triple casting, you can easily "tag along" and be available to help as needed.

AIDS FOR ORGANIZATION

One of your main concerns with story dramatization will be, "How will I keep things organized?" It is a legitimate concern, but with some careful planning, many problems and difficulties can be alleviated.

Following are a number of organizational suggestions for you to consider. All of them have been utilized in the lesson plans included, so you need not be overwhelmed by them. In fact, they will evolve quite logically as you work with the stories. In time, you will find the techniques that work best for you and for your children, and for the stories that will become your particular favorites.

a. Organize space carefully.

Usually you will want to have the major scenes take place in the middle of the playing circle or in front of the classroom. However, other areas of the room, such as the corners, will be useful for additional scenes. When there are several scenes in a story, it is sometimes helpful to place the scenes around the circle or the room, sequencing them in the order of their appearance in the story.

You will need to think this organization through ahead of time. Later, as you feel more comfortable, you will want to consult the children about their ideas on mapping out the scenes. Sometimes it is helpful to create specific locations using classroom furnishings.

A story corner is often a good place to play a circle story.

For example, the teacher's chair can become "the king's throne"; a story rug might become "a city."

b. Use the children's desks/tables whenever possible. Often these can be "homes" for the citizens of the town, "pens" for animals in a story, "stores" for shopkeepers, and so forth. Try also to keep the children at their desks (or seated on a rug) until "their scene" is ready to be played. During these "sitting out" periods, you can refer to the children as the *audience*.

c. Look for the natural controls within the story. Often the characters take a nap or rest. Sometimes characters are in an immobile position due to enchantment or other reasons. Often characters "return to their homes," or desks. Capitalize upon these moments to give legitimate quiet periods.

d. Designate characters in some way so you—and they—can remember who is playing which part. An easy method is to create simple nametags or paper bands for the head, perhaps with pictures of the characters on them. Simple costuming (hats, props, pieces of fabric) is also useful but may take more time. You may wish to add these after initial playings and when you are sure the children will want to continue playing.

e. All of the above controls are helpful so that not all of the class is moving and talking at the same time. Separating and grouping the children in various parts of the classroom as well as the nametags will help you (and them) see the layout of the story and remember the characters in groups.

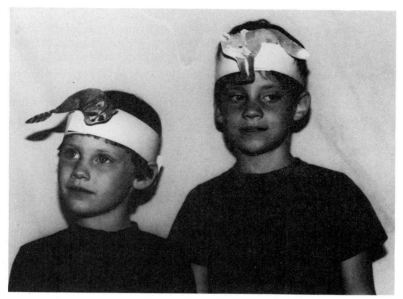

Paper headbands with pictures of the characters being played help leader and children keep track of who is playing what part.

ORGANIZATION THROUGH NARRATION
AND CHARACTER ROLE (REVIEW)

Two additional techniques (both of which have been discussed in previous sections) will be indispensible to you in playing the story. They are *narration* and *playing a character role.* Narration will help you guide the story from the outside. If you play a character role in the story, you can guide the playing from within. And, you can use both techniques interchangeably in the same story dramatization.

Ways to Guide Using Narration

1. Open the story.
    "Once upon a time there was . . . "
2. Guide the story if it lags or if the children forget the sequence of events.
    "And then the peddler went down the road, singing."
3. Control the action if problems arise.
    "Finally, the animals decided to stop arguing and returned to their homes."

4. Add pantomime ideas if the children need suggestions.

"The magicians worked far into the night stirring up their brew. They checked their magic books, and they poured potions from bottles into the cauldron, stirring everything very carefully."

5. Provide transitions for scenes, indicating passage of time or change of environment.

"The next morning, she woke up and went downstairs to see what was under the Christmas tree."

6. Close the story.

"And they all lived happily ever after."

Ways to Guide by Playing a Character Role
What Role Do I Play?

a. You can play the main role either by yourself or with perhaps one or two of the children. This technique can be useful with very young children or with children who need considerable help. Even when children are experienced, you may be able to help revitalize a story by playing a character role.

b. You may choose to play a secondary role, such as a king's prime minister or a friend to the central character. If these roles do not already exist in the story itself, they can usually be easily added.

c. You may step into a scene in a spontaneously invented role and assist if children have forgotten the sequence of events or to reactivate the children's involvement if the playing is becoming perfunctory.

What You Can Do in a Character Role

1. Carry the dialogue, initiating the interactions.

"I'm looking for someone to help me with my chores here on the farm. Can you help?" (or, if playing a role with some children) "We've got some things to sell. Would you buy something from us?"

2. Give directions and assistance in character to help the story along.

"Let's see, where did we put that whistle? Do you know where it is?" "I don't know about you, but I'm awfully tired. I think I'll take a nap here under this tree."

3. Control the action and discipline.

"As the king's prime minister I must remind you that you cannot go into the throne room until you are quiet. And you must bow before the king before you speak. Are you ready?"

4. Reactivate involvement, offering new situations for children to react to and new challenges for the children to solve.

"Say, excuse me, but do you have a peddler's license? I'm the

Teacher assists children in dialogue by playing
a character role. *(Kalamazoo Gazette)*

inspector here in this town, and we don't allow door to door
peddling unless someone has a license. I'll have to ask to see
yours."

Now, let us look at a very simple way to play easy stories.

SIMPLE STORY DRAMATIZATION
WITH CIRCLE STORIES

Young children love to dramatize stories. They want to play as many parts as they
can and act out all the excitement they know so well. Many stories can be dramatized
very simply, easily, and quickly. For many groups this will be desirable, especially
if the children are eager to see immediate progress in their efforts at making a play.

One useful technique I call "Circle Stories." If you visualize a story being dramatized in a circle, it will be relatively easy to organize. The circle may be seats in
a circle, children sitting in a circle on a carpeted area, or a circle around the outer
aisles of the room. Even very young children understand and sense an orderliness
about a circle and will usually be most cooperative. They will also quickly learn the
procedure and will be able to adapt it themselves to new stories.

With "Circle Stories," we are focusing on the easiest and most orderly method
to involve all the children in playing the action or basic story line. This technique
is more like organizing a game since little emphasis is given to characterization,
emotion, and sensory awareness. (You will learn other procedures in the next chap-

ter.) The method is also useful for run-through playing in order to set a framework to build on in further replayings.

Generally, stories that fit this method best have one or two main characters and an indefinite number of one other character type. For example, in *Millions of Cats,* there are the old man and his wife and millions—and billions and trillions—of cats.

Other stories that fit this method best have one or two main characters and a series of different characters who are met. The dialogue is simple and usually repetitive. Often these stories are called "cumulative." *Mushroom in the Rain* is a classic example of this type.

In playing "Circle Stories," you, with perhaps one or two other children, may play the main part initially. This gives you the opportunity to move the story along, to initiate dialogue, and to role model the playing. You will often alternate between being a narrator and playing your role. The rest of the children will sit in a circle and become the other characters when they appear in the story.

Following are lesson plans for several circle stories, with some added hints on playing them. Feel free to add your own touches and additions to the suggested instructions and to adapt the methods to similar and favorite stories of your own.

SAMPLE LESSON PLANS FOR CIRCLE STORIES

Ask Mr. Bear, Marjorie Flack.
New York: Macmillan, 1932

Synopsis

It is Danny's mother's birthday and he does not know what to give her. The Hen suggests eggs; the Goose recommends feathers for a pillow; the Goat offers milk for cheese; the Sheep has wool; the Cow says milk and cream; but Danny tells them his mother has all these things. The Cow suggests that he ask Mr. Bear. Mr. Bear whispers a secret and Danny returns home to give his mother a big, bear hug.

1. *Casting:*

  a. You play Danny with perhaps one or two other children.

  b. As many as three children can be each of the animal characters: Hen, Goose, Goat, Sheep, and Cow, all seated or stationed in a circular pattern. You can just name off the various characters around the circle.

  c. Two children each can play Mr. Bear and Mother. One child playing the Mother should be verbally confident enough to do the guessing at the end.

2. *Action:*

  a. Danny goes around the circle to each of the various animals.

  b. The animals all follow Danny in a little parade until he goes to see Mr. Bear. Note that everyone skips, then hops, then gallops, and then trots. When Danny is told to see Mr. Bear, the animals decide to let Danny go by himself. Here you can narrate, "And all the animals went back to their places in the barnyard—the Hens, then the Geese," and so forth, and all return to their seats.

  c. Danny goes alone to Mr. Bear, running and then walking.

  d. To include the animals again in the end, you can add a line of narration, "And all the animals were glad that Danny had finally found a gift for his mother." Then lead them in clapping, or let each animal make its sound on cue from you ("The Hens cackled, the Geese honked, . . . " and so on.

3. *Dialogue*

  a. The Dannys talk together about how they do not know what to get Mother for her birthday.

    b.   The dialogue is repetitive (''Good morning, _____. Can you give me something for my mother's birthday?'' The children need only remember what gift is logical for each animal. They will enjoy saying the repetitive line, ''Let's see what we can find then.''

    c.   At the end, Mother's guesses repeat each of the gift ideas Danny encountered.

Bartholomew and the Oobleck

Dr. Seuss. New York: Random House, 1949

Synopsis

King Derwin of Didd complains to his page boy, Bartholomew, that he is bored with the weather. The problem is turned over to the Magicians who suggest that "oobleck" would be a good solution, though they have never made it before. As the "oobleck" begins to fall the following morning, the King is delighted and declares a holiday. But the joyousness is shortlived when it is discovered that the oobleck is green, sticky, and falling in greater abundance hourly. Only the King's magic words, "I'm sorry," stop the oobleck and restore sanity to the Kingdom once again.

1. Casting

a. You can play Bartholomew with perhaps one or two other children. (I like to use a boy and a girl.)

b. Three to five students can play the Magicians. Three students can play the Bell Ringer, three more the Trumpet Blower, and another three the Captain of the Guard.

c. Two can play the King, or, if you prefer, you can have a King and a Prime Minister or a King and Queen.

d. The rest of the students can be divided into townspeople and people in the palace. The book's illustrations show various occupations in the kingdom and mention is made specifically of musicians, the laundress, and a cook in the palace. Students will feel more special if you give them specific jobs or have them choose an occupation. They will be acting out their routine tasks when they become stuck in the oobleck.

2. Action

a. Before starting the story, place the students around the room in the circular pattern. The throne room is at the front of the classroom. On the King's right (as he sits on his throne) are the Magicians in the corner as if "offstage." On the King's left are the three Bell Ringers. In the back corners of the room are the three Trumpet Blowers and the three Captains of the Guard. Seated at the back desks are the people of the kingdom and at the front desks are the people of the palace.

b. In the opening scene the King complains about how boring the weather is. You can narrate a brief opening like, "Once upon a time, in the Kingdom of Didd, there lived King Derwin who was bored with the weather. One day he was overheard complaining to his pages." A pause and usually the King picks up the cue and begins complaining. Or, as Bartholomew, you can open the scene by saying to the King, "Your majesty, isn't it a beautiful day today? Just look at the sun . . . ''

c. If the King does not remember to call the Magicians, you (as Bartholomew) can suggest it. The pages can also legitimately escort them to the palace with the admonition to be sure to bow before speaking to the King. The dialogue here is simple enough, but if needed, you can tell the Magicians what it is the King wants. The Magicians can be escorted back to their workplace.

d. Here you can narrate how the Magicians work late into the night. If they need help thinking of actions to perform, you can sidecoach/narrate how they take down bottles from the shelves, pour and stir the different ingredients, whisper magic chants, and so forth. Narrate/sidecoach that everyone in the kingdom goes to sleep, including the King and Bartholomew. Finally, the Magicians, too, are finished with their task and go to sleep.

e. (Continue narrating) "The following morning, the King got up early and looked out the window and was delighted with what he saw. But Bartholomew woke up, looked out the window, and wasn't sure how to react. Small little green specks dotted the sky. It was the oobleck. The King called for Bartholomew and declared a holiday." Now you can join the Bartholomews and either exchange some brief dialogue with the King or make your way over to the Bell Ringers to declare a holiday.

f. The Bell Ringers will not be able to ring the bell because of the oobleck, and now you realize that there is not cause for a holiday. Instead, you must warn the people of the Kingdom.

g. Move to the Trumpet Blowers and the Captains of the Guard. Students usually remember what to do and say as the characters in f and g. Your job as Bartholomew is just to ask for help and be surprised when oobleck gets in the way. Standard lines like, "Oh, dear, what's the matter?" or, "Uhh, I don't think I'd do that if I were you," will probably come naturally to you as the students play their parts.

h. Now, as Bartholomew talking to the other Bartholomews, you can suggest, "We'd better get back to the palace." As you go through the back desks in the classroom, comment on the various people in the kingdom, the jobs they are doing, and how they are stuck in oobleck. You can even stop and talk briefly to a few, "What happened to you?" "How long have you been stuck like this?"

i. As you approach the front desks, you can do the same with the people in the palace.

j. As you go to the throne room (front of classroom) the King (and partner) will also be stuck. Here there is an exchange of a little bit of dialogue. You can talk about how bad things are in the kingdom; the king tries to think of some magic words; you shame the King into saying he is sorry. (If the King has trouble here, you can narrate, "And, If you listened closely, you could hear the King say very softly, "I'm sorry.")

k. Narrate an ending like, "And no one knows why, but as soon as those magic words were spoken, the oobleck began to melt, until it finally disappeared altogether. And then there was cause to celebrate. The bells rang, the trumpets blew, and the guards marched and everyone cheered. ('Hip, hip, hooray!') in honor of the day the oobleck came *and left*." Lead the class in applause for themselves and return to seats.

3. *Dialogue:*

a. The King complains about the weather; calls for Magicians; declares a holiday; and says "I'm sorry."

b. The Magicians usually have no trouble remembering to suggest oobleck and the fact that they have never made it before.

c. The Bell Ringers, Trumpet Blowers, and Captains of the Guard usually have no trouble remembering their difficulties with the oobleck.

d. The dialogue with people of the Kingdom and the people in the palace is optional.

The Captain of the Guard in a Dr. Seuss story gets his mouth stuck when he tries to eat "oobleck."

"The Cat and the Parrot,"

Sara Cone Bryant. (3) (35)

Variations

Fat Cat, by Jack Kent (New York: Parents', 1971).

The Greedy Fat Old Man, Paul Galdone (New York: Clarion, 1983).

Synopsis

A parrot is the dinner guest of a cat. A meager meal is served, but the parrot returns the invitation and serves a feast. The greedy cat eats everything, including his host, and casually sets out for home. On the way he meets, one by one, an old woman; and old man with a cart and a donkey; a wedding procession including a newly married prince, his wife, soldiers, and many elephants walking two by two. The cat tells everyone he meets to get out of his way. When they refuse he eats them "Slip! slop! gobble!" He finally eats two land crabs who pinch a hole in his stomach, and everyone escapes. The cat is left to sew up his coat.

1. Casting

    a. You play the cat with one or two other children.

    b. Go around the circle naming all the other characters that are met.

2. Action

    a. Begin playing when the cat eats at the parrot's house.

    b. To designate that they have been eaten, characters can line up behind the leader and continue the journey in a follow-the-leader fashion. Here it is fun to play a follow the leader game. The cat might decide to skip (the children must do the same since they are in the cat's stomach). Then walk across a swinging bridge very carefully, and so forth. In a first playing it is best to stay in a circle as much as possible.

    c. After the cat falls asleep under a tree, the children escape from the stomach and tiptoe back to their "homes" or seats, one by one. Here you may assume a narrator's voice and direct this part if needed.

3. *Dialogue*

a. The dialogue is repetitive.

b. You might let the children say "slip, slop, gobble," each time someone is eaten.

"The Conjure Wives,"

Frances Wickes, (40) *

Synopsis

On a Halloween night a group of conjure wives (or evil spirits) are gathered around a fire cooking their supper and casting spells. The wind howls and there is a knocking at the door. The spirits repeatedly ask who it is, and the answer repeatedly (in a chant) says the voice is one who is tired and cold and hungry and asks for food. The spirits tell the "voice" to go away. Finally they decide to give the stranger the smallest piece of food imaginable. But the little piece of food grows mysteriously and enormously and when the witches try to escape the door is shut tight. They become scared, grow small with big eyes, and the voice tells them to fly out the window because they have been turned into owls. (Note: the story is written in dialect, but is exciting enough to have appeal in Standard English, too.)

1. Casting

    a. You can be the leader of the spirits, along with two other students.

    b. Three students can be the mysterious voice and can be hidden.

    c. The rest of the class can be the witches seated in the circle.

2. Action

    a. Narrate a brief opening like, "Once upon a time, on a Halloween night, a lot of old conjure wives sat by the fire cooking their meal. They talked about the spells they were planning to cast that evening." You can encourage witch-like movements and cooking of food.

    b. The major part of the story is the inquiry and reply. At the end, the witches grow small and the voice tells them to fly out the window. Tell students beforehand that they are to circle their desks once and then sit back down to signify owls sitting in trees. They can continue their subtle bird movements and wide-eye blinking as you close the story with narration, "And now, as you walk through the woods, you can hear the conjure wives calling "Whooo?" But stay away from them on Halloween night, 'cause they turn back into conjure wives weaving their spells."

---

*Also in: Harper, Wilhelmina, ed., *Ghosts and Goblins*. New York: E. P. Dutton, 1965 and Sechrist, Elizabeth H. ed., *Heigh-Ho for Halloween*. Philadelphia: Macrae, 1948.

3. Dialogue

a. At the beginning of the story, you, as leader witch, can ask what kinds of spells your "fellow witches" are planning to cast.

b. The Voice's request and response, as well as the witches' request and response, are repetitive. You might shorten them into simple, rhythmic chants or write them out on a chalkboard. It is more effective if the three people playing the Voice and the witches can speak their lines in unison.

Optional

Halloween type background music playing softly in the background can help create an appropriate mood. It is also fun to darken the room and have a flashlight inside a jack-o-lantern in the center of the circle for an even spookier atmosphere.

King Rooster, Queen Hen

Anita Lobel. New York:
Greenwillow, 1975.

Synopsis

A Rooster and a Hen decide they want to go to the city and become king and queen. An old shoe becomes a carriage, and Mice become their horses. On their way they meet a Sparrow who asks to be the Queen's maid; a Duck wants to be their cook; a Crow plans to be their butler. They meet a Fox who has other ideas and invites them to his home to stay the night. The Sparrow gets the Fox to open the window and they all escape. Deciding this life is too dangerous, all the animals return to their old ways.

1. Casting

  a. Leader plays Rooster along with another child.
  b. Two more play the Hen.
  c. As many as six can be the Mice.
  d. Sparrow, Duck, and Crow can be two players each.
  e. Three players can be the Fox, perhaps linked together to indicate bigger size.

2. Action

  a. Rooster and Hen travel around the outside of the circle once, meeting the Sparrow. Take another trip around the circle and meet the Duck. Another trip around the circle and the Crow is met.
  b. You might use "traveling music" to help children keep together. A simple record of march music will help keep a group in step, if that seems necessary. Or, sing a song: "Hi, ho, hi, ho, it's off to town we go. We'll dress up fine and have a good time. Hi, ho, hi, ho, hi, ho. . . . "
  c. The Fox's home can be the inside of the circle, so all go in and are seated in a smaller circle. After the Fox asks the Rooster to sing, the Sparrow, who notices that the table is set for only one diner, says the room is too stuffy for singing and asks the Fox to open the window. The Sparrow leaves first, followed by the Rooster, Hen, Duck, Crow, and Mice. (You may need to narrate the exiting.) All run around the circle together once and stop.
  d. Each animal decides to leave the Rooster and Hen and return home to a safer existence (back to seats). You may need to nar-

rate this if children do not initiate dialogue for it. The Rooster and Hen are left scratching the dirt in the barnyard, as in the beginning. You can say an ending line like, "Ah, me, well, it was fun while it lasted!"

3. *Dialogue*

    a. Dialogue is repetitive in meeting all the animals; they need to remember what job they want to do for the King and Queen.

    b. Fox initiates the invitation to dinner and to sing.

The Little Rabbit Who Wanted Red Wings.

Carolyn Bailey.
New York: Platt & Munk, Publishers, 1978.

Synopsis

A little rabbit is not happy with himself and wishes to be different. Mr. Groundhog advises him to go to the wishing pond. Little Rabbit sees a red bird and wishes for red wings. But after he gets his wish, he finds that no one recognizes him. Only Mr. Groundhog will take him into his house where he spends a miserable night. The next day the wise Groundhog tells him he can wish his wings off again. He does so, and Mother takes in the Rabbit she knows and loves.

1. Casting

a. Leader can play Rabbit's Mother (with another child).

b. Little Rabbit can be double cast.

c. Mr. Bushy Tail, Mr. Porcupine, Miss Puddle Duck, Mr. Groundhog, and the Red Bird can also be double cast.

Little Rabbit must sleep at Mr. Groundhog's house.

d.   The rest of the children can link hands and form the circle for the wishing pond.

2. *Action*

a.   The animals that Little Rabbit admires can take their walk around the inside of the circle and then return to their seats.

b.   Mr. Groundhog walks into the circle with Little Rabbit to tell him about the wishing pond and then returns to his seat.

c.   Little Rabbit can walk around the outside of the circle (to indicate walking into the woods) while the Wishing Pond and Red Bird take their places. He enters the circle again.

d.   While the Pond and Bird return to their seats, Little Rabbit can again walk around the outside of the circle.

e.   Now he goes to Mother and each of the other animals (in their seats) who do not recognize him. He stays with Mr. Groundhog at his home (seat).

f.   He returns to the wishing pond again to wish off the wings. (Repeat earlier procedure.)

g.   Finally he returns to Mother who takes him in.

3. *Dialogue*

a.   Rabbit has to remember what he likes about each of the characters and wishes he had.

b.   Groundhog's dialogue is the most demanding.

c.   Animals have to remember not to let the Rabbit in for the night.

Optional Costuming   Each of the animals' distinguishing characteristics can be represented with simple costumes and props. Bushy tails (pieces of white Christmas tree garlands), porcupine quills (pieces of dark shag carpet) can be pinned on. Red socks can be Duck's red feet. Red wings can be on a headband. Mother might wear a kerchief and apron.

Millions of Cats,

Wanda Gag. New York:
Coward-McCann, Inc., 1956.

Synopsis

A very old man and a very old woman are lonely and decide to get a cat. The man journeys over the hills and finds "hundreds of cats, thousands of cats, millions and billions and trillions of cats." Since he cannot decide on the prettiest, he brings them all home. The couple realize they cannot keep them all, so let the cats decide which one is the prettiest. The cats argue and eat each other up. Only one scrawny cat remains, and the couple take such good care of it that it does, indeed, become the prettiest.

1. Casting

a. Leader plays the man and another child (or even two or three) is the wife.

b. All the rest are the cats. (You may wish to double cast each of the specifically mentioned cats.)

2. Action

a. The cats all follow you as you walk around the outside of the circle.

b. Cats return to seats to indicate that they arrive at the house.

c. To indicate that they have been eaten, they can, one by one on your cue, go behind their seats or sit on the floor in front of their seats.

d. The quarrel is the trickiest part. Cats (who are still in their seats) can pantomime biting, scratching and clawing the air in front of them—not with each other.

Dialogue

a. On a cue from you, all cats could say "Mew, mew! We are thirsty!" as well as the line, "Mew, mew! Now we are hungry!"

b. Use a sound arrow to indicate when they may argue over who is the prettiest and how loud they may argue. Establish that they must be silent on cue.

Optional costuming Use appropriately decorated head bands for the white cat, the black and white, the grey, the black, and the brown and yellow stripes. A red band might be used for the cat who remains at the end.

Mushroom in the Rain,

Mirra Ginsburg. New York: Macmillan, 1974.

Variations

"The Little House" Valery Carrick, (3)
The Mitten, Alvin Tresselt. Lothrop, Lee & Shepard, 1964.
My Red Umbrella, Robert Bright. Morrow, 1985.

Synopsis

A mushroom expands when numerous animals seek shelter under it. First is an ant followed by a variety of other animals, each bigger than the last. They are all sure the mushroom is too small to let in another animal, but somehow everyone is able to squeeze in.

1. Casting

   a. You probably do not need to play a role in this story, but be prepared to step in and help.
   b. You can double or triple cast the various animals.
   c. Rest of children play the mushroom.

2. Action

   a. Begin this story with the children who represent the mushroom in a tight huddle. The rest of the children are in a circle on the floor.
   b. As the children playing the ant approach, the "mushroom" joins hands and expands to let the ant in. Do the same with each of the other characters.

3. Dialogue

   a. Each animal pleads to be let in. If necessary, you can join each of the characters seeking shelter, in order to help the verbalizing along.
   b. At the end, after you narrate the question, "And do you know what happens to a mushroom when it rains?" all the children will want to answer, "It grows," perhaps raising their arms as a kind of final salute.

Option. You might want to use a band of stretch fabric for the mushroom.

Where the Wild Things Are,

Maurice Sendak. New York:
Harper & Row, Pub., 1963.

Synopsis:

When Max misbehaves, he is sent to his room. There a forest grows and an ocean appears. A boat takes him to Where the Wild Things Are. Max tames them and they ask him to be their King, but he declines, returning home to find his supper waiting for him.

1. Casting

 a. You play Max with one or two other children.

 b. The rest of the children in the circle can become the trees in the forest growing, the waves of the ocean (hold hands and undulate arms in toward the circle and back) and the Wild Things.

2. Action

 a. Begin the playing with Max in his room.

 b. Max gets in the boat and sails around the circle and reaches the land of the Wild Things.

 c. Wild Things stay in their seats and only roll eyes and show claws. They are not to touch each other.) When Max tames them by saying "Be still!" they must freeze.

 d. Max announces the wild rumpus, and the dance begins. Play music and let all wild things dance in front of their seats. Or, if you prefer, divide them into three groups and let only one group at a time dance a short dance. They may dance only while the music plays. One foot may be "rooted to the floor" as in the Caught in the Act game in Chapter 4.

 e. As Max sails away, Wild Things can wave goodbye and may even want to shed a tear or two. Then they become the ocean again, and the trees, as Max sails home.

3. Dialogue

 a. Wild Things can say their entreaty to Max as a chant: "Oh please don't go. We'll eat you up, we love you so."

 b. When Max sits down to his supper, you narrate the closing lines.

Option: This story is perfect for use of masks, too.

CIRCLE STORY AS PART OF LONGER LESSON PLAN

There may be times when you will want to make a Circle Story part of a more extended lesson plan. Two lesson plans of popular folktales are presented here for your use, "The Elves and the Shoemaker" and "The Gingerbread Man." (*Note:* Each of these stories will also be presented in the next chapter, using the "Segmented Story Lesson Plans," so you can compare the two methods. "The Elves and the Shoemaker 2" begins on p. 190, and The Gingerbread Man 2" begins on p. 192.)

The Elves and the Shoemaker 1

Introduction

Option A.   Begin with a discussion of elves. What are they? What do they look like? You might have some pictures of elves to share.

Option B.   Or, you might choose to talk about shoes. What different kinds can they name? How are shoes made? You might have some shoemaking tools to show, even an awl and large-sized needle or perhaps a piece of suede-like fabric cut like the sole of a shoe with needle holes indicated.

Warmup

Option A.   Have an elf dance in a circle, taking half the class at a time. (Or, they might just dance at the side of the desks.) Use a light and lively record such as "Dance of the Sugarplum Fairy" from Tchaikovsky's *Nutcracker Suite.* Since elves do not want to be discovered, they must stop dancing whenever the music stops.

Option B.   Use "The Journey" from Arnold Lobel's *Mouse Tales* (New York: Harper and Row, 1972), changing the mouse to an elf. This story can be narrated while the children, at their desks, pretend to be the elf going on a journey to his mother's house.

Option C.   For the shoemaking introduction, you might have the children pretend to be making shoes by hand. Guide them through some pantomiming at the desk—cutting out leather, threading a needle, sewing shoes, and perhaps even polishing them. Make a pair of giant shoes with giant tools (the way it might be for the elves using the shoemaker's tools). Make very tiny shoes with tiny

The elves work hard all night long making shoes.

tools (the way it might be for the shoemaker and his wife when they make the clothes for the elves.)

Presenting the Story
Tell or read your favorite version of the story, emphasizing the pantomime and the dialogue.

Playing a Circle Story

1. Casting

    a. Select perhaps five shoemakers and five shoemakers' wives. Each pair has its own little space in the center of the circle.

    b. The rest are elves. Ask them where they hide at night so they will not be seen by anyone, perhaps a flower, a stone they hide under, or a matchbox bed they sleep in. Their desks become that place.

    c. Someone may want to be in charge of lights, turning them on and off to indicate daytime and evening.

2. Action

    a. Narrate the story, giving the shoemaker and his wife plenty of action to do. When they go to sleep at night, they return to their place in the circle.

b. The elves come out of their hiding place to the center of the circle on a music cue. They must be very quiet so they do not wake anyone. After they do their work, they return to their seats when it is morning.

c. Now the shoemakers and wives awake and return to their shops. They pretend to sell all the shoes and make a lot of money. They cut out the shoes they will sew the following day. This time they return to seats but pretend they are hiding behind a curtain instead of sleeping so they can watch to see who is sewing the shoes for them.

d. The elves visit a second time and return home.

e. The shoemakers and wives return to the circle to make the little clothes for the elves. They hide a second time.

f. For the final visit the elves discover the clothes, put them on, and joyfully dance back to their homes never to be seen again.

3. Dialogue

a. If you narrate, this story can be played without any dialogue at all.

b. You can also cast some customers to come into the shop and buy shoes.

(*Note:* Even if you add more dialogue in subsequent replayings, you may still need to continue to narrate the elves' visit and to use music to control it. As the playing becomes more sophisticated, the children may want to see fewer elves and have more dialogue between the shoemaker and his wife.)

Evaluation

Have a brief discussion of what they like best. Check any trouble spots. They will, however, be anxious to repeat the playing and switch parts.

Replaying

You will need to repeat the playing until all children have had a chance to be the shoemaker or wife and an elf, since most children will demand it. Ideally, it is best to complete this process in one drama session.

Quieting Activity

Bring all children back to their seats.

Narrate a brief paragraph about a little elf getting ready for bed. "This one sleeps in a shell. He/she fluffs up a bit of soft moss for a pillow. A soft leaf serves as a blanket. Snuggle down. Close your eyes. Dream of the next good deed you'll do for someone. And go to sleep." (Play soft music such as Brahms' "Lullaby.")

The Gingerbread Man 1

Sources:
The Gingerbread Man, Ed Arno. New York: Scholastic, 1967.

Selected Variations:
Journey Cake Ho! Ruth Sawyer. New York: Viking, 1953, 1970. Appalachian setting.
"Johnny-cake," Virginia Haviland. (15) English version.
The Pancake, Anita Lobel. New York: Greenwillow, 1978. Swedish version.
"The Wee Bannock," Virginia Haviland. (16) Scottish version.

Warmup:

a. Have children pantomime making gingerbread cookies: Stir the batter, adding all the extras like raisins and nuts. Shape the dough on the board, cutting out the cookies or shaping each part. Decorate them their own way. (You comment on what the children seem to be pantomiming: putting on face, decorating with frosting, and so forth.) Have them put cookies in the oven. "Smell them baking. Take out and taste—carefully, they might be hot! Enjoy!"

b. Tell the children *they* are the dough and you are going to shape *them* into gingerbread boys and girls. You might talk to yourself as you stir up the batter (of course, they have to pretend to be the batter being stirred), adding all the extras like raisins and nuts. Now shape the dough on the board, rolling a little ball (they become a little ball) and pressing it into a head, (their body parts emerge.) then shape the body, the arm, and so on. Add the eyes, nose, mouth. Decorate with some frosting "buttons." Put into the oven to bake. Little ones will love it if you go around touching each one to test doneness and pretend they are hot—almost done—and so forth.

Presenting the Story
Tell or read the story. Encourage the chanting of the refrains. You might have the refrains written on the chalkboard or a chart.

Playing a Circle Story

1. Casting

a. Designate the parts, the little old woman, the little old man, the gingerbread man (can use two or three), and the rest of the class divided into all the people and animals he meets. (These characters will depend on the story version you choose.)

    b. Be sure you know who is playing which part and that the children all know who they are. (Example: "Group 1, you'll be the farmers working in the field;" or "Cows, here are your nametags.")

2. Action

    a. Have the children sit in a large circle. The running will be done around the inside of the circle.

    b. Explain that the running is to be done only on a drumbeat (or other signal). When the drumbeat stops, they must freeze. (You may wish to practice this.)

    c. In some versions of the story, the chasers, each in turn, get tired and stop to rest. You may want to do this (especially in a first playing) instead of having a cumulative parade of everyone chasing. Since everyone gets to say the chant, the whole class is still involved in the story.

3. Dialogue

    a. Chant may be said by everyone.

Narrate the beginning of the story, the little old man working in the garden and the little old woman making the gingerbread people. The little old woman opens the oven door and the gingerbread people hop out and begin running. (Drum-Freeze) The old woman chases them. (Drum-Freeze)

"So, the old woman gets tired and has to sit down and rest. But the gingerbread people run on." (Drum-Freeze) "They see the little old man and call out (Chant) and they run while the little old man chases them." (Drum-Freeze), and so forth until the end of the story.

Evaluation

Have a brief discussion of what they liked best. Check for any trouble spots. They will want to repeat the playing, switching roles.

Replaying

You will need to repeat the playing so all children have a chance to be the Gingerbread Man. But this may take more than in one session.

Quieting Activity

Bring all children back to their seats.

Narrate a brief paragraph about the Gingerbread Man falling into water and getting very soft and mushy—feet first and then all the way to the head—until they are just a mushy mass at their desks. "Oh, poor Gingerbread Man."

Story Dramatization: Segmented Stories

11

In the last chapter you learned about story dramatization with "circle stories." In this chapter, another method (I call them "segmented stories") is used. Because this method takes more time to experience, it is probably best suited to third grade and perhaps some second grades.

For segmented stories, a story becomes a stimulus for creating numerous separate (or segmented) drama activities. Both pantomime and verbal activities are considered. Each of these categories is then divided into solo activities and group activities.

Once you have made your listing of activities, it is fairly easy to select ones which would be most meaningful for your group to try out. Since there are far more activities than you would play in one session, you can pick and choose, as from a menu. Each story will thus give you several lesson possibilities, should you care to try all the activities.

You can begin the lesson with some solo activities, both pantomime and verbal, at the desk. For pantomime solo activities, the children all play simultaneously. For verbal solos, call on as many volunteers as you wish. If there are more volunteers than you have time for, you can pair the students and let them share their ideas with each other.

Then you can move to the group pantomimes and finally to the group dialogue scenes. For these, divide the class into small groups. You may wish to assign one activity to each group, although the children will probably want to play them all eventually. In the pair and group verbal activities, you may want to let the children rehearse a bit and then share the scenes as in the method described on page 130. To end the lesson, you can return to one of the desk activities for a quieting activity.

Notice that many of the activities extend beyond the original storyline and may introduce new characters or new situations. Often children get so interested in the uniqueness of these activities that they do not even consider "putting the story together." The exploration into the various aspects of the story is often satisfying by itself.

But it is also true that you have really rehearsed the story in bits and pieces after playing the various activites. So, then it is very easy to select the ones you and the children like best, arrange them chronologically as they appear in the original story, and use them as a basis for creating your own improvised play from beginning to end. Either way you choose, you are bound to have much fun!

Charlotte's Web
E. B. White.
New York: Harper and Row, 1952

Synopsis

A little farm girl named Fern is responsible for saving the runt pig of a litter. Later, it is a spider, Charlotte A. Cavatica, who befriends Wilbur and with the assistance of other barnyard creatures such as Templeton the Rat, saves his life again.

The following activities are only some of the many that can be created from a book-length story.

Pantomime (solo at desks)

1. "You are taking care of Wilbur the little runt pig the way Fern would do. You are giving him a bath, and he's so dirty! Scrub hard. Dry him off well. Now show how you put on Wilbur's bid and feed him his bottle. Rock him gently until he falls asleep."

2. "Be Wilbur eating the 'slops' Lurvy has put in the trough. As I read the passage describing all the food, you think like Wilbur about how delicious they all are, as you carefully taste each one."

3. "Now you are Charlotte. A fly has just flown into your web. Creep up on it carefully, inject it with your poison, and then wrap your silk around it. Do this to the count of ten in slow motion."

4. "It took four weeks for the goslings to hatch. Pretend you are an unborn gosling all scrunched up in your egg. Now it is time for you to hatch. Start pecking at the inside of your shell and keep going until you finally poke your head out. I'll count slowly, and by the time I reach ten, you will be hatched."

5. "Be the goose who's hatching the eggs. Get up off your nest and get a drink of water. Now waddle back and settle back down, but be careful not to break any of those precious eggs!"

Verbal (solo at desks)

1. "You're Templeton the Rat, a born complainer. What is it that happened in your lifetime that makes you such a complainer?"

2. "Charlotte once told Wilbur a bedtime story about a spider who built a web across a stream in order to catch a fish. Think of another bedtime story Charlotte could tell Wilbur and tell it to us." (This could be done round-robin style.)

3. "You are Wilbur. There are many wonderful things about Charlotte you like very much. Tell us about some of them and explain why she is such a special friend of yours."

4. "You're Lurvy the farmhand. There's a lot of fuss being made over this pig, and you're getting tired of it. Tell us how you're feeling. Have you got any plans to try to change this? Why or why not?"

5. "Everyone came from miles around to see Wilbur and Charlotte's web. Tell us who you are, where you live, and why you've come to see this unusual event."

Pantomime for Pairs and Groups

1. "When Fern comes home after school, Wilbur follows her around. One of you be Fern and the other Wilbur, doing three things you might do after school." (Count slowly to three).

2. Build a place (see p. 107). "Create Zuckerman's barn and surrounding barnyard. Some things to include could be the pig trough, Templeton's rat hole, the rotten egg, Charlotte's web, the goose nest, the swing in the hayloft, and the goose's nest as well as various kinds of farm equipment." Other places to build might be the Fair tents, the midway, the farm kitchen.

3. "Create a frozen picture of the day Wilber got loose and everyone tried to catch him." (Use five people.)

4. "A very important moment occurs when Templeton cuts down Charlotte's magnum opus (egg sac) and Wilbur carries it safely home in his mouth. In pairs, be Templeton and Wilbur performing this very serious and delicate business."

5. "After the miracle occurred at Zuckerman's farm, a newspaper photographer came to take a picture of Wilbur and his friends. In groups of five, be the animals posing for your picture. Be sure we can tell which animal you are."

6. Count Freeze Activities. "Guess which rides Fern and Avery are on at the fair." "Guess the word Charlotte is gracefully spinning in her web."

7. "In groups of six to eight, become one of the amusement rides at the fair. When I play the carnival music, you may demonstrate your ride."

Verbal in Pairs and Groups

1. "In pairs be Fern convincing her father not to kill Wilbur the runt pig. Father is reluctant at first and then gives in."

2. "When Wilbur first moved to Zuckerman's farm, he was very lonely. He asked the goose, the lamb, and Templeton the rat to play with him. In groups of four, when Wilbur asks you to play, make up some excuse why you can't."

3. "Suppose it's Wilbur's birthday, and his barnyard friends decide to have a surprise party for him. In groups of five, be the friends talking over your ideas of what to serve for refreshments, the games you could play, and the party decorations you could make. As I come by your group, you may speak up so we can hear your plans."

4. "Some visitors have come to town. They've heard the story about the miraculous pig but don't believe it. In groups of four, two people who have seen the webs and know the story will try to convince the visitors that it's all true."

5. "You are a panel of Charlottes (perhaps five students seated in the front of the classroom) who will give counsel to other barnyard animals in the audience. Perhaps the goose is worried about Templeton attacking one of her baby goslings. Or perhaps Templeton is beginning to care that the barnyard animals don't seem to like him. Whatever your questions and concerns, now is your time to ask the expert, Charlotte. Raise your hand if you have a question to ask."

6. "In groups of five, create a television commercial that will convince people that Wilbur is, indeed, quite a remarkable pig. You may use slogans, jingles, or whatever else you think is necessary to promote good feelings for Wilbur."

7. "In pairs, one is Wilbur and the other Charlotte. You've just met, and Wilbur is still a little afraid of the spider and her bloodthirsty ways. Have Charlotte try to convince a reluctant Wilbur of her virtues."

The Elves and the Shoemaker 2

Pantomime (solo at desks):

1. "You are the shoemaker or his wife, cutting out a pair of shoes from the leather." (To add conflict and tension, you could say, "You're working carefully, but you have many orders to fill and you don't have much time.")

2. "You are the shoemaker or his wife, hiding behind the curtain in the workshop at night, waiting for the elves. Now they enter, and you watch them carefully, but you mustn't let them see or hear you. I'll play some music to indicate that the elves are busy at work, and you show your reactions."

3. "You are the shoemaker or the wife, sewing the new clothes and making the new shoes for the elves. Remember how very tiny they are."

4. "You are the elves making the shoes. Let's see you doing this, cutting out the leather, piercing the holes, threading the needle, and sewing the shoes. But, remember that the shoes are much bigger than you are, and so are the tools."

Verbal (solo at desks):

1. "You are the poor shoemaker (or wife). Tell how poor you are and how very difficult it is for you to make a living."

2. "You are an elf who specializes in making shoes. Tell us how you learned your craft."

"Pretend to be an elf making shoes. . . . "

3. "You are the shoemaker. In front of you is a pair of the most wonderful shoes you ever made. Show the quality and workmanship to us and tell us what is so wonderful about them."

Pantomime in Pairs and Groups

1. Ten count freeze (see p. 102) of the different kinds of shoes the shoemaker and his wife must make. "Make the shoe and then put it on and try it out." (Possibilities: ballet shoes, hunting boots, hiking shoes, sandals, and so forth.)

2. "Do the mirror game. In pairs, be the elves trying on their new clothes."

3. Build a place (see p. 107). Create the shoemaker's workshop.

4. "In groups of five, create the clock that strikes midnight." (Perhaps the clock has little figures in it that do certain actions on the hour.)

5. Groups of five to eight. "Create an assembly line of elves making shoes. Each worker should perform a different task." (Play music).

Verbal in Pairs and Groups

1. "In pairs, be the shoemaker trying to make a sale and a customer who is very difficult to satisfy."

2. Pairs. "The landlord who owns the shoemaker's shop has come to collect the overdue rent. The shoemaker tries to put you off—again. The scene ends when you agree, reluctantly, to let the rent go for one more month."

3. Experts Game (see p. 127). "You are a group of elves who are specialists in shoemaking. Answer questions from the audience about your work."

4. "The elves return to 'Headquarters' to receive their next assignment. Where will the Chief Elf and Assistant decide to send the elves and what will their job be? But the elves feel they deserve a vacation since they did such a good job for the shoemaker. How will this problem be worked out to everyone's satisfaction?"

The Gingerbread Man 2

Pantomime (solo at desks)

1. Do either or both of the baking pantomimes in "The Gingerbread Man I" p. 182.
2. "You are the gingerbread cookie being devoured by the fox, one part at a time. As I count to ten, you slowly disappear until you are totally eaten."
3. "You are the fox watching the gingerbread cookie running over the countryside. As your eyes follow him around, you lick your chops hungrily."
4. "Think of three things the little old man or the little old woman might do while they wait for the gingerbread people to return. I'll count slowly to three while you pantomime each of the three things."

Verbal (solo at desks)

1. "You are the gingerbread person. Why are you planning to run away from everyone? Where are you trying to go?"
2. "You are the little old woman. How do you suppose it happened that the cookies you baked came alive?"
3. "You are the little old man. Do you think the gingerbread people should be punished for running away? Why? How would you punish a cookie?"
4. "You are the animal that captures the little gingerbread person. How do you think you were able to succeed when everyone else failed?"

Pantomime in Pairs and Groups

1. "In groups of six, create the oven and, on my signal, open the door and let the gingerbread people out."
2. "Do a count freeze (see p. 102) of one of the people or animals who chased the gingerbread man, doing what they were doing the moment the gingerbread man passed them."
3. Build a Place (see Chapter 7). "The gingerbread person wants a gingerbread house to live in. Create the one room house with its furnishings, all made of cookies and candies."

Verbal in Pairs and Groups

1. Groups of four. "Be the little old man and little old woman trying to convince your doubting neighbors that you baked gingerbread people that came alive."

"I'm the Gingerbread Man, and I can run away from you, I can, I can!"

2. "You are a panel of expert judges at a baking contest. The audience wants to ask you some questions about cookies that come alive. Perhaps they'd like to have a recipe for making them. You have the answers for all their questions."

3. "In pairs, be the little old man and little old woman discussing whether you should bake any more gingerbread people. One of you wants to go ahead, but the other is afraid. What will you finally decide to do?"

4. Groups of three. "Suppose the Gingerbread Man doesn't get eaten and eventually returns home. He wants a second chance. The old man and woman aren't sure they want to go through the trouble again. How will he convince them that he will mind and that they should let him return home?"

Jack and the Beanstalk

Sources:
Jack and the Beanstalk, Walter de la Mare. Alfred A. Knopf, 1959.
"Jack and the Beanstalk," Virginia Haviland. (15)

Pantomime (solo at desks)

1. "You are one of Jack's magic beans. As I beat the drum, grow from a tiny seed into a tall bean plant that slowly gets larger and larger until it is a giant stalk."
2. "Think of three things Jack might do at the fair. Number them 1, 2, and 3. As I call out the numbers, you be Jack doing these three things."
3. Same as above with chores on the farm.
4. "Pretend you are Jack stealing the magic harp while the Giant sleeps at his table. Be very careful not to awaken him. Go out the door and climb down the beanstalk."
5. "You are the Giant who smells a human being about. Think of three places he might be hiding, and look for him in each place as I count to three slowly."
6. "You're the Giant eating your meal. By your actions we should be able to tell what you're eating. Remember, you eat a lot and probably aren't very neat about it." (You might pretend to be the Giant's wife or a servant grumbling about how she/he has to cook so much for him and clean up afterwards.)

Verbal (solo at desks)

1. "You are Jack's cow and don't like the idea of being sold. Tell us why."
2. "You're the Giant's wife with a grocery list in hand. Tell us some of the items on your list."
3. "You are Jack explaining to the Giant's wife why she should let you in. What will your story be?"
4. "You're the man who traded the beans for Jack's cow. How is it that you know Jack's name, and why did you want a cow instead of the magical beans?"
5. "You're the Giant. Tell how you got all your wealth, including the hen that lays the golden eggs and the singing harp."

Pantomime in Pairs and Groups

1. Build a Place (see p. 107). "Create the one-room cottage that Jack and his mother live in. Remember the time period we're in and the fact that Jack and his mother were poor."

2. "In groups of four, show the Giant's wife fetching a bag of gold, the hen, and the singing harp. A person plays each of the Giant's treasures."

3. Count-Freeze Pantomime (see p. 102). "Be a performer at the fair (acrobat, juggler, fortune teller). We'll try to guess who you are."

Verbal in Pairs and Groups

1. Create these scenes in pairs. "Jack tries to find work but no one will have him. What jobs does he apply for and why won't anyone hire him?"

2. "In pairs be Jack explaining to his mother the great bargain he made at the fair. Mother is angry and upset; Jack is puzzled why his mother doesn't see how wonderful magic beans would be."

3. Groups of four. "Some neighbors notice the giant beanstalk and talk about some of the crazy things Jack has done in the past. What might they say to each other?"

4. "At the end of the story, Jack marries a princess. In pairs be Jack explaining to a King why he is worthy of a princess' hand in marriage."

STORY BIBLIOGRAPHY

The materials are arranged in alphabetical order according to title. The numbers in parentheses refer to the numbered anthologies at the end of the book. The age level the stories might be best suited for is indicated in the left hand margin. Annotation includes suggested themes and/or curricular topics the stories might be correlated with.

K-2 "The Adventure of Three Little Rabbits," author untraced. (40) Little rabbits get stuck in some spilled syrup and almost become rabbit stew. You can use circle mapping with two or three little old couples. Good story for spring or for a science lesson in how syrup softens and melts when heated.

3 "Anansi and the Fish Country," Philip Sherlock. (2) Anansi tries to trick fish by pretending to be a doctor in this African trickster tale.

3 "Anansi Plays Dead," Harold Courlander and Albert Kofi Prempeh. (22) Anansi pretends to die so he will not have to go to jail, but the villagers trick him. This African folk tale shows how those who trick are often outwitted themselves.

3 "Anansi's Hat-Shaking Dance" Harold Courlander and Albert Kofi Prempeh. (22) Anansi makes a show of mourning for his mother-in-

law and is shown for the boaster he is. This African folk tale shows we are eventually seen for what we really are.

3 *Anatole and the Cat*, Eve Titus. New York: McGraw-Hill, 1957. A clever mouse outwits the cat who hampers his work as a cheese taster in Duval's cheese factory. It has a French setting. Other Anatole stories may also be of interest.

3 *Angus and the Mona Lisa*, Jacqueline Cooper. New York: Lothrop, Lee, and Shepard, 1981. Angus, a cat of French ancestry, takes a trip to Paris, and with the help of Antoinette, a cat who works for Interpol, prevents two thugs—Pigeon and Turtle Dove—from stealing the Mona Lisa from the Louvre. French vocabulary and references to places in France offer a language and geography lesson in addition to an exciting mystery.

K–1 *Are You My Mother?* P. D. Eastman. New York: Random House, 1960. A baby bird hatches and goes off in search of its mother. But, since he does not know what she looks like, he mistakes other animals and even a steam shovel for her. This easy-to-read book with limited vocabulary is easy to play as a circle story.

3 *The Cock, the Mouse, and the Little Red Hen*, Lorinda Bryan Cauley. New York: G. P. Putnam's, 1982. It retells the story of the Little Red Hen who does all the work. In this one she saves the Cock and Mouse from being the Fox Family's dinner. It has easy dialogue and beautiful illustrations. Mouse and Cock do lots of "grumbling," which can be mimed or elaborated in great detail.

3 *The Country Bunny and the Little Gold Shoes,* DuBose Heyward. Boston: Houghton-Mifflin, 1937. A little country girl bunny proves that she can grow up to be an Easter Bunny. This is an old favorite that can be played as a circle story, particularly for the scenes with the twenty-one little bunnies. Because it is a longer story, you should allow more than one session to play.

3 *The Cuckoo's Reward*, Daisy Kouzel and Earl Thollander. Garden City, N.Y.: Doubleday, 1977. A cuckoo helps save the grain from fire in this Mexican folktale. Helpfulness of the animals toward humans is presented.

2–3 *Drakestail*, Jan Wahl. New York: Greenwillow, 1978. A very clever duck, with the help of some unusual friends, outwits a greedy ruler and becomes king in this traditional French folktale.

3 *The Elephant's Child*, Rudyard Kipling. New York: Walker, 1970. The elephant's child, who has "'satiable curtiosity," finds out some answers to his questions but gets a long nose doing it. After he discovers all the advantages of having a long nose, his relatives decide they want one, too. It is a mythical explanation of the elephant's trunk. See also (24).

3 *The Fence*, Jan Balet. New York: Delacorte, 1969. A poor family in Mexico is taken to court by a rich family because they sniffed the delicious aromas from the kitchen of the rich family's house. The Judge outwits the greedy, rich family, using their own logic.

3 *Fin McCool*, Tomi dePaola. New York: Holiday, 1981. Giant Fin is afraid of an even bigger giant, but his wife saves the day with a bit of trickery. The cast is small, but children enjoy this popular tale.

K–3 *Gillespie and the Guards*, Benjamin Elkin. New York: Viking, 1956. Three brothers with powerful eyes become guards of the kingdom. The King offers a reward to anyone who can get past them. Gillespie, a young boy, tricks them in an unusual way, giving an example of problem solving.

3 *Granny and the Desperadoes*, Peggy Parish. New York: Macmillan, 1970. Granny captures some desperadoes and turns them over to the sheriff, but not before she gets them to do chores for her.

2–3 *Hansel and Gretel*, Elizabeth D. Crawford. New York: Morrow, 1980. This is the classic Grimm fairy tale of two children left alone in the woods who meet a witch. See also the version by Rika Lesser, New York: Dodd, Mead & Co., 1984.

3 "How Jahdu Took Care of Trouble," Virginia Hamilton. (50) Jahdu tricks Trouble and frees everyone from the huge barrel they have been caught in. This is a trickster tale.

3 "How the Animals Got Their Fur Coats," Hilda Mary Hooke. (48) All the animals get lovely new coats except Moose, who gets the leftovers. Charming characters appear in this Canadian Indian legend.

3 "How the Birds Got Their Colors," Hilda Mary Hooke. (48) Delightfully funny tale of how all the birds get colorful feathers except the Sapsucker in a Canadian Indian legend.

3 "How the Little Owl's Name Was Changed," Charles E. Gillham. (5) Brave Little Owl takes fire away from evil men in this Alaskan Eskimo folktale.

3 *How the Sun Made a Promise and Kept It,* Margery Bernstein. Scribner's, 1974. In this retelling of a Canadian myth, the sun is captured and the animals take on the task of freeing it.

3 *Jim and the Beanstalk,* Raymond Briggs. Reading, MA: Addison-Wesley, 1970. In this new version of an old tale, the Giant wants a set of false teeth, a pair of glasses, and a red wig. Children might like to make up their own new version of an old tale after experiencing this one.

3 *King Midas and the Golden Touch,* Al Perkins. New York: Random House, 1969. The Greek mythological tale of the king who loved gold too much.

Little Red Riding Hood meets the Wolf.

K–2 *The Little Engine That Could,* retold by Watty Piper. New York: Platt & Munk, 1954. A little engine is able to take the stalled, larger train over the mountain to deliver Christmas toys. Perseverance pays off. Even smaller persons can help the larger and more powerful.

K–2 *Little Red Riding Hood,* numerous editions. A little girl finds a surprise when she visits her grandmother.

1–2 *Little Toot,* Hardie Gramatky. New York: G. P. Putnam's, 1939, 1967. Little Toot is a tugboat who would rather play than work. He is challenged to prove himself and does so by rescuing a stranded ocean liner. Much of this story can be narrated, but children also like to play the other tugboats and add dialogue. At least one playing should be solo narrative pantomime so that everyone can have a chance to be this popular character.

K–3 *Loudmouse,* Richard Wilbur. New York: Macmillan, 1968. A mouse with a very loud voice turns out to be an effective burglar alarm. Our weaknesses can sometimes turn out to be our strengths.

3 *Lyle, Lyle, the Crocodile,* Bernard Waber. Boston: Houghton Mifflin, 1965. A crocodile who is more human than animal has remarkable adventures. Other Lyle stories may be of interest.

2–3 *Madeline,* Ludwig Bemelmans. New York: Viking, 1939. Madeline lives in a Paris convent with eleven other little girls. After she is rushed to the hospital for an appendectomy, she becomes the envy of her friends. Sequels are available.

2-3 *Mike Mulligan and His Steam Shovel*, Virginia Lee Burton. Boston: Houghton Mifflin, 1939. Mike Mulligan's unique solution to collecting the money for digging the basement of the town hall with his steam shovel, Mary Anne, makes an old story remain ever-popular.

3 *No Help At All*, Betty Baker. New York: Greenwillow, 1978. This humorous Mayan Indian legend is about West Chac, the rain god of the West, who helps a young boy one day and then asks for his help in return. But everything the boy does is "no help at all," except by accident.

2-3 *Not This Bear!* Bernice Myers. New York: Four Winds, 1967. A little boy in a furry hat and coat is mistaken for a bear by a bear family. He has to convince them that he is not one of them.

3 *Once Upon a Dinkelshühl,* Patricia Lee Gauch. New York: G. P. Putnam's, 1977. In a retelling of a medieval German legend, the city's gatekeeper's young daughter and her friends confront the invading soldiers and save the town from being plundered and burned.

2-3 *Petunia*, Roger Duvosin. New York: Knopf, 1950. Petunia, a goose, thinks she has knowledge because she owns a book, even though she cannot read. Children will delight in knowing what Petunia does not—that "firecrackers" does not spell "cake."

K-1 *Runaway Marie Louise*, Natalie Savage Carlson. New York: Charles Scribner's, 1977. A little mongoose runs away when her mama spanks her for being naughty. For various reasons none of the other animals will take her in. She goes to a witch toad who wisely sends her back home. You are still loved even though you may be punished.

K-2 *The Saggy Baggy Elephant*, K. and B. Jackson. Racine, WI: Western Publishing Co., 1947, 1974. A little elephant is teased by a parrot for his loose skin. Sooki, as the little elephant calls himself, does not know what animal he is until a herd of elephants welcome him as one of their own. Perfect for a circle story and an elephant parade, perhaps accompanied by Henry Mancini's "Baby Elephant Walk" music.

K-2 *The Three Billy Goats Gruff*, Marcia Brown. New York: Harcourt, Brace, Jovanovich, 1957. This is the age-old story of the goats who outwit the Troll under the bridge. This is considered one of the best versions.

K-2 "Three Little Pigs," several editions. This is the story of two foolish pigs and one smart pig who outwits a greedy wolf.

K-2 "Ticky-Picky-Boom-Boom," Philip Sherlock. (2) Tiger is chased by yams from Anansi's fields and tries to find hiding places with his friends. This African folk tale has an enjoyable repetitious chant that everyone will want to say. Children can do chasing around circle or tapping hands on thighs.

The Troll fishes while the Little Billy Goat Gruff trip traps over the bridge.

"Little pig, little pig, let me come in. . . . "

2–3 *Two Hundred Rabbits*, Lonzo Anderson and Adrienne Adams. New York: Viking, 1968. A rabbit watches, and tells the story of, a young boy who wishes to entertain the king for the castle festival. A rabbit parade solves the boy's problem. This is perfect for circle story playing since most of the children can play the forest animals and the rabbits. The parade can be accompanied by march music or "The Bunny Hop."

3 *Tye May and the Magic Brush*, Molly Bang. New York: Greenwillow, 1981. This is a retelling of a Chinese fairy tale in which a young girl has a magic paintbrush she uses to help the poor. A greedy king tries to get it from her, but she outwits him. Another version, *Liang and the Magic Paintbrush*, by Demi (New York: Holt, Rinehart, and Winston, 1980), has a boy as the hero.

1–2 *Where Can an Elephant Hide?* David McPhail. Garden City, N.Y.: Doubleday, 1979. Morris the Elephant wants to be able to hide like the other animals. But their methods of camouflage do not work for him. He finally finds a place to hide—and just in time to escape the hunters. It is a good science lesson.

K–3 "Why the Bear is Stumpy Tailed," George Webbe Dasent. (4) The Bear is tricked into fishing in the ice with his tail and loses it. This myth explains animal characteristics and is a good story for winter. If you play this as a circle story, children can form the lake that freezes over. Other characters can be ice skaters skating, fish swimming, and even a sun that slowly sets.

12 Extended Drama Lesson Planning

Throughout this resource guide you have been given many ideas for drama activities and even some lesson plans. As you have seen, single activities can be incorporated into your classroom teaching at any time and with various curricular subjects. Lesson plans for some of the longer activities can range from fifteen or twenty minutes to forty-five minutes. Sometimes it has been recommended that a lesson plan cover two class periods.

You may find that you want to take a given topic or theme and create an extended drama lesson around it. Perhaps you would like an extended lesson plan to last over a few days' time, spending about twenty or thirty minutes each day on an activity. This chapter is designed to help you in this planning.

1. Our first consideration is the theme or topic which will tie the activities together in a unified plan. Like most teachers, you are probably pressed for time, and will want your drama lessons to fit other areas of the curriculum. Perhaps you want to cover seasons of the year, pilgrim life, or a story in a basal reader. Or, perhaps your class has a particular interest in animals, motorcycles, or a favorite author and you want to center a lesson on a topic of high appeal.

2. Next consider your goals and objectives. Ideally, you will want to emphasize, as often as possible, the three goals identified at the outset: drama, personal development, and subject matter.

3. You then might make a list of activities you could do, trying to include as wide a range as possible: beginning activities, narrative pantomime, verbal activities, creative stories, and so forth.

4. Now you are ready to sequence the activities.

    a. The first activity is generally a warmup. This material should not be overly challenging in order to put the class in a relaxed mood and ready for further work together. If children are overly excitable, the opening material will need to be highly structured and controlled. It may also be helpful to use an activity that expends children's excess energy in order to calm them down and focus on the task.

    b. As the activities progress, they should become more challenging. To analyze the level of difficulty, consider the sequence chart on p. 12.

        For example, you might choose to do a pantomime game from the many listed in Chapter 7. According to variable 3 on the chart, pantomimes are easy activities compared to verbal. But, they are also advanced, according to Variable 8, since they require an audience of guessers. At the same time, it would probably be easier for children to perform a pantomime of their favorite sport in a Count Freeze Pantomime (p. 102) than it would be to participate in creating a Group Frozen Picture (p. 105) of a current event. The former relies on the children's individual and personal interest (Variable 4: solo playing) and something they are familiar with (Variable 7: informational content), while the latter requires group decision making (Variable 4: pair and group work) and a knowledge of current events (Variable 7: higher data content). Each activity is a pantomime for guessing, but the other variables change the levels of difficulty.

        While you need not slavishly adhere to a thorough analysis of each activity you choose to do, an overall consideration will help you sequence your activities so that children will experience maximum success.

    c. Finally you end with a relaxing or quieting activity.

    d. (optional) As a personal preference, I like to include some alternative possibilities to my activities so that I have more flexibility to make changes.

On the following pages are three extended lesson plans for you to begin on, adapt from, or simply use as stimulus for your own ideas.

EXTENDED LESSON PLAN
"Winter" (Snow)

Objectives

a. Gain an understanding of the winter season and the various activities connected with it.

b. Experience creative movement in enacting winter activities.

c. Communicate and interpret nonverbal messages through pantomimes for guessing.

d. Dramatize a folktale with opportunities for pantomime and verbal interaction.

e. Experience characterization of selfish and generous qualities in the trees and the helplessness of the wounded bird.

Preparation and Materials

a. Copy of *The Snowy Day,* Ezra Jack Keats (New York: Viking, 1962).

b. Copy of the folktale "Why the Evergreen Trees Keep Their Leaves in Winter" by Florence Holbrook (40).

c. (optional) Pictures of people engaged in various wintertime activities.

d. (optional) Paper headbands for characters in the story dramatization of the folktale.

e. Length of Unit: Four separate days of approximately 30 minutes each.

Warmup Activity: Snowy Day (play at desk or other limited area)

a. Open session with comments about winter and snow appropriate to the experiences of the children.

b. Read and show pictures from the book, a narrative pantomime story about a small boy who has his first memorable experience in the snow.

c. Narrate/sidecoach the story which includes dressing for snowy weather, building a snowman, making a snow angel, and being a mountain climber. The ending is the return indoors, taking off outdoor clothing, going to bed, and dreaming of a wonderful day in the snow. (Suggestion: End playing with Peter in bed so children are seated. Omit playing the book's ending of going outdoors again on the following day.)

Half and Half Pantomime: Snow Activities (pantomimers in front of class, guessers at desks)

a. Discuss with children snow or winter activities not included in *Snowy Day*. Show pictures of people engaged in winter activities such as ice skating, skiing, feeding birds, and so forth. Children add their own ideas to the discussion.

b. Divide class in half. One group performs a winter activity for the other group to guess. Depending on the maturity of the children, you may tell them what to pantomime or let them decide. Or, have activities written on a few cards and let them draw one card.

c. Switch groups perhaps three times.

Story Sharing: "Why the Evergreen Trees Keep Their Leaves in Winter" (at desks or story corner)

a. Tell or read this folktale of a little bird with a broken wing who cannot fly south with the other birds as winter approaches. When it seeks shelter in the trees, it is rejected as being too small and unimportant. Only the evergreens offer help. When the wind blows in the winter, the Frost King tells it to spare the leaves of the evergreen trees because of their kindness to the little bird.

b. End with a brief discussion of their reactions to the story and the various characters.

Story Dramatization

a. Review story if you read it on a previous day.

b. Act out the sensory and emotion pantomimes and some of the brief verbal interaction from the story (at desks or in a circle).

    1. Children are the various birds flying south for winter. You briefly sidecoach and narrate a few words about the birds' takeoff, soaring to higher altitudes, circling around one more time to encourage the little bird to join them or to say goodbye.

    2. (Continue side-coaching.) "Now you're the little bird with a broken wing trying to fly, sadly watching your friends leave. You feel the cold and puff out your feathers to protect yourself from the wind."

    3. "Now you are the trees, the birch, oak, or the willow, standing proudly, feeling very important. You don't like strangers. Oh, oh, it looks as if someone's coming."

    4. Children continue to play the trees. You play the little bird (either by yourself or with a couple of children you choose

The wounded bird asks the maple trees for shelter.

quickly) and approach some of the trees and ask for permission to make a home in their branches. Some children will forget that they are the trees that say "no" to the little bird. (They may feel very sorry for the bird, especially if you are convincing). If this is the case, you can say, "Oh, you must be one of the friendly evergreen trees."

5. Now you can narrate/side-coach the trees briefly through the experience of having the cold and wind touch their leaves, making them shake loose and fall a few at a time. You can play the wind yourself, coming near them and touching a few trees at a time ("this row," or "this table") This is a nice control feature as the trees must wait until you give them a signal. (Note: Little children may literally fall to signify the leaves falling. Be prepared to sidecoach a slow motion fall.)

6. "Now you are the friendly evergreen trees who are much kinder to the little bird. They offer their branches, protection from the north wind, and even berries to eat. And here comes the little bird with the broken wing." Again, you (by yourself or with two more children you select quickly) play the bird and interact briefly with a few of the trees.

7. To end these "warmups," you can narrate briefly the ending of the story. "And, so, the little bird was protected by the friendly evergreens and the Frost King rewarded them. And that's why, to this day, evergreen trees keep their leaves in winter."

c. If the children want to continue, you may wish to put the story together as a small playet.

Cast (in order of appearance)

Wounded Bird:	played by two children (you may choose to play with them)
Birds:	played by three children
Unfriendly Trees:	groups of two or three each for an oak, a birch, and a willow
Wind:	two children
Wind sound effects:	played by same three children who were the birds
Frost King	two children

Discussion/Evaluation

a. "Was the story clear?"

b. "Could we see a difference in the two kinds of trees—the selfish and the generous?"

c. "How could we tell the bird was wounded?"

d. Other changes or additions.

Replaying of Story, Switching Parts

Other Additions for Future Playing

If the children enjoy playing the story and repeat it several times, you might wish to encourage them to consider additions like the following:

a. A scene showing how the bird's wing was wounded.

b. A scene between the birds when the wounded bird's problem is discovered.

c. A scene at the end, showing the return of the birds in the spring who discover the young bird well again.

Quieting Activity: Melting Snowman
(may be used at desks or in larger areas)

Children are snowmen melting in the warm sun. "Your right arm melts the fastest and starts to slide down your round body. Now your left arm starts to slip. The sun gets higher in the sky and starts to melt your head. Your face starts to run and your head begins to roll off. Then your shoulders begin to slump and your back begins to curve. You're only about half as tall as you once were. The sun is getting warmer and now you are beginning to melt faster. You sink into a large lump. Now the lump starts to spread out until you are just a puddle of water.''

If children are in larger areas of space, after a moment of re-laxation, you (as the Frost King) touch the children, one by one, as a signal to return to desks.

EXTENDED LESSON PLAN
"Emotions"
Objectives

a. Gain an understanding of what emotions are.

b. Learn how emotions can be conveyed through facial expression, body posture, gestures, and tone of voice.

c. Identify and express a variety of emotions from pictures and pantomime activities.

d. Act as characters in stories who experience a variety of emotions in the many situations they encounter.

Preparation and Materials

a. Copy of *Frances Facemaker* by William Cole (New York: World Publishing Co., 1963).

b. Pictures of children experiencing a variety of emotions. You probably have a number of these already collected and in use for other purposes. Many magazine advertisements feature children in interesting situations that are suitable for an emotion discussion.

Other suggested sources:

Berger, Terry. *I Have Feelings*, New York: Behavioral Publications, 1971

Tester, Sylvia. *Moods and Emotions*, Elgin, Ill.: David C. Cook, 1970. Includes sixteen poster-size photos illustrating various emotions.

c. Copy of Maurice Sendak's *Where the Wild Things Are* or a story of your choice to dramatize.

d. Copy of quieting poem of your choice. Or, if available, Guatemalan "worry" dolls.

e. Optional: Copy of "What Was I Scared Of?" by Dr. Seuss (37).

f. Length of Sessions: A number of options are available in this unit. Most activities will take anywhere from 15 to 20 minutes. For the story dramatization, you may prefer to read the story one day and enact it the next. The dramatization itself will need from 30 to 40 minutes for almost any story you select.

Warmup Activity (played at the desk)

a. Discuss emotions with children. What emotions can they name? List on the chalkboard. Look at some pictures of children expressing different emotions. Can they guess the emotions? What clues tell when someone is feeling a particular emotion?

b. Sing the traditional action song ''If You're Happy and You Know It.''

If you're happy and you know it, clap your hands (clap, clap)
If you're happy and you know it, clap your hands (clap, clap)
If you're happy and you know it, then your face will surely show it
If you're happy and you know it, clap your hands. (clap, clap)

Additional verses can have whatever emotions and actions you wish. For example, you might use: sad—wipe a tear; angry—stamp your feet; surprised—say ''oh, oh''; cheerful—whistle a tune; sorry—hang your head, and so forth. Children will have ideas to add, too.

Narrative Pantomime: Face Making (play at the desk)

Narrate/side-coach the story *Frances Facemaker.* If you give just a little introduction explaining what the story is about, you probably do not need to read it before playing.

Children can make the faces Frances does when the book says, ''You do it.''

Option: Play ''Pass the Face'' (p. 43).

Sculpting (play in space around the room)

a. How are emotions expressed with the rest of our bodies as well as our faces? Look at pictures showing people/children expressing different emotions in a variety of ways.

b. In pairs, children mold a partner into an expression of a particular emotion. They may mold the face as well as the body posture. You may specify the emotion or let children choose their own. Children may tell what the emotion is or let the rest of the class guess each statue.

Option: Play in pairs Dr. Seuss' story ''What Was I Scared Of?'' (37) A typical Seuss character is frightened of a pair of pants with nobody in them, until it finds the pants are afraid of it!

One-Liners with Pictures (played at desk)

a. Discuss how we can tell how people are feeling by the sound of their voice. Ask children to remember when they talked with someone over the telephone. Even though they cannot see the person's face, they can usually tell how the person is feeling.

b. Next try a game of emotion guessing. You say something with your back to the class, expressing it happily (sadly, angrily, etc.) Use just a single word like ''Hello,'' or ''Oh.'' Next let volunteers say the same or different words, expressing a variety of emotions.

Option: Put emotion words on one set of cards. Make another set of cards with single words or even sentences. Children draw a card from each stack and say the word or sentence with the emotion they drew.

c. Using large pictures from books or ones you have collected and mounted yourself, show to the children and ask them to think of something the person in the picture might be saying. Volunteers should say the line the way they think the person would say it. Note that they are now creating dialogue for a situation as well as expressing it in an appropriate manner.

Story Dramatization: *Where the Wild Things Are* (see lesson plan p. 178)

Optional: Most stories for dramatization have characters involved in exciting or interesting situations that encourage a variety of emotional expressions. Therefore, you may select any story in Chapters 10 or 11 to use for a lesson on emotions. Emphasize the emotions as you tell the story, saying how the characters feel in their situation. Or, specifically ask children at the end of the storytelling: "How do you think_____felt when he or she_____?"

Worry dolls of the Guatemalan Indians

There should be some room for interpretation; not all children will identify the characters' emotions in exactly the same way.

Quieting Activities (at desk or in circle)

a.   "Tired Tim," Walter de la Mare. (4) Poor Tim is just too tired to move.

b.   "Slowly," James Reeves. (52) Everything moves very slowly in this poem.

c.   An ancient Indian legend of Guatemala tells how children assign their worries and cares to little "worry people," or dolls, (see photo 211) so they can assume the children's problems at night when the children are asleep. "Let's pretend we're putting our worries on these dolls, one by one, and now we can go to sleep, free of care."

EXTENDED LESSON PLAN
"Circus"
Objectives

a. Gain an understanding of an ancient form of entertainment and occupations related to it.

b. Experience creative movement and pantomime of various circus acts.

c. Experience verbal activities related to circus history and circus stories.

Preparation and Materials

a. Copy of *Harold's Circus* by Crockett Johnson (New York: Harper and Row, 1959).
(Optional: enlargements of the pictures from the text.)

b. Pictures of various circus acts for the pantomimes for guessing. In additon to your own collection of pictures, the following sources are useful:

Harmer, Mabel. *The Circus*. Chicago: Childrens Press, 1981. This is an easy-to-read, basic introduction to the circus with color photographs.

Krementz, Jill. *A Very Young Circus Flyer. New York: Alfred A. Knopf*, 1979. In this fascinating book, complete with color photographs, a nine-year-old trapeze artist tells of his family's life as they travel and perform with the circus.

McGovern, Ann. *If You Lived with the Circus*. New York: Four Winds, 1972.

Schenck de Regniers, Beatrice. *Circus*. New York: Viking, 1966. Colored illustrations of the circus are presented in this picture-book.

c. Sequence cards for the verbal sequence game.

d. Copy of Robert Leydenfrost's *The Snake That Sneezed* (New York: G. P. Putnam's, 1970) for story dramatization.

e. Source material for clown antics activity.

f. Copy of *The Chimp and the Clown* by Ruth Carroll (New York: Henry Z. Walck, 1972) for storytelling quieting activity.

g. Length of Sessions: Most activities will take about 30 to 40 minutes. Time will vary depending on how much information children already have about the circus. A number of options are also presented throughout.

Warmup Activity: Harold's Circus (play at desk or other limited area)

a.   Discuss the circus. What do the children already know about circuses? What information can they share? If children seem quite unfamiliar with a circus, you might want to begin first with some brief action and sensory pantomimes of various circus activities. For example: walking a tightrope, clowns juggling, eating cotton candy, riding a circus horse, and so forth.

b.   Read and show pictures from the book *Harold's Circus*. This book is quite small and may be difficult to share with a large class without enlarging the pictures on an opaque projector. Or, copy the pictures to transparencies for an overhead projector or redraw them on larger, heavy paper. This is relatively easy to do as the pictures are simple line drawings.

c.   Narrate/sidecoach the story, letting everyone play Harold tightrope walking, riding a horse, being a clown, and even getting a lion returned to its cage.

d.   Options: Use *Curious George Rides a Bike* by H. A. Rey (Boston: Houghton-Mifflin, 1952), edited for solo playing. Or, use *Andy and the Lion* by James Daugherty (New York: Viking, 1966). Play in pairs beginning with Part II.

Count Freeze Pantomimes: Circus Acts

If children know enough about circuses, they may be able to demonstrate some circus acts for others to guess. The acts may be solo, pairs, or small groups. You might have a number of pictures of various circus acts the children could choose from to enact if they need ideas. (See source books listed above for pictures of circuses.)

Verbal Sequence Game

In this game circus history is based on information in *The Circus* by Mary Kay Phelan (New York: Holt, Rinehart and Winston, 1963). (*Note*: to prepare sequence cards, each line below will need a cue line. See p. 117 for additional information on verbal sequence games.)

(*Pretend to use a megaphone*) Announcing: The Greatest Show on Earth!

(*Pretend to use a megaphone*) Ladies and Gentlemen! And children of all ages . . .

Listen closely! Here's some history about the circus!

The circus is very old. Some say it began over 4,000 years ago!

(*Say very quietly*) I think that's before I was born.

What's that, my child? Before you were born? Why, that's even before there was a United States!

Excuse me. That's even before America was discovered.

May I continue? Thank you. The circus we see today is much like the Circus Maximus in Rome.

What's "Circus Maximus?"

(*Pretend you are very smart.*) In Latin, *Circus* means "circle," and *maximus* means "big."

(*Say very quietly.*) Oh. Thank you.

That means there was a big circle of seats where thousands of people could sit and watch the show.

That sounds a lot like a big football stadium.

It was. Only you didn't watch football. It started off with a big parade. And there were acrobats. (*Do a somersault or other acrobatic trick.*) And jugglers. (*Pretend to juggle.*) And animal acts. (*Roar like a lion.*)

But I want to know about circus here in the United States.

I can tell you one thing. In the pioneer days, sometimes a fur trapper would tame a wild bear and have it do tricks for people. And when ships sailed back and forth across the ocean, sometimes the captains would bring strange animals from different countries. A lion was one of the first animals brought over.

Gosh, I'll bet no one had seen anything like that before.

You're right! Did you know that George Washington saw the first real circus in the United States in 1793?

Sure! And he saw a clown and a tightrope walker. The circus owner performed the main act doing some trick riding. His horse, Cornplanter, would jump over the back of another horse.

(*Say in a loud whisper.*) Now that's what I call a good trick!

(*Say in a loud whisper.*) I wonder if George liked it?

Hush, just listen. Circuses grew bigger and bigger. A man named Barnum collected strange and different things for people to see.

He had an elephant named "Jumbo." It was the biggest one

in the world. Jumbo became very famous. And now the word "jumbo" means anything that is very large.

Mr. Bailey started a circus that used the first electric lights. Barnum and Bailey put their two circuses together to make the first three-ring circus in America.

Then five boys named Ringling started a circus in their back yard. They charged people a penny to see an old billy goat.

They worked very hard to make the biggest circus they could and called it the "Greatest Show on Earth."

Let's hear it for the circus. *(Clap your hands.)* Thank You.

Story Dramatization

Enact a Circle Story (see Chapter 10) with Robert Leydenfrost's *The Snake That Sneezed,* New York: G. P. Putnam's, 1970. In this story, a snake named Harold sets off to seek his fortune with the advice, "Don't bite off more than you can chew." He meets various animals and eats them all. A sneeze pops them all out, and just in time to join a circus. This story can be played in a similar fashion to "The Cat and the Parrot" (Lesson Plan, p. 168). It is additional fun to end with a circus parade, using a recording like *Merle Evans Directs the Ringling Brothers Barnum and Bailey Circus Band* (Decca).

Option: Dramatize William Pène du Bois' *Bear Circus.* New York: Viking, 1971. In this picturebook koala bears show their gratitude to kangaroos, who aided the bears when grasshoppers destroyed their food, by performing a circus show. This story gives a chance to create many circus acts, since the bears rehearse for seven years with costumes and equipment they find aboard a circus plane.

Clown Antics

After a study of clowns, their costumes, makeup, and their various pantomime skits they do, children can create their own pantomime skits in small groups. This can expand into several lessons if there is interest enough to do a clown unit by itself.

Quieting Activity

Do round-robin storytelling based on the wordless picturebook *The Chimp and the Clown* by Ruth Carroll (New York: Henry Z. Walck, 1972). A clown's chimpanzee runs away from the circus parade

After a visit from a real clown, this class made up clown skits, created their own clown makeup, and shared their fun with others. (*Kalamazoo Gazette*)

The old "pie-in-the-face" routine—in mime. (*Kalamazoo Gazette*)

and goes off on his merry adventures with the clown in hot pursuit. They get back together again just in time for the circus performance.

LESSON PLAN REFERENCE CHART

Following is a list of some of the topics or themes covered by the various materials and activities in this book. The left-hand column gives the topics and titles, the center column lists the type of drama activity they are, and the final column gives the page references.

The intent of the chart is to help you begin to make a variety of lesson plans by presenting some possible themes and then listing some of the activities and materials under that heading that are found in this book. In some cases the listing is only a reference; in other cases, lesson plans(*) are provided.

No attempt has been made to include every reference in this text, nor is the chart designed to provide an inclusive list of themes for each activity or literary selection.

TOPIC/TITLES	TYPE OF DRAMA ACTIVITY	PAGE
AFRICA		
"Anansi and Fish Country"	story dramatization	195
"Anansi Plays Dead"	story dramatization	195
"Anansi's Hat Shaking Dance"	story dramatization	195
The Elephant's Child	story dramatization	196
Elephants of Africa	narrative pantomime resource	86
"Ticky-Picky-Boom-Boom"	story dramatization	199
Who's in Rabbit's House?	group narrative pantomime/	82
	masks	245
ANIMALS (Fiction)		
"The Adventure of Three Little Rabbits"	story dramatization	195
Alligators All Around	action pantomime	38
Anatole and the Cat	story dramatization	196
Andy and the Lion	paired narrative pantomime	72
Are You My Mother?	story dramatization	196
Ask Mr. Bear	circle story	163
The Bear and the Fly	storytelling	124
*"The Bear Hunt"	action story	37
"The Bear in a Pear Tree"	paired narrative pantomime	72
The Bears on Hemlock Mountain	narrative pantomime resource	85
The Bears Who Stayed Indoors	group narrative pantomime	77
"Boa Constrictor"	action pantomime	38
"Cat"	action pantomime	39
*"The Cat and the Parrot"	circle story	168
**Charlotte's Web*	segmented story	187

Puppets, Shadow Plays, and Masks 13

Saying the word "puppets" today probably conjures up the image of the "Muppets" in the minds of most people. The popularity of *Sesame Street* Muppets, as well as the Muppet television shows and films, have made Jim Henson's creations a household word and one that is almost synonymous with puppets.

But puppets are as ancient and as varied as history itself. Different cultures have evolved their own kinds of puppets, many of which have been passed down from generation to generation and are still in existence today. There are puppets manipulated by strings, by rods, and by hand. They may require only two fingers on the hand of one person, or they may require the manipulator's entire body or the cooperative manipulation of several puppeteers. They may be a "found object" (a wooden spoon, a feather), the hand by itself, or a person in a costume. Their size can range from being larger than a person to being as small as a finger puppet. And, of course, they can represent abstract beings as well as humans and animals. In short, their versatility knows no bounds.

But basic to all puppets is the puppeteer/manipulator or actor. While actors usually do not consider themselves puppeteers, puppeteers consider themselves actors—in disguise. Although the attention is on the puppet during the performance and even after, it is the actor manipulating the puppet who is the real performer and theatre artist. Even though we adults may recognize Jim Henson's voice when Kermit speaks or Frank Oz as Miss Piggy, we still think of the two puppets as people

227

in their own right. The puppeteer/actor has created that magical illusion of character creation for us.

It is this aspect of puppetry magic that makes the fascination of puppets so universal and appealing to all ages. The puppeteer's power to do this magic may also explain why the motivation for creating theatre with puppets is so strong. It also helps to explain why many children can play with puppets, making them say and do things they would be too shy or too inhibited to express on their own. The therapeutic and educational value is almost a given. Who can ignore these personages who seem to have a life of their own? No one, it seems. And, least of all, your students.

HOW TO BEGIN

There is no one way to begin working with puppets. In fact, you may find yourself choosing one method for one class and taking a totally different approach with another. It is important for you to feel free to experiment with the method you use. Therefore, several approaches will be mentioned so that you will begin to see some of the choices available to you.

There are some *cautions*. First, be sure that you do not spend more time making the puppets than you and the children spend using them. Frequently puppet-making is used as an art project, but that is often just where it stops. And if the puppet making is an elaborate process, children may become tired of the puppet before

Beautifully crafted puppets of well-known folk tale characters will almost guarantee a puppet play.

they ever have a chance to give it life. For this reason, some teachers prefer to have puppets already made (purchased, collected by children, or made by room mothers) and waiting for the children to use. Sometimes this can also be a way to assess the children's interest and readiness for puppetry.

If you take the above approach and buy or make your own puppets, be sure to consider how the puppet is manipulated. The size should fit the child's hand rather than the adult's. The materials used should be durable and perhaps even washable. There are many beautiful and elaborate puppets available for purchase, but some are also extremely expensive. Do not waste money on a puppet collection that only you or a puppet collector will appreciate.

It is also useful to think in terms of a cast of characters as you collect or make your puppets. If you have three pigs and a wolf, for example, a simple story is ready and more likely to be played out. Or, a king, queen, and various other court characters might inspire the enactment of "Sleeping Beauty" or "Thurber's *Many Moons*. Familiar stories are almost always easier for children to enact than are originals, though that, too, is possible.

MAKING PUPPETS

If you are ready to have children make their own puppets, it will be important to determine what type your children will be able to manipulate. For children whose hand dexterity is not well developed, it is necessary to focus on simple puppets. The following puppet types are described in the order of their ease of manipulation.

FACE PUPPETS

A cardboard circle or paper plate made into a face with a cardboard stick to hold it with, is one of the easiest to make and easiest to use. The child simply holds up this rod-type puppet and moves it slightly, makes a sound for it, or speaks for it. In some cases the puppet may be held in front of the face and used similarly to a mask.

Since these puppets are not capable of much movement, they will work best with simple stories having numerous characters of the same type. For example, *Millions of Cats* by Wanda Gag (see lesson plan p. 176) can be enacted with many cat puppets. The narrative pantomime story, *Caps for Sale* by Esphyr Slobodkina (see page 72), has many monkeys. The children can use their puppets in playing these stories, making the simple sounds of the animals.

HEAD PUPPETS

Similar to the paper-plate puppets, head puppets are those which focus on a three-dimensional head. These can be made from wooden

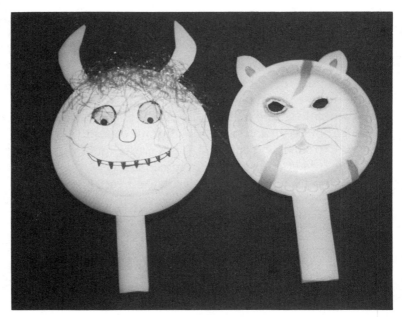

Paper plates can be made into masks or puppets on a stick. (Left) *Where the Wild Things Are;* (right) *Millions of Cats.*

spoons (the handle is built in), rubber balls, styrofoam balls, stuffed paper bags, or more elaborate materials like papier maché. A dowel, with a square piece of fabric over it for the puppet's costume, may be inserted into the head. The child then easily manipulates the puppet by holding onto the handle.

Another type of head puppet can be made from a paper cup, a small cereal or instant soup box. In this case, the hand goes into the head, and the movement of the head is controlled by the child's wrist.

As children gain hand dexterity, they can manipulate the head puppets made from the rubber or styrofoam balls by inserting a finger into the head. Sometimes the insertion of a small cardboard tube as a finger stall makes the manipulation easier.

PUPPETS WITH MOVEABLE MOUTHS

Hand puppets whose mouths move are often easier to manipulate than those with moveable arms and hands. Many are made so that the fingers operate the upper jaw while the thumb operates the lower. The following are some possibilities:

  a. **Paper bag puppets** are one of the most familiar. You need a bag that has a flat bottom. When that is folded over at its natural crease,

A papier maché head puppet.

Puppets with moveable mouths.

and the fingers are enclosed inside, the bottom becomes the upper jaw of the puppet, which moves up and down against the thumb or the palm of the hand for speech. This "mouth" is enhanced by painting or gluing teeth, tongue, and other human or animal features to the upper and lower jaw. The rest of the puppet can be decorated to any extent desired.

b. **Sock puppets** also allow for moveable mouths. Put the sock on your hand and then put the fingers in the toe and the thumb in the heel. Again, the mouth features can be enhanced as above. The rest of the puppet can also be decorated to any extent desired. Unlike the bag puppet, however, you can more readily sew the sock puppet, adding pieces of fabric, buttons, yarn, and so forth. A sock puppet is also more durable and can, if care is used, be made washable.

c. **Paper envelopes** can also make an interesting mouth puppet. Fold the flap inside and then place the hand inside the envelope with the fingers in one of the bottom ends and the thumb in the other. Then tuck and bend into the middle of the bottom of the envelope to form a sort of beak. This can be decorated in a variety of ways by stapling, gluing or taping other features to it. The more decorating or painting you want to do, the sturdier the basic envelope should be.

DIALOGUE ACTIVITIES FOR PUPPETS

When using the moveable mouth puppets, it is not necessary to keep the mouth constantly opening and closing as it speaks. In fact, the mouth need only open and close at the beginning and end of the speech to create the illusion of speaking. And, if the mouth appears to be constantly "yapping," it will only distract from what the puppet is "saying."

With these mouth puppets, children may like to explore some of the earlier verbal activities. The following are some suggestions:

a. Try the Verbal Sequence Games with Literature using puppets. (See p. 119) Children should raise their puppets high enough for their classmates to see "it" speaking the lines.

b. Also in Chapter 8, Verbal Activities, the students might want to try the One-Liners and Storytelling with puppets.

c. Consider also the Verbal Games from Chapter 8, Verbal Activities. A panel of puppets ("on stage," if desired) may be questioned by students; puppets may question a panel of students; or the entire game may be played with puppets.

PUPPETS WITH MOBILE BODIES

Puppets that are the most challenging for early elementary children to manipulate are those whose heads and arms/hands move. There are at least three ways to manipulate these puppets:

a. The head is the index finger; the thumb and middle finger are the two arms. The last two fingers fold down into the palm of the hand. (This is the most used method.)

b. The head is the middle three fingers; the thumb and little finger are the two arms. (With this method the head or torso of the puppet has to be large enough to accommodate three fingers.)

c.   The head is the index finger; the thumb and the little finger are the two arms. The middle and ring finger fold down into the palm of the hand.

Let children find their own preferences for these methods, depending on what seems easiest for them to do. Not all will select the same method.

These puppets are simply made as follows:

a.   **Handkerchief puppet.** Put a square cloth (like a handkerchief) over your hand. Decide which fingers you want for the head and put a rubber band around them. (You can even stuff a little cotton into this head for a more rounded appearance.) Holes can be made in the cloth for the arms, or they can work freely.

b.   **Ball puppet.** Put cloth over your hand as above. Cut hole for the head finger(s) and insert into a styrofoam or rubber ball.

c.   **Costume puppet.** This is simply a puppet that is made of fabric, sewn in the shape of the hand, with a head and two arms indicated.

With these puppets, children can explore much more body movement. While these puppets can "speak," their mouths do not move. Their speech can be enhanced, however, by nonverbal body movements.

Exploring Puppets' Body Movement

The following activities can be fun for the children to do at their desks with their puppets in order to explore body movements. These activities will be easier to do once the children have performed them themselves. In other words, it is easier to make a puppet perform a certain action if you have tried it with your own body first. As a side point here, children are learning a basic anatomy lesson in working with puppets.

Classes will vary in their abilities, so be sure you are not pushing too hard. Do not try to do all the activities at once, and use them only if the children find them fun to do. Be sensitive to children becoming tired or frustrated in attempting to make their hands do what may simply be too difficult for them. Encourage children to discover and share their own "tricks" for their puppets to do.

Head: looking up, down, side to side.
Seeing: watching birds flying overhead, looking for something lost on the ground, watching a parade going by.

Hearing: a loud siren, a clock striking 3:00.

Smelling: fresh cookies baking, a skunk, a sweet-smelling flower.

Tasting: bitter medicine, licking an ice cream cone, eating an ear of corn

Hands: clapping, waving, pointing, scratching.

Touch: touch something hot, something cold, pantomime petting a dog.

Waist: Bow, rotate, touch toes.

Legs: How does your puppet look when it walks, marches, jumps, skates, stamps its feet, etc?

Narrative Pantomimes

At this point you may want to have students explore a variety of movements presented in some of the stories or poems listed under "Solo Narrative Pantomimes," Chapter 5. Let children share with each other the ideas and techniques they discover for movement exploration. It is doubtful that you will want to try pair or group playing, as your children may not be able to do them successfully. This decision will be left to you and to your judgment of your class's abilities.

PUPPETS AND NONVERBAL DIALOGUE

The puppet can say a great deal nonverbally. For example, it can move its head up and down to indicate "yes." The puppet may also be able to point to indicate "There." Or, it may be able to clap its hands to show a joyful reaction or to scratch its head as if thinking.

The following activities can be fun to try: (You may simply wish to demonstrate some of these ideas with a puppet yourself and have the children guess the puppet's feelings and expressions. Then allow children to try them in a later lesson.)

a. Movements for the Head. What does the puppet appear to be "saying" if the head drops forward? (tired, bashful, sad) If the head moves to one side? (listening, thinking)

b. Movements for the Hands. Clapping, waving, pointing, scratching, rubbing hands together, patting stomach, putting hand to mouth, hand to cheek, hand behind ear. What might each of these gestures say?

Remember that there can be different interpretations of nonverbal ideas. Not all children will think the puppet is saying the same thing. Allow for flexibility in these explorations.

STORY DRAMATIZATION WITH PUPPETS

Eventually children will want to work with entire stories, turning them into puppet plays. The same simple stories listed earlier can also be performed with puppets. Again, you may note that once children have acted the stories out themselves, the easier it will be for them to play them as puppet plays.

PUPPET STAGE

Simple stages are often the best. A table turned on its side with children kneeling or sitting on low chairs behind it is sufficient. If children insist on more formal staging, you have several options. However, the smaller the stage, the fewer number of children can use it at one time. You may, in this case, need to allow a small group of children on their own to work out their own stories.

Smaller stages can be made from cardboard boxes, wooden boxes, an old folding screen and even a cast-off television set with the insides and screen removed. Curtains are not necessary, but are simple enough to add.

Scenery is more difficult, not to make but to work with. Furthermore, if the location of the story keeps changing place, you will need to make and change scenes. If a story has one location, a simple backdrop painted on paper and taped to the inside back wall of the box should probably satisfy.

A table turned on its side is all you need for a simple puppet stage.

SHADOW PLAYS

Shadow plays work on the same principle of making shadow pictures with your hands on a wall. Instead of a wall, however, we will suggest three different shadow play methods.

METHOD I

Younger children will enjoy simply making shadows with their hands and bodies on a projector screen. You can use the projector light or one or more overhead projectors for the strong light needed to cast shadows. With this method they can see the results of their work. Allow for experiementation and let children discover on their own the many possibilities. You may suggest poetry like Robert Louis Stevenson's "My Shadow," (3)(4)(35) to act out.

METHOD II

Shadow puppetry for young children is easiest to do by using an overhead projector. The cutouts of the puppets are made and then laid flat on the glass surface of the projector. The shadows are then projected on the screen. This method is easy for them to do and also allows them to see their work. There will be some confusion, at first, with the reverse directions of what is seen on the projector and its projection on the screen.

A tug-of-war game is played behind a sheet with a back light.

METHOD III

A third method suitable for third grade children involves using a screen of thin, white fabric (an old sheet does nicely). This may be stretched tightly over a frame. Behind the screen (away from the audience) and shining on it is a very bright light. The puppets are flat and, when pressed against the screen, create a strong shadow outline or silhouette.

The screen is elevated, often on a table, so that the puppet operators can stay below it. (You want to see the puppets' shadows, not the shadows of the puppeteers.)

MAKING SHADOW PUPPETS

The puppets are cutouts which can simply be attached to a stick or rod. Several of the group stories in Chapter 5, Narrative Pantomime can be made into shadow plays. Since most of these group stories come from picturebooks, the illustrations will give you many ideas for interpretation.

If you make a number of cutouts of each character, using the various positions of the characters on different pages of the book, you will have additional movement and a more interesting presentation of your play. You can also turn the puppet over so it can be shown facing the opposite direction.

You can make groups of people or animals as one large puppet. This makes it much simpler to enact stories with many characters.

If you use thick or dark cardboard for your puppets, they will

Authentic Asian shadow puppets made of animal hide.

appear as a very solid, black shadow. This can be very effective and dramatic. But you may also want to cut away some of the cardboard so that light can show through and create simple facial features or bits of costuming. If you then cover the cut out areas with colored tissue or cellophane, you will get color in your puppets.

If you wish more color, you can use light-weight cardboard or a heavy paper and apply the color you wish. Then, to stiffen it and protect it, cover it with several thicknesses of clear, plastic adhesive paper. This creates an almost translucent puppet, similar to those made of thin animal skins centuries ago in many countries around the world.

Attaching the Rod

To hold the puppet, you will need a rod or stick. Thin wires from craft stores work well. Rods can also be made from coat-hanger wire, although these are a little heavier. If you tape the end of the wire or attach a bit of foam rubber, you can make a handle that will be easier to hold.

The wires are attached to the puppet either in a flat position or in a hinged position. If the wire is flat, you will have to hold it directly against the screen. If you bend the wire a bit at one end and use a heavy piece of plastic tape to secure it, then you can hold the puppet against the screen even though you are standing several inches away. This allows you to have a bit of shelf space on your table to lay the puppets on when they are not "on stage."

More elaborate puppets are hinged to enable more sophisticated movements. Generally, it is the arms and legs of the puppet that are made to move. Simply cut legs and arms to overlap the torso or body of the puppet. Then make a small hole and thread a string through, knotting it on each side so the arms and legs are free to move. Sometimes the arms and legs are simply allowed to dangle or move of their own accord. Older children may wish to attach rods to the arms and legs and control these movements.

SCENERY

For Method II, p. 236

When using the overhead projector, you can draw scenery on overhead transparencies with a felt pen. The transparencies come in different colors which can give you some variety of mood and setting.

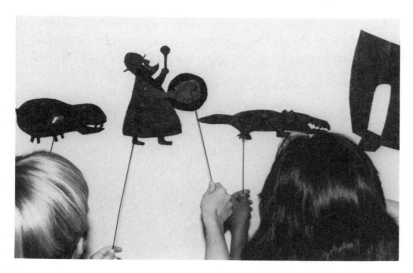

Shadow play of Emberley's *One Wide River to Cross* behind the scenes and from audience's viewpoint.

For Method III, p. 237

You can also create scenery for your shadow plays that use the sheet screen and light. However, you do not want to clutter the screen up with too many extraneous details. Remember that the puppets are the most important part of your play. Also, if your story changes scenes frequently, you will spend all your time changing the scenery rather than operating the puppets.

Scenery can be very simple and, if possible, put in place prior to the showing of the play. A "ground row," for example, can be a horizontal strip of cardboard taped along the bottom of the screen. It is shaped to look like grass, a hill, a floor, or whatever is needed.

At the side might be a tree, or at the top might be a sun, clouds, and so forth. If these are taped or attached to the frame of the screen, they will leave the center of the screen free for the puppets' actions.

DRAMATIZATION WITH SHADOW PUPPETS

Since shadow plays are so versatile, it is possible to use a variety of sources. The following picturebooks are suggested because of the many pictorial images they utilize.

3 *Hailstones and Halibut Bones,* Mary O'Neill. Garden City: Doubleday, 1961. This contains poetry about various colors and the things they portray and symbolize.

3 *Hansel and Gretel,* William Wiesner. New York: Seabury Press, 1971. This is a shadow puppet picture book that includes instructions for staging the story as a shadow puppet play.

1-2 *May I Bring a Friend?"* Beatrice Schenk de Regniers. New York: Atheneum, 1965. A small child is invited to have tea with the King and Queen, and each day he brings another animal friend. On Saturday, the child and all his animal friends invite the King and Queen to tea at the zoo.

3 *Once a Mouse,* Marcia Brown. New York: Charles Scribner's, 1961. An East Indian hermit/magician befriends a mouse. To save the mouse's life, the man turns him into progressively larger and more powerful animals until the mouse becomes too proud and is returned to his former state.

2-3 *One Wide River to Cross,* Barbara Emberley. Englewood Cliffs: Prentice-Hall, 1966. An old folk song of Noah and the Ark is brought to life. Because black woodcuts are used in this book, reading it is almost like watching a shadow play.

3 *Papagayo the Mischief Maker,* Gerald McDermott. New York: Windmill, 1980. Papagayo, a parrot, is too noisy for his jungle friends. But when the ghost of ancient monster dog comes to eat away at the moon, Papayago teaches all the animals to use their sounds to scare him. This contains brilliant colors and vivid pictures of the animals.

3 *Peter and the Wolf,* Erna Voight. New York: David R. Godine, 1980. This beautifully illustrated musical story of a young boy's adventure with a duck, a cat, a bird, and a wolf can be narrated with Serge Proko-fieff's music in the background.

3 *The Rooster's Horns: A Chinese Puppet Play to Make and Perform,* Ed Young with Hilary Beckett. New York: Collins and World, 1978. This is a story with instructions to children for making and performing their own shadow puppet play. It includes puppet pieces to trace.

2-3 "The Strange Visitor," Joseph Jacobs in *English Fairy Tales.* New York: G. P. Putnam's, 1904. An old woman sits spinning and wishing for company. A visitor arrives, but the body parts enter one at a time.

1-2 *The Very Hungry Caterpillar,* Eric Carle. New York: Collins Publishers, 1969. A voracious caterpillar eats through something new each day on its way to becoming a butterfly.

Puppets created for the story "The Cat and the Parrot." (See circle story lesson plan on pp. 168–69.)

MASKS

Because children enjoy making and wearing them, and because they can be used effectively in many dramatizations, we include a few words about masks.

Masks and dramatic rituals and plays have had a long history. Masks were believed to give power to the wearer by allowing him or her to be someone else. Perhaps the wearer might be an animal to be killed in some future hunt, and the wearer/hunter would have power over the animal. Or, perhaps the mask symbolized some god or superior entity or being.

Children, of course, associate masks with Halloween and with other sorts of dress up events. But, similar to the experience of manipulating a puppet, wearing a mask can also hide a person and encourage expression anonymously. Shy children, or those who need self confidence for other reasons, may find mask wearing a particularly satisfying activity.

MAKING MASKS

Masks can be made in a variety of ways. We shall focus on the most simple ways. As with puppets, for drama experiences it is more important to make use of the mask than to spend inordinate amounts of time making them only as art projects to be looked at or hung on a wall.

Paper Bag Mask

a. This type is worn over the head, with places for the eyes, nose and mouth cut out.

b. The mask should be of a size to fit snugly so that it can turn when the children move their heads. It may be helpful to cut slits in the bottom four corners of the bag or as a fringe all around so that it will fit down over the children's heads.

c. Now the bag can be decorated in any manner the children wish.

d. You may wish to cut out the bottom half of the bag so that the face is covered only as far as the mouth in order to make speaking easier, should that be desirable.

Paper Bag Mask/Costume

a. Make this from a large grocery bag. Turn the entire bag upside-down over the child's head.

b. Cut holes for the facial features and holes for the arms. (Or you can make long cutouts on the sides of the bag, so just a shoulder portion is left remaining.)

c. Sometimes children prefer to have a hole cut for their face and put decorations on the bag around the face.

d. If you cut a hole in the top so the child can poke his or her head through, the bag becomes a costume you can decorate and use along with another mask.

Paper Plate Mask

a. These masks are made simply by attaching a stick or other type of holder to the edge of the plate so that the mask can be held up in front of the face. Eye holes are cut in the appropriate places.

b. If you wish to attach the mask to the face, then you will want to cut nose and mouth holes. Some children will want to put their own noses through the nose hole in order to get a three dimensional effect.

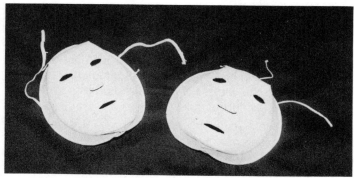

Masks made of paper plates, with stapled darts for chin and forehead, and string or elastic for ties.

    c.   To attach the mask to the face, you can make holes in the paper plate near the ears. Then knot a length of heavy string in each hole and tie in back of the head. You can also use rubber bands or pipe cleaners (curved over the ears like a pair of glasses).

    d.   If you want to shape the paper plate, just make slits in the edges of the paper plate, overlap the pieces and staple together as if you are making darts or tucks in clothing. A two inch dart for the chin and three inch dart for the forehead is suggested.

    e.   You can decorate the paper plate any way you wish. Extra noses and ear, horns, or fringed hair make interesting extensions in the masks. Covering the mask with aluminum foil can create interesting robot-type characters.

Fear and rage—expressing emotions with expressionless masks.

DRAMATIZATION WITH MASKS

The following stories are suggested for dramatization with masks.

2-3 *The Funny Little Woman,* Arlene Mosel. New York: E. P. Dutton, 1972. A giggling little Japanese woman chases a rice dumpling past some Jizos (statues of gods) to the wicked onis (troll-like creatures). Masks can be used for the Jizos and the onis.

3 *The Loon's Necklace,* William Toye. New York: Oxford University Press, 1977. An illustrated retelling of an Indian legend involving a loon and a medicine man. Authentic Indian masks are used to dramatize the story in a film by Encyclopedia Brittanica, Chicago, Ill. Color, ten minutes.

K-1 *Millions of Cats,* Wanda Gag. New York: Coward-McCann, 1928, 1956. Use masks for the many varieties of cats. (See lesson plan p. 176)

2-3 *The Hobyahs,* Simon Stern. Englewood Cliffs, N. J.: Prentice-Hall, 1977. Masks can be used for the little hobyah creatures. The grocery bag masks will allow you to create your own version of a hobyah.

A grocery bag makes an oni character for *The Funny Little Woman* by Arlene Mosel.

K-2 *Three Billy Goats Gruff,* Marcia Brown. New York: Harcourt, Brace & World, 1957. Use masks for the troll. Children may want masks for the Billy Goats, too.

K-2 *Where the Wild Things Are,* Maurice Sendak. New York: Harper and Row, 1963. Use masks for all the monsters. (See lesson plan p. 178).

3 *Who's in Rabbit's House?* Verna Aardema. New York: Dial, 1977. Caterpillar takes over Rabbit's house and will not come out. This picturebook shows all the characters in masks performing a play.

SELECTED REFERENCES
ON PUPPETRY, SHADOW PUPPETRY, AND MASKS

Alkema, Chester J. *Mask Making.* New York: Sterling Press, 1981. Extensive instructions are given for making a variety of masks.

Champlin, Connie. *Puppetry and Creative Dramatics in Storytelling.* Austin, TX: Nancy Renfro Studios, 1980. This well-illustrated, easy to follow book uses many stories and drama ideas that relate nicely to this text.

Hunt, Kari and Bernice Carlson. *Masks and Mask Makers.* New York: Abingdon Press, 1961. Many unusual masks are illustrated in this book for children.

Lynch-Watson, Janet. *The Shadow Puppet Book.* New York: Sterling Publishing Co., 1980. This explains shadow puppetry in detail.

Mendoza, George. *Shadowplay.* New York: Holt, Rinehart and Winston, 1974. Black and white photographs show the hands of Prasanna Rao of India, a foremost shadowplay artist, creating shadow images from swans to witches. Although not about shadow puppetry, this fascinating book explains a related art form that will be of interest to children as well as adults.

Ormai, Stella. *Shadow Magic.* New York: Lothrop, Lee & Shepard, 1985. This book for children tells of shadow entertainment as well as many science concepts about light.

Price, Christine, *The Mystery of Masks.* New York: Charles Scribner's Sons, 1978. The author describes for student readers the many purposes masks have served in ancient times and still today. It is extensive, but readable. Documentation is accompanied by detailed pencil illustrations.

Renfro, Nancy. *Puppetry and the Art of Story Creation.* Austin, TX: Nancy Renfro Studios, 1979. This is an excellent book for showing numerous simple techniques for creating puppet and puppet shows.

Ross, Laura. *Puppet Shows Using Poems and Stories.* New York: Lothrop, Lee & Shepard, 1970. In this extremely useful book, explanatory notes are given for using forty-six literature selections for puppetry.

14 Going to the Theatre

For many children in today's world, going to the theatre is a unique experience. No doubt, your students have spent many more hours in front of a television screen or even attending films than they have in going to the theatre. And, in fact, the same is probably true of most adults.

There are several obvious similarities between live theatre performances and television and film performances. For example, what appears on film and television screens is what has traditionally been performed live. Many artists do their work in all three media. There are scripts used in all three. There are actors involved as characters in dramatic situations, and directors who supervise the actors' work.

But the differences between a live theatre performance and television and film performances are quite significant. The theatre is live actors performing in front of an audience. Many children who have never seen a play before will comment on and be amazed by the realization that there are "real people up there." Sometimes after a children's play, the actors, in their costumes and makeup, will form a receiving line in the theatre lobby so the children can meet them. This experience makes children even more aware of the aliveness of the performers.

Most importantly, theatre performers develop a communication with the audience. They can hear the laughter, the gasping, and the other responses of the audience. This feedback stimulates the performers, helps them to know if the audience is understanding the play and the dramatic situations in it. On the other hand, when films are made, usually only the other actors and film crew are watching. The per-

A well-produced children's theatre play can bring children's literature alive. A scene from *Charlotte's Web*. Kalamazoo Junior Civic Youth Theatre.

formers never know what an audience's response will be until they sit in the audience themselves, watching themselves on screen in the completed film. Television sometimes has studio audiences and shows that are "taped before a live audience," but these are rare and comprise only a fraction of the audience that will eventually see the show. Frequently, professional actors and actresses comment on their desire for the live audience contact that is missed when they perform in film and television. And it is the reason many actors and actresses go back to acting in a play from time to time in order to renew the feeling of communicating with a live audience.

It is this communication between the performers and the audience in a live theatre performance that children need to be made aware of, particularly if their experiences have been limited to television and film. There is a theatre etiquette that is demanded, or everyone's enjoyment of the event will be spoiled. The following list will be a starter for you to discuss with the children:

THEATRE ETIQUETTE

a. One should arrive on time for the scheduled theatre performance. (If your school is going to the theatre by bus or walking, departure and arrival times must be carefully coordinated.)

The Prince Street Players, a professional touring children's theatre company, performs their musical version of *Pinocchio*.

b. Going to the bathroom and getting drinks of water while a performance is in progress are both difficult and disturbing for others. Children need to understand the importance of having this taken care of before the play begins. (Most children's plays are short enough to make intermissions unnecessary.)

c. One should be considerate of others in the theatre audience. Talking during the performance disturbs the actors as well as the rest of the audience. Before the performance begins, the audience may talk quietly, but it is not acceptable to walk around in the theatre, play punching games, fuss with seats and clothing, kick the seats in front of you, or engage in other such behaviors.

d. Unlike television or film viewing, neither food nor drink is allowed in the theatre.

e. A theatre audience shows respect and appreciation for the performance by giving their full attention to the play and by applauding at the end. Loud whistling and shouting may be appropriate at a ball game outdoors, but is not acceptable in a theatre auditorium.

f. Dimming of house lights and blackouts of stage lighting are often a part of many performances. Children should understand this theatrical technique and remain calm when the lights go out.

g. When the performance is over, the audience does not rush to the exits but patiently waits its turn to leave the theatre.

THEATRICAL CONVENTIONS

Theatrical "conventions" are those common practices in the theatre which are accepted by all in attendance. "Conventions" may also be the devices the theatre uses to encourage the audience to accept the play as reality. Many of these conventions are traditionally accepted by the audience, even children, without question. Some may need explaining or discussion. Following is a list of some of the more common conventions:

PERFORMANCE SPACE

Performers are always physically separated in some way from the audience. Often they perform on a stage, on platforms, or in some other specifically defined area. The audience sits outside that area. (In some plays, the actors will come into the aisles of the theatre or may even interact with the audience. But they are still characters in the play; and if they encourage responses from the audience, they do it in accordance with their character.)

USE OF CURTAIN

In most cases, if a play is in an auditorium on a stage, a curtain raising or opening is the signal that the performance has begun. When

Simple but effective costumes used in formal plays can give you ideas for classroom use. This dragon's costume can be imitated with a decorated grocery bag (stuffed with newspaper), three yardsticks (crosspiece at top) and large strip of material. (Kalamazoo Junior Civic Youth Theatre)

it is lowered or closed, either the play has ended, or an intermission is indicated.

INTERMISSION

An intermission is a pause in the performance, lasting anywhere from five to fifteen minutes, during which time the audience members may stand up, go to the bathroom, get a drink of water, or talk quietly. Many children's plays are short enough in length so that an intermission is unnecessary.

USE OF LIGHTS

a. Blinking of auditorium lights is a signal for the audience to take their seats and that the play will begin in about five minutes.

b. Dimming of auditorium lights is a signal that the play is about to begin. As soon as the house lights go down, the stage lights go on, and the curtain is open or raised.

c. Blackouts (all lights out briefly) are used as a special effect or to show the passing of time at the end of a scene or an act.

APPLAUSE

In the theatre, the audience shows its appreciation of the performance by a polite clapping of hands. Usually applause comes at the end of scenes, acts, the end of the play, and for the curtain call. If a particularly exciting moment or special effect occurs during the play, an audience may spontaneously applaud.

PROGRAM

A theatre program gives written information about the production. It lists the cast of characters as well as an acknowledgement of the playwright, director, actors, designers, and technicians. It may also include an explanation of the plot. A program is also a souvenir. (Some children's theatre companies have a practice of not distributing programs for fear that the child audience will not be able to handle them quietly.)

CURTAIN CALL

At the end of the performance, all the actors come back on stage to take their bows and acknowledge the audience's applause.

STUDY GUIDES

Most children's theatre companies provide study guides for their productions. These guides vary considerably, but most will contain some or all of the following:

plot summary
information about the script, source of material, theme
information about the author, cast, the producing company
discussion of play setting, historical period, style, staging techniques
pre- and post-discussion questions
pre- and post-activities
bibliography

Often the experiences related to the play will incorporate creative drama as well as music, visual art, creative writing, or creative movement activities. There may also be a number of suggestions for integrating the play into other areas of the curriculum such as science, language arts, or social studies.

THEATRE, TELEVISION AND FILM

At first, children may be confused with the differences between theatre and other entertainment forms like film and television. This chapter has discussed some of the conventions of theatre and why children's behavior in a theatre audience has restrictions on it. The chief difference, of course, is that theatre is *live*. Although a play has been rehearsed for many days and weeks, it is happening at the very moment the audience is seeing it.

The theatre is an ancient art form that has been a part of every culture in the world almost since the beginning of time. Film and television are relatively new when compared to the centuries that theatre has been in existence. They are part of what is called the "electronic media," dependent upon highly developed technology to make them available to audiences.

Film, which is a little older than television, is literally *moving pictures* or *"movies."* The series of pictures on film, when run through a projector, actually creates the movement of the actors on the screen. Cartoon films are drawn or "animated" pictures. The more movement that is drawn in the pictures, the more movement there will be when the film is projected. Of course, the more animation in the pictures, the more the film will cost.

When live action films are made, they are "shot" in a studio on a "set" or "on location.'' The ''set'' is much like the scenery in the theatre. ''On location'' means the place the film crew go to in order to create, as realistically as possible, special scenes that are needed: a desert, mountains, city, or a farm, for example. These scenes would be too difficult to recreate in a studio.

Many scenes are shot and reshot during the filming period. Sometimes dozens and even hundreds of ''takes'' of one particular scene may be shot before the director and other artists feel satisfied. After the film is developed, it is previewed and the best scenes are selected for the final copy. Sometimes as much as half to ninety percent of the film is rejected. This fact, plus the many other expenses involved, is the reason that film budgets of well-publicized films that children hear about are so costly.

In the early days of television, the shows were performed ''live''; that is, they were actually happening as the home audience watched. Many mistakes would be seen although the performers often ''covered,'' or made up for, the errors so the audience would not be as aware of them. Now most shows are pre-recorded or filmed for later viewing. ''Live'' shows today are very rare.

Sometimes live studio audiences watch the videotaping being done. Often it is this audience's response and laughter that we hear in the background when the tape is eventually ''aired'' or played for the home audience. If a show does not have a live audience, sometimes ''canned laughter'' will be added to the tape. This artificially-reproduced laughter is supposed to encourage the audience to respond appropriately. Viewers who are watching at home alone are helped to feel that they are part of a larger audience, the way one would feel at a theatrical performance or in a movie theatre. Depending on the careful selection of ''canned laughter,'' it sometimes adds to the show. Often it seems unnatural and quite phony.

While there are many other similarities and differences in theatre, film, and television, it is the ''live'' audience aspect that is the most significant and notable in any comparison. In the theatre the audience gives an immediate response; in film and television it is often delayed. But it is usually the audience's reaction, over time, that eventually determines the success or failure of all material produced by these three entertainment forms.

SUGGESTED CLASS ACTIVITIES FOR DEVELOPING AWARENESS OF DIFFERENCES IN THEATRE, FILM, AND TELEVISION

1. Borrow a film from your school media center or local library. Taking care not to damage it (wear white cotton gloves), hold up a section of the film (or view it with an overhead projector) so children can see the series of pictures that make a film.

2. Have the class study Sunday newspaper cartoons. How are the pictures sequenced in order to tell a story? How is this similar to the pictures on film?

3. Select a children's picture book that has had a film made of it. (Weston Woods film company in Weston Woods, Connecticut, 06883 is an excellent source.) Have the class make a comparison of the two. Using the idea in #1 above, let children see how the pictures in the book must be made many times in order to achieve animation.

4. Have children make "flip books." These have many small sheets of paper stapled together. The pictures, made like simple cartoon drawings, should be slightly different from each other so that when the book is flipped, the characters appear to be moving.

5. Have children make a simplified type of film. Select a series of pictures that tell a story. Use Sunday newspaper cartoons, cut up an old picture book, or let children draw their own pictures. Glue the pictures, in sequence, to a strip of paper rolled around two dowels. The "film" may go from side to side or up and down. By rolling the paper from one dowel to the other, you can create a simplified version of a film. The film may also be shown by using a cardboard box with two slits cut at the sides for the paper to go through and a large hole cut in front for viewing.

6. Check with children to see if they or someone they know makes films or has a video camera. Invite these resource people into the classroom to explain their work or hobby to the class.

7. If a video or a film camera is available to you, use it to record creative drama activities. Let children view their work and evaluate. Compare the differences they see in watching the activities "live" and on tape.

SELECTED READINGS FOR CHILDREN
ON THE THEATRE

There are a number of books for children which focus in some way on theatre. You may wish to make them available to your class for independent reading.

K–3 *Backstage*, Robert Maiorano and Rachel Isadora. New York: Greenwillow, 1978. A young girl, whose mother is a ballerina, goes backstage in the theatre during a rehearsal of Tchaikovsky's *The Nutcracker* ballet, taking the reader with her through the pictures. Although the performance is a ballet, the backstage details are similar to those for theatre.

2–3 *The Bionic Bunny Show*, Marc Brown and Laurene Krasny Brown. Boston: Little, Brown, 1984. This is a humorous behind-the-scenes look at how a fictitious television show, "The Bionic Bunny," is made. Focus is particularly on showing how the star, a rather ordinary bunny, is made to look heroic. The book cleverly cuts from what is seen on the television screen to what is seen on the actual television set. A glossary of television terms is included.

2–3 *The Duck with Squeaky Feet*, Denys Cazet. Scarsdale, NY: Bradbury Press, 1980. This is a humorous story about a mouse who tries to write a play for a duck with squeaky feet, a toothless alligator, and other assorted animals who keep appearing on stage. But the play turns out to be too silly for words.

2–3 *Hattie the Backstage Bat*, Don Freeman. New York: Viking, 1970. Hattie, a bat who lives in the theatre, makes a dull mystery play exciting when she flies out of hiding and into the lights casting a huge shadow. Illustrations show scenery being built, stage lighting, back of a set, and stage relationship to auditorium.

3 *Here Come the Purim Players*, Barbara Cohen. New York: Lothrop, Lee & Shepard, 1984. Purim players in Prague, in medieval tradition, perform the Biblical story of Queen Esther's bravery.

2–3 *Jesse and Abe*, Rachel Isadora. New York: Greenwillow, 1981. Set in the 1920's, Jesse's grandfather is a doorman at Brown's Variety Theatre. Every night Jesse gets to watch the theatrical acts from the wings. This gives a glimpse at an era when vaudeville was at its peak.

3 *The Little Moon Theatre*, Irene Haas. New York: Atheneum, 1981. A caravan theatre travels all around giving tailor-made performances and meeting an assortment of people, including a fairy godmother. Though whimsical in treatment, the book does give an interesting look into the traveling show.

K–3 *The Marcel Marceau Alphabet Book*, George Mendoza. New York: Doubleday, 1970. This is an interesting look at a famous mimist who recreates the alphabet in this book of photographs. It gives children an exposure to the art of stylized mime.

K–3 *Sing, Pierrot, Sing: A Picturebook in Mime*, Tomie de Paola. New York: Harcourt Brace Jovanovich, 1983. Drawing from French and Italian folklore, this wordless picturebook features the traditional characters from the commedia del arte—Pierrot, Columbine, and Harlequin—in a tale of love of the highest order.

Story and Poetry Anthologies and Books for Dramatization

15

ANTHOLOGIES

Throughout the text, numbers in parentheses have referred to these correspondingly numbered anthologies and children's novels.

(1) *All the Silver Pennies*, Blanche Jennings Thompson. New York: Macmillan, 1967.

(2) *Anansi, the Spider Man*, Philip M. Sherlock. New York: Thomas Y. Crowell, 1954.

(3) *Anthology of Children's Literature*, (5th ed.), Edna Johnson, Evelyn R. Sickels, Frances Clarke Sayers, and Carolyn Horovitz. Boston: Houghton Mifflin Company, 1977.

(4) *The Arbuthnot Anthology of Children's Literature* (4th ed.), May Hill Arbuthnot, rev. by Zena Sutherland. Glenview, Ill.: Scott, Foresman, 1976.

(5) *Beyond the Clapping Mountains,* Charles E. Gillham. New York: Macmillan, 1964.

(6) *The Blackbird in the Lilac*, James Reeves. New York:Dutton, 1959.

(7) *Catch a Little Rhyme*, Eve Merriam. New York: Atheneum, 1966.

(8) *Catch Me a Wind*, Patricia Hubbell. New York: Atheneum, 1968.

(9) *Children's Literature for Dramatization: An Anthology*, Geraldine Brain Siks. New York: Harper & Row, Pub., 1964.

(10) *Cinnamon Seed*, John T. Moore. Boston: Houghton Mifflin Company, 1967.

(11) *The Crack in the Wall and Other Terribly Weird Tales*, George Mendoza. New York: Dial Press, 1968.

(12) *The Dancing Kettle and Other Japanese Folk Tales*. Yoshiko Uchida. New York: Harcourt Brace Jovanovich, 1949.

(13) *Eleanor Farjeon's Poems for Children*. Philadephia: Lippincott, 1951.

(14) *Eric Carle's Story Book; Seven Tales by the Brothers Grimm*. New York: Franklin Watts, 1976.

(15) *Favorite Fairy Tales Told in England*, Virginia Haviland. Boston: Little, Brown, 1959.

(16) *Favorite Fairy Tales Told in Scotland*, Virginia Haviland. Boston: Little, Brown, 1963.

(17) *Favorite Stories Old and New*, selected by Sidonie Matsner Gruenberg. Garden City, N.Y.: Doubleday, 1955.

(18) *Fingers Are Always Bringing Me News*, Mary O'Neill. Garden City, N.Y.: Doubleday, 1969.

(19) *Fire on the Mountain and Other Ethiopian Stories*, Harold Courlander and Wolf Leslau. New York: Holt, Rinehart & Winston, 1959.

(20) *Grandfather Tales*, Richard Chase. Boston: Houghton Mifflin Company, 1948.

(21) *Gwot! Horribly Funny Hairticklers*, George Mendoza. New York: Harper & Row, Pub., 1967.

(22) *The Hat-Shaking Dance and Other Tales from the Gold Coast*, Harold Courlander and Albert Kofi Prempeh. New York: Harcourt Brace Jovanovich, 1957.

(23) *The Hare and the Bear and Other Stories,* Yasue Maiyagawa. New York: Parents' Magazine Press, 1971.

(24) *Just So Stories*, Rudyard Kipling, illustrated by Victor Ambrus. New York: Rand McNally, 1982.

(25) *"Let's Marry, Said the Cherry,"* N. M. Bodeker. Atheneum, 1974.

(26) *A Light in the Attic*, Shel Silverstein. New York: Harper & Row, Pub., 1981.

(27) *Mouse Tales*, Arnold Lobel. New York: Harper & Row, Pub., 1972.

(28) *Night Noises and other Mole and Troll Stories*, Tony Johnston. New York: G. P. Putnam's, 1977.

(29) *Now We Are Six*, A. A. Milne. New York: Dutton, 1927.

(30) *Oh, What Nonsense!* selected by William Cole. New York: Viking, 1966.

(31) *Once the Hodja*, Alice Geer Kelsey. New York: Longmans, Green, 1943.

(32) *On City Streets*, Nancy Larrick (ed.), New York: M. Evans and Co., Inc., 1968.

(33) *Piping Down the Valleys Wild*, ed. Nancy Larrick. New York: Dell Publishing, 1968.

(34) *Reflections on a Gift of Watermelon Pickle*, Stephen Dunning, Edward Lueders, Hugh Smith (eds.), Glenview, Ill.: Scott, Foresman, 1966.

(35) *The Riverside Anthology of Children's Literature*, 6th edition, Judith Saltman (ed.), Boston: Houghton Mifflin, 1985.

(36) *The Sea of Gold and Other Tales from Japan*, Yoshika Uchida. New York: Charles Scribner's, 1965.

(37) *The Sneetches and Other Stories*, Dr. Seuss. New York: Random House, 1961.

(38) *Some Haystacks Don't Even Have Any Needle*, compiled by Stephen Dunning, Edward Lueders, Hugh Smith, Glenview, Ill.: Scott, Foresman, 1969.

(39) *Storytelling*, Ruth Tooze. Englewood Cliffs, N.J.: Prentice-Hall, 1959.

(40) *Stories to Dramatize,* Winifred Ward. New Orleans, LA.: Anchorage Press, 1981.

(41) *Take Sky,* David McCord. Boston: Atlantic-Little, Brown, 1962.

(42) *Tales from the Cheyennes*, Grace Jackson Penney. Boston: Houghton Mifflin Company, 1953.

(43) *Tall Tales from the High Hills,* Ellis Credle. Camden, N.J.: Thom. Nelson, 1957.

(44) *That's Why*, Aileen Fisher. Camden, N.J.: Thom. Nelson, 1946.

(45) *There Is No Rhyme for Silver*, Eve Merriam. New York: Atheneum, 1962.

(46) *The Thing At the Foot of the Bed and Other Scary Tales*, Maria Leach. New York: The World Publishing Company, 1959.

(47) *Thirteen Danish Tales,* Mary C. Hatch. New York: Harcourt Brace Jovanovich, 1947.

(48) *Thunder in the Mountains: Legends of Canada*, Hilda Mary Hooke. Toronto: Oxford University Press, 1947.

(49) *The Tiger and the Rabbit and Other Tales*, Pura Belpré. Philadelphia: Lippincott, 1965.

(50) *The Time-Ago Tales of Jahdu*, Virginia Hamilton. New York: Macmillan, 1969.

(51) *Time for Poetry* (rev. ed.), May Hill Arbuthnot. Glenview, Ill.: Scott, Foresman, 1959.

(52) *The Wandering Moon*, James Reeves. New York: Dutton, 1960.

(53) *Where the Sidewalk Ends*, Shel Silverstein. New York: Harper & Row, Pub., 1974.

(54) *Why the Chimes Rang*, Raymond Macdonald Alden. Indianapolis, Ind.: Bobbs-Merrill, 1954.

(55) *The Wicked Tricks of Tyl Uilenspiegel,* Jay Williams, New York: Four Winds, 1978.

(56) *Windsong*, Carl Sandburg. New York: Harcourt Brace Jovanovich, 1960.

(57) *World Tales for Creative Dramatics and Storytelling*, Burdett S. Fitzgerald. Englewood Cliffs, N.J.: Prentice-Hall, 1962.

(58) *Yertle the Turtle and Other Stories*, Dr. Seuss. New York: Random House, 1958.

BOOKS FOR DRAMATIZATION

The following longer books are highly recommended for extended dramatization work. They are only a representative sampling of the fine literature available for today's children. Some are older classics that remain as viable today as they were when first printed. Others have been selected for their historical and geographical settings, relationship to other areas of the curriculum, social themes, and their variety of heroes and heroines.

The books are listed alphabetically according to title. Suggested grade levels are indicated in the left-hand margin.

(59) 1–3 *A Bear Called Paddington,* Michael Bond. Boston: Houghton Mifflin, 1958. A charming humanlike bear arrives in London and is adopted by a family. Life becomes full of adventures that border on the disastrous. Sequels also available.

(60) 3 *The Borrowers,* Mary Norton. San Diego: Harcourt Brace Jovanovich, 1953. The adventure of the little people who live under the floorboards of the house and borrow small objects to furnish their home are presented. Sequels are also available.

(61) 3 *Carolina's Courage,* Elizabeth Yates. New York: Dutton, 1964. Carolina, a pioneer girl on a wagon train, is able to assist in the advance through Indian territory.

(62) 3 *Charlotte's Web,* E. B. White. New York: Harper & Row, 1952. Wilbur the pig, with the help of his barnyard friends and most particularly Charlotte the spider, develops into a most unique pig.

(63) 3 *Christmas on the Mayflower,* Wilma P. Hays. New York: Coward, McCann & Geoghegan, 1956. A dramatic conflict is presented when the crew of the Mayflower wants to return to England before the safety of the pilgrims is assured.

(64) 2–3 *The Courage of Sarah Noble.* Alice Dalgliesh. New York: Scribner's, 1954. This is the true story of a little girl who bravely accompanies her father into the Connecticut territory in the early 1700's.

(65) 2–3 *The Drinking Gourd,* F. N. Monjo. New York: Harper & Row, 1969. A New England boy learns of the Underground Railroad in the 1850's.

(66) 3 *The Great Quillow,* James Thurber. New York: Harcourt Brace Jovanovich, 1944. Quillow outwits a giant and saves his town.

(67) 3 *James and the Giant Peach*, Roald Dahl. New York: Knopf, 1961. Inside the magic peach, James finds many insect friends, and together they have a fantastic journey across the Atlantic from England to New York.

(68) 3 *John Billington*, Clyde Robert Bulla. Thomas Y. Crowell, 1956. This is a historical fiction account of a young boy who was one of the passengers on the *Mayflower*.

(69) 2–3 *The Little House in the Big Woods*, Laura Ingalls Wilder. New York: Harper & Row, Pub., 1959. This is the true story of an American pioneer family in Wisconsin. Many books in the "Little House" series.

(70) 1–3 *Little Pear*, Eleanor Frances Lattimore. New York: Harcourt Brace Jovanovich, 1931. The amusing adventures of a little Chinese boy are presented.

(71) 3 *Mary Jemison: Seneca Captive*, Jeanne Le Monnier Gardner. New York: Harcourt Brace Jovanovich, 1966. This is the exciting biography of a courageous white girl who was captured and adopted by Indians in the late 1700s.

(72) 3 *Mr. Popper's Penguins*, Richard and Florence Atwater. Boston: Little, Brown, 1938. Still a favorite, this story tells of Mr. Popper who, after writing of his interest in South Pole expeditions, receives a gift of a penguin from Admiral Drake. With a zoo's gift of a mate for the penguin, they increase to twelve. The Poppers train and take the penguins on the theatrical circuit in order to make enough money to care for them.

(73) 2–3 *The Mouse and the Motorcycle*, Beverly Cleary. New York: William Morrow, 1965. A mouse has interesting adventures with a toy motorcycle. Sequels are available.

(74) 3 *Peter Pan*, Sir James Barrie. New York: Scribner's, 1950. This is the classic story of a boy who does not want to grow up.

(75) 2–3 *Pinocchio*, adapted by Freya Littledale. New York: Scholastic, 1979. The adventures of a puppet who wants to become a real boy are presented.

(76) 3 *Pippi Longstocking*, Astrid Lindgrin. New York: Viking, 1950. Pippi, a superhuman girl, lives by herself and is independent. Her adventures are unorthodox and very appealing to children. Sequels are also available.

(77) 2–3 *Rabbit Hill*, Robert Lawson. New York: Viking, 1944. The small animals are concerned about the "new folks" who are moving into the empty house.

(78) 3 *Sam, Bangs and Moonshine*, Evaline Ness. New York: Holt, Rinehart & Winston, 1966. Sam, a fisherman's daughter, makes up fanciful stories. Trouble begins when she tells her friend about her mermaid mother.

(79) 3 *Sarah Whitcher's Story*, Elizabeth Yates. Dutton, 1971. Based on a true account, this story is of a little pioneer girl in New Hampshire who becomes lost in the woods for four days.

(80) 1–3 *Squaps, the Moonling*, Artemis Verlag. New York: Atheneum, 1969. A shy moonling hangs on the suit of an astronaut and is taken back to earth. He can only say "squaps," he likes the rain, and he can float when there is a full moon. This story will be particularly enjoyable to E.T. lovers.

(81) 2–3 *Sumi's Prize,* Yoshiko Uchida. New York: Scribner's, 1964. Sumi, a little Japanese girl, is the only girl to enter a kite-flying contest.

(82) 3 *This Time, Tempe Wick?* Patricia Gauch. New York: Coward, McCann and Geoghegan, 1974. A true story about Tempe Wick, a girl who lived in New Jersey during the Revolutionary War. Forgotten and disillusioned Pennsylvania soldiers try to rob Tempe of her horse so they can return home, but she outwits them in a clever way.

(83) 2–3 *Thy Friend, Obadiah*, Brinton Turkle. Viking, 1972. A young early American Quaker boy tries to reject a friendly and persistent seagull.

(84) 3 *While the Horses Galloped to London*, Mabel Watts. New York: Parents', 1973. On his carriage ride to London, Sherman guards a cooking pot which he uses to outwit the outlaw, Rough Roger.

(85) 1–3 *Winnie the Pooh*, A. A. Milne. Dutton, 1954. Winnie, a stuffed bear, and his animal friends have many delightful days. Sequels are also available.

Glossary

aesthetic discipline   The ability of an artist to focus on the requirements and demands of his or her art form.

character   A person, animal, or entity in a scene, story, or play with distinguishing physical, mental, and attitudinal attributes.

children's theatre   Plays performed, either by children, adults, or a combination of the two, for audiences of children.

choreography   Staged dancing; the arrangement of dances for performance.

climax   The moment in a play of the highest dramatic or emotional intensity.

conflict   An essential ingredient of most plots, in which the central character or characters meet opposition that must be resolved.

concentration   The ability to focus and keep one's attention on one's work, excluding all distractions.

creative drama   An improvisational, nonexhibitional, process-centered form of theatre in which participants are guided by a leader to imagine, enact, and reflect upon human experiences.

cue   The final words or actions of one character which signal the next character to begin his own.

dialogue   The words used by the characters, or improvised by the actors, to communicate thoughts, feelings, and actions.

double casting   Using two people to play the part of a single character.

emotional awareness   Creative drama activities used to heighten understanding of feelings.

evaluation   In creative drama, the appraisal of one's own work and the work of others after engaging in dramatic activities.

freeze To stand completely still as if for a picture. Also used as a command to students to stop their dramatic enactments.

frozen picture Name given to activity in which students, usually in groups, create interesting visual scenes to emphasize certain important moments or emotional situations.

imagination The process of visualizing what is not physically present or has never been experienced.

imitative movement Activities in which children imitate the characteristic movements of animals, people, objects, and the like.

improvisation The act of spontaneously inventing characters, action, dialogue, or plot during rehearsal or performance of dramatic materials.

motivation a. An activity or discussion which stimulates and prepares the students for the drama activity or lesson to follow, helping them identify with the characters and situations.

b. The psychological rationale that contributes to a character's behavior.

pair playing Any number of players interacting as two different characters in a scene. All couples play at the same time.

pantomime The performance of dramatic action without words.

playing in role A technique used by the drama leader during the playing, in which the leader pretends to be a character, appropriate to the situation, for the purpose of heightening and advancing the playing.

plot The storyline of a drama. Plot structure usually includes a beginning, middle, and end with a problem that is resolved in some way by the time the drama is completed.

project or projection To increase the size of the voice and movement so that it can be seen and heard by everyone in the audience.

properties or props Set props: all that is added to the scenery on stage such as furniture. Hand props: any article or object used by the actor in the playing of his/her part.

proscenium arch The opening of a stage through which the audience views the performance.

puppetry The artful animation of objects, from hands to larger-than-life figures, creating characters for dramatic enactments.

quieting activity An activity that physically and mentally calms down the students at the end of a drama lesson and prepares them to continue school work in a controlled and relaxed manner.

reader's theatre Staged readings of dramatic materials.

replaying Enacting a scene or story again for the purpose of changing roles, adding to, or improving upon the dramatic work.

role playing Enacting a character other than oneself in any dramatic material.

script The written lines spoken by the actors.

sensory awareness Perception of one's environment through the senses. To develop the actor's sensory awareness, activities and experiences are used to focus on and sharpen perceptions.

shadow play A form of puppetry using flat puppets, actors' hands, or actors' silhouettes presented behind a backlit screen.

sidecoaching   A technique used by the drama leader during the playing, in which the leader offers verbal suggestions or comments from the sidelines to heighten and advance the playing.

simultaneous playing   Several students, and often the entire class, playing the same character or story at the same time.

skit   A short scene of dialogue or pantomime.

solo or individual playing   Any number of players performing by themselves in their own playing space, all at the same time.

spectacle   The visual staging, such as sets, props, lighting, and costumes, to clarify and enhance the audience's understanding of the plot and characters of a drama.

story dramatization   The making and performance of an informal play from a story.

studying the script   The process of careful reading and rehearsal in interpreting the action and dialogue in a playscript.

triple casting   Using three people to play the part of a single character.

"waiting in the wings"   Expression to describe actor's readiness for entry onto the stage.

warmup   An activity designed to limber up actors' bodies/voices as well as positive mental attitude toward further drama work.

wings   Off-stage space to the left and right of the playing area where actors await their entrances and props and small set pieces are kept until needed.

Theatre Arts for All Children: Making Considerations for Children with Special Needs

A child in a wheelchair participates in a story dramatization. He is aided in moving about the room by a classmate who is double-cast in the same character role. A drama leader tells a story, making sure that her lips and face can be seen by a child wearing a hearing aid. A child with special talents has written a story that a small group of her classmates are dramatizing. And a child with behavior difficulties is making a noticeable effort to restrain his outbursts in order to play a drama activity with his classmates and be a part of the group.

Today's elementary classroom has students with a multitude of different needs. Caring for these needs is mandatory if we are going to provide equal opportunities to all. In conducting drama activities, we look at children's special needs in order to help them participate as fully as possible. However, while there may seem to be certain aspects of drama some children may not be able to participate in fully, children frequently will see ways to solve the problem creatively on their own. Focusing on the children's abilities rather than their inabilities will encourage these attempts.

And even though we generally consider the teacher responsible for identifying the various needs children have and for implementing compensatory learning experiences, the classroom can also become a community of learners who willingly assist each other and help each other succeed. Many goals can be achieved by establishing a "buddy" or support system. A child who speaks a different language, for example, can be aided by the child who is bilingual. The academically gifted, in addition to pursuing their own interests, may be able to assist those who need special tutoring. Children can assist handicapped classmates; in fact, some handicapped children can assist others whose handicaps are different from theirs. All of these experiences can give children a needed sense of responsibility and importance in serving the classroom community.

GENERAL DRAMA TECHNIQUES THAT ARE USEFUL

Two drama techniques that have been used throughout this text should be helpful for a number of special needs. One is *simultaneous or unison playing.* When all children are playing an idea at the same time, they are automatically part of the group. They can also see other children participating and learn from this modeling and demonstrating. Yet there is no undue attention on the children themselves, and they can participate and blend into the activity at their own pace.

A second technique is *multiple-casting of roles,* used most frequently in story dramatization. Almost any role in a story can be double-cast, allowing two children to work together, one supported by the other. Some character parts can use even more than two players. This technique can allow any child to play any part because of the assistance from a partner.

Finally, it is helpful to remember that drama encourages participants to get *outside of themselves.* Much of the stress we feel in our lives is the result of inward focus, and children who have been made aware of their special differences no doubt carry an extra burden. By extending ourselves in the world around us and "losing ourselves" in activities like drama, we experience a therapeutic release. This release can help us put life back into its proper perspective and render us healthier for future tasks.

ADDITIONAL SUGGESTIONS FOR SPECIFIC SPECIAL NEEDS

Following are some additional suggestions for working in theatre arts with children of varying needs and abilities. They are not all-inclusive but merely intended to encourage your thinking. Eventually you will discover many more options yourself that will fit your own and your classroom's particular needs.

BILINGUAL-BICULTURAL

1. Many drama activities in this resource guide are based on folk literature, a universal literary form. Some folktale plot lines (for example, "Cinderella") have been found to exist in almost every language and culture. Take special note to include stories from your classroom's language and culture heritage. Encourage the children to bring such stories to your attention for drama activities.

2. Movement, pantomime, and nonverbal communication are also universal languages. They can take over when words fail or are inadequate to express needs. Bilingual children will enjoy the focus on pantomime activities particularly.

3. Another universal activity is puppetry. Crafting a puppet, making it move, and giving it a personality can all be done without verbal language. Some children may have knowledge of special kinds of puppets from their country or culture that they can share with the class.

4. Incorporate references to special cultural holidays, customs, and experience in drama activities, from simple sensory activities to more elaborate story dramatizations. Utilize the rich multiethnic resources your students can provide for you and for each other.

5. Many story dramatizations, particularly the circle stories, can be a good vehicle for learning vocabulary. Headbands or name tags can be made for characters (i.e. dog, king, man, and so on) using both the English word and the second-language words.

MENTALLY HANDICAPPED

1. These children will need to deal with concrete experiences as much as possible. Pictures, props, and other aids will be necessary for them to understand information and concepts.

2. Pantomime is also valuable for the slow learner, whose verbal skills may not be advanced enough to engage fully in the dialogue and improvisational activities. Include plenty of pantomime activities in each drama lesson.

3. The graded materials in this text should assist in finding literature these children can handle successfully.

4. The roles these children play in drama activities should not tax them beyond their academic skills; and the same time, they can often surprise us with their concentration and involvement, their careful observation of classmates, and their contentment in participating with their peers in a group activity.

ACADEMICALLY GIFTED AND TALENTED

Academically gifted children, who have high IQ scores, are ahead of their classmates mainly in the use of language. However, there are other talents that children can be gifted in, such as music, athletic abilities, or even interpersonal skills. Therefore children can be gifted or talented in some areas but not in others.

Enriching experiences are usually required for gifted and talented youngsters, who can bypass the kind of drill work other children may need.

1. In drama, gifted children will probably excel in dialogue and improvisation. They will particularly enjoy verbal encounters and debates. They may find it easy to invent all manner of dialogue in story dramatization.

2. Some gifted and talented children may be interested in creating drama materials. They may even wish to develop some of the activities discussed in this text, from narrative pantomimes to sequence games to segmented story activities. Encourage

these activities, perhaps letting them work with the many bibliographic references in this text.

3. Gifted children may also want to try their hand at leading drama activities. They may wish to narrate a narrative pantomime story for the class or for a small group to perform. They may show directorial skills by visualizing interesting ways for their classmates to interpret stories.

4. Gifted children may also be encouraged to try their hand at playwriting, creating puppet shows, or even leading a small group to perform dramas for other classrooms in your school.

5. Other avenues of enrichment for these children may include working with film, television, or appropriate community theatre activities. They may be interested in reading further about theatre and sharing their findings with the rest of the class.

PHYSICAL DISABILITIES

1. A partner can assist in moving a wheelchair or in making an area accessible to the child.

2. These children may be partial to verbal and dialogue activities if they are limited in bodily movement. Be sure to give plenty of opportunity for such activities in each lesson.

3. Remember that nonverbal communication (pantomime) is conveyed by all parts of the body—from body posture to facial expression and from hand gestures to the way we move our feet. Depending on the impairment, focus on pantomime activities that can be done with the children's most mobile parts of the body. Facial expression can be focused on for those whose arms and legs are impaired. Or, gestures can be focused on if the hands and arms are mobile.

4. People in wheelchairs tend not to receive as much supportive touch as other children, probably because the chair itself acts as a barrier. Be alert to this fact and give reassurance and emotional tactile support to these children as often as you do to the rest of the class.

VISUAL IMPAIRMENTS

1. Try to paint word pictures and clear details of what you are talking about. Describe pictures, and props, and tell stories with great detail to create mental pictures for the visually impaired.

2. Recorded music is valuable in aiding the mood or environment you are trying to create.

3. Let visually impaired children explore through touch as much and as often as possible. If you are using props, for example, they will want and need to touch and handle them.

4. Abstract concepts and ideas may not be easily understood by these children. Consider this as you plan a lesson in order to make sure you cover all points clearly.

5. Touch, carefully monitored, can assist in calming, directing, or assisting the child and can give moral support and encouragement.

6. A partner can help explain quietly the points that may be missed.

HEARING IMPAIRED

1. Be sure these children can see your face and particularly your lips if they are trying to lip read. There is no need to exaggerate your speech; in fact, that will distort the sounds they have been trained to observe. Also try not to stand with a window behind you, as this will cast a shadow over your face.

2. Repeat comments made by children whose voices are too soft to be heard easily.

3. Visual cues, pictures, props, gestures, directions on cards, are very helpful for these children. Use them generously.

4. These children generally enjoy and are successful with pantomime activities particularly.

5. A partner can repeat directions or explanations quietly whenever the child needs additional assistance.

SPEECH IMPAIRED

Speech impairments generally include articulation disorders, stuttering, phonation problems, and delayed or limited speech.

1. Generally, the classroom teacher can assist with speech difficulties by providing an open and relaxed atmosphere that encourages rather than inhibits these children in their speech. Since children usually consider drama fun, they tend to forget about their speech difficulties during drama class.

2. Pantomime experiences will be particularly enjoyable for these children.

3. Being able to play with oral activities is useful for the speech impaired youngster. They need opportunities to speak and to hear others engaging in language.

4. Engaging in rhythmic activities, choral-type speaking in unison, and character role-playing often lessens stuttering behaviors.

EMOTIONALLY HANDICAPPED

Emotionally handicapped children may have difficulty controlling themselves, but some may be very quiet and withdrawn.

1. Because these children often have short attention spans, they will need to move frequently from one task to another. Be alert to their responses and to the fact that you may need to cut activity short and go to another for variety's sake.

2. At the same time, extending their periods of concentration on a task is also desirable. Move by slow increments in this goal for maximum success.

3. Movements of larger muscles is often successful. Body movement activities and pantomime should be particularly useful for them.

4. A secure, consistent, and supportive environment is important for these children. They also need to experience success and feel good about themselves. Initially, using a series of short activities that they can feel competent in doing should provide a good foundation to build on.

Finally, it is important to remember that there are more similarities than differences between children with "special" needs and their classmates. We are all human and we all have the need to love and be loved, to communicate, to learn, and to feel successful.

The subject of drama is the subject of life. And because it provides a variety of avenues for all to express their specific talents in unique ways, drama has often been called a great "leveler" of persons. No one is considered any greater or lesser than anyone else in drama. And this is as it should be in life itself.

Evaluation in a Theatre Arts Curriculum

In teaching a theatre arts curriculum in the elementary grades, we provide opportunities for children to participate in dramatic games, pantomime, verbal games, storytelling, story dramatization, puppetry or any one of the myriad of activities covered in this book. It is important, however, to assess children's progress along the way. Only then will you know the successes of your program and be able to plan the direction of subsequent lessons.

CAUTIONS IN EVALUATING

While it cannot be argued that teachers must check the students' progress in all educational ventures, there are some cautions you should remember. First of all, many educational goals are difficult to pinpoint, let alone define. Drama is no exception. Often in the process of explorative learning, undefined goals emerge and are achieved unexpectedly. Ironically, those serendipitous goals or objectives may turn out to be even more significant than any of your predefined ones.

In addition, if you design a drama activity around or limit it to only one or two skills or objectives, you may overlook the larger goals of instruction, the chance to explore drama experiences that emerge spontaneously, or even the opportunity to just play with ideas in a creative way. Furthermore, as is the case with many educational goals, many drama goals will be beyond precise measurement. In the attempt to measure a skill in a precise way, you could lose sight of other possible outcomes.

Being alert to these cautions can save you considerable time and frustration. The mark of a creative and effective teacher is one who lets the children and their needs define the direction of the lessons rather than the other way around. You should also be alert to the learnings the children make *when they happen* rather than looking for them *only* when you schedule yourself to do so.

TEACHER EVALUATION

Every teacher's situation is different and probably will require a little different format. For greater effectiveness and satisfaction, you are encouraged to develop your own personal drama/theatre evaluation checklist or evaluation forms. School systems or groups of teachers may wish to combine efforts to make an evaluation instrument that works for your particular circumstances.

The following checklist is presented as a *sample* only. It is not intended that all items are needed for any one activity or lesson. Nor is the list complete for all activities. You can draw additional items from the objectives listed in the Scope and Sequence section. The list also does not include specific curricular objectives. For example, if you have studied pioneer log cabins and the students play "Build a Place," constructing a cabin in pantomime, you will probably expect that students will include furniture and household goods appropriate for the setting and the time period. You may then wish to include that objective in that day's evaluation. Finally, many of the goals will also need special consideration or adaptations depending on individual children's needs, such as the gifted, those with handicaps, or those with other individual differences.

Since you will be involved with the children during the drama lessons, it will be necessary for you to evaluate them at a later time, preferably as soon as possible after a lesson has been taught. A periodic assessment is usually as effective as keeping a daily record and should enable you to see students' growth and progression more readily.

You may choose simply to *check* the items you see a child demonstrating favorably and record a *minus* for those that are not favorably performed. What is not applicable may simply be left blank. Or you may choose to use a rating scale (example: 1 poor, 2 fair, 3 good, and 4 superior) for each item, marking only those that are applicable.

By placing all the students' names lengthwise along the top of the paper, you should be able to make your report easily on one sheet. Another option is to focus on only a few students at a time in any one assessment. This should be less overwhelming than trying to evaluate every student after each lesson.

DRAMA SKILLS AND BEHAVIORS CHECKLIST

Date: Lesson Title:	Students' names (placed lengthwise)								
Body Movement and Pantomime Skills demonstrates coordination and control									
reacts with appropriate sensory awareness									
uses appropriate gestures/facial expression									
communicates ideas and concepts through pantomime									
"reads" others' nonverbal communication									
with acceptable accuracy									
Verbal Expression speaks clearly and distinctly									
uses vocal variety and inflection									
improvises dialogue appropriately									
Concentration follows directions; focuses on tasks									
sustains involvement in playing									
Imagination contributes original ideas									
responds spontaneously									
Evaluation and Critical Analysis makes constructive contributions									
incorporates suggested improvements into playing									
Social Awareness and Cooperation contributes to group effort									
listens/observes with appreciation									

CHILDREN'S SELF EVALUATION

In addition to the teacher's evaluation instrument, it is important that the children's self-evaluation, as individuals and as a group, be encouraged. Aesthetic judgments are developed as they are given voice. Children need opportunities to make and defend their points of view with each other. And since not even so-called educated critics of the arts would agree with each other, children may not either. Neither should group consensus be considered the final word in the matter. Lone defenders of a viewpoint are often proved more accurate or insightful at a later date.

Likewise it is also true that tastes change and develop. Over a period of time, we all change our minds and directions about what appeals to us and what bores us. We may adopt the popular style of the day and then later reject it with as much energy as we first embraced it. Children, too, need opportunities to experiment with varying artistic ideas before they can come to any conclusions about their judgments.

For **self evaluation,** young children may be questioned orally in a brief conference. However, it is also possible to have older students write a periodic self-evaluation. Students may:

a. circle "usually," "some of the time," "hardly ever" for each item.

b. write out their answers, perhaps even indicating "why" or "why not."

Questions might be similar to these:

1. Do I participate and contribute to the activities?

2. Do I stay focused and concentrate when I am playing?

3. Am I a good observer/audience member for my classmates?

4. Do I participate and contribute to group planning?

5. Am I careful to consider my classmates' feelings?

6. Do I offer original ideas?

It is hoped that these evaluation formats will not result in teachers using creative drama as a routine drill. Rather, drama experiences should be enriching to the entire curriculum and enjoyable for all.

Prentice-Hall Correlation to the Essential Elements Theatre Arts, Grades 1–3 (Teacher Resource Book)

Creative Drama Resource Book for Grades K–3 is designed to aid teachers in guiding younger elementary children in creative drama experiences, puppetry, and appreciation of theatrical events.

This book is intended for use either by an elementary school theatre arts specialist or a classroom teacher with limited training in theatre arts. While specialists will be familiar with many of the concepts presented, they should find the structure of the book helpful in curriculum planning. Over 400 selections of children's literature are suggested and over 20 sample lesson plans are presented. Along with over 100 games and activities, these should augment the specialists' own collection of drama materials. The classroom teacher with limited formal training in theatre arts should find the book readable and easy to follow. Each chapter builds on the previous one (specifically Chapters 3–12), and each chapter begins with easier activities that progress to the more difficult. Thus, the teacher can learn along with the children the skills to be mastered.

Creative Drama Resource Book K–3 is based, in principle, on a successful college text by the same author. However, for this resource book, the format has been simplified and designed for easier reading and reference. It has been considerably expanded with new chapters, new materials, and updated resources. Over 20 sample lesson plans have been included to help teachers experience success and to assist them in designing their own materials.

ESSENTIAL ELEMENTS

Teacher resource books for Grades 1–3 shall include material on:

1. Expressive use of the body and voice
   1.1 develop body awareness and spatial perception using;
   rhythmic and imitative movement

   sensory awareness

   pantomime

   1.2 imitate sounds and dialogue

   1.3 recall sensory and emotional experiences

2. Creative drama
   2.1 dramatize limited-action stories and poems using:
   simple pantomime
   puppetry
   2.2 dramatize literary selections using:
   shadow play

CORRELATION

See particularly activities in Chapter 3, "Getting Started," pp. 32–47. Imitative movement is encouraged throughout most creative drama activities and in the Resource Book progresses in skill-building particularly through Chapter 4, "Using More Space," pp. 49–62, Chapter 5, "Narrative Pantomime with Children's Literature," pp. 63–82, Chapter 6, "Further Uses of Narrative Pantomime," pp. 83–99.

See particularly 40–43; 44–47; 52–58 (selected activities)

32–47; 49–62; 63–82; 83–99; 100–112; 136–154. In addition, pantomime activities are included in all sample lesson plans and story dramatizations. See, for example, pp. 163–182, 187–201; and 204–217.

66; 74–75; 113–117; 156; 160. Simple dialogue in story dramatization lesson plans can be found on pp. 163–164; 167–168; 170; 173, 175–178; 181; and 183. Simple, improvisational dialogue is covered on pp. 123; 126–128; progressing to activities on pp. 128–135. Additional improvisational activities in story dramatization can be found on pp. 187–189, 190–191; 192–193; 194–195.

25–26; 40–47; 52–58 (selected activities); 109; 205; 209–212; 220; 224. Since recalling of sensory and emotional experiences is needed in playing pantomime, sections on "pantomime" may also be considered.

34–39; 63–82; 83–99
83; 234; 235; 240

236–241

ESSENTIAL ELEMENTS	CORRELATION
pantomime	63–77; 83; 84–90; 141; 163–182; 187; 188; 190; 191; 192; 194–195
imitative dialogue	74; 119–122; 156; 163–164; 167; 169; 171; 173; 175–178; 181; 183

3. Aesthetic growth through appreciation of theatrical events
   3.1 view theatrical events emphasizing:

player-audience relationship	Chapter 14, "Going to the Theatre," pp. 246–251
audience etiquette	247–248

ADDITIONAL FEATURES OF CREATIVE DRAMA RESOURCE BOOK FOR KINDERGARTEN THROUGH GRADE THREE (with page references)

1. A rationale for studying theatre arts in the elementary curriculum	1–9
2. Theatre vocabulary	7–8; 73–77; 246–250; 259–261
3. Background information needed to teach the specified theatrical concepts and skills	1–9; 11–12; 42; 46–47; 52; 246–250
4. Background information that explains the creative drama process and teaching strategies for presenting the instructional material	11–28; 32–33; 49–51; 63–68; 71–72; 73–77; 90–92; 100–101; 111–112; 113–114; 117–119; 122–123; 126–127; 128–129; 131–133; 136–140; 140–146; 155–160; 161–162; 185–186; 202–203
5. Suggestions for effective theatre arts class organization and management	11–28; 32–34; 47–48; 49–59; 100–101; 139–140; 157–160; 161–162; 185–186
6. A clearly defined scope and sequence of student learning objectives for theatre arts in Grades 1–6	Chapters 3–12 carefully progress from simpler to more complex activities. See "Scope and Sequence of Student Learning Objectives for Theatre Arts: Kindergarten Through Grade 6."
7. Imaginative experiences and activities for achieving objectives, appropriate for students of varying ability, sequenced according to complexity for the designated category (Grades 1–3 or Grades 4–6)	34–47; 52–59; 69–71; 72–73; 77–82; 84–90; 102–111; 113–128; 129–135; 136–137; 163–182; 187–195; 202–213; 232–234. Grade levels are given for all entries in annotated bibliographies of children's literature recommended for drama activities.
8. Quality literature appropriate for the concepts and activities being presented	See specific bibliographies on pp. 36–37; 38–40; 47–48; 52–53; 69–71; 72–73; 77–82; 84–90; 115–117; 119–122; 124–125; 136–137; 173–184; 187–201; 204–218; 218–226; 240–241; 244–245; 251–252; 253–258

ESSENTIAL ELEMENTS

9. Instructional strategies and procedures for adapting instruction to accomodate students will varied interests, abilities, and special needs

10. Suggestions for correlating creative drama experiences with instruction in such subjects as English language arts, other languages, social studies; art; music; and physical education

11. Model lessons with suggestions as to how the teacher might extend the concepts and create various other lessons

CORRELATION

See "Theatre Arts for All Children." See also pp. 12–23; 23–29; 49–52; 63–68; 71–72; 73–77; 100–102; 111–112; 128; 131–134; 138–140; 140–146; 155–162; 185–186; 202–203; 233–234; 236–237; 241.

8–9; 42; 43; 46–47; 63–82; 84–99; 102–112; 114–117; 119–122; 124–126; 129–130; 136–138; 141–142; 147–154; 163–184; 187–201; 202–226; 240–241; 244–245

59–61; 64–82; 147–154; 161–184; 185–201; 202–226

Lesson plans alphabetized by title, include:

Adventures (beginning activities), 59

An American Colonial Child's Morning (narrative pantomime), 96–99

Animals, 59 (beginning activities)

Ask Mr. Bear (circle story), 153–164

Bartholomew and the Oobleck (circle story), 165–167

The Borrowers (creative story building), 151–154

"The Cat and the Parrot" (circle story), 168–169

Charlotte's Web (segmented story), 187–189

Circus (extended lesson), 213–218

"The Conjure Wives" (circle story), 170–171

"The Elves and the Shoemaker" (circle story), 179–181

"The Elves and the Shoemaker" (segmented story), 190–191

Emotions (extended lesson), 209–212

"The Gingerbread Man" (circle story), 182–184

"The Gingerbread Man" (segmented story), 192–193

Harold and the Purple Crayon (creative story building), 147–150

"Jack and the Beanstalk," (segmented story), 194–195

The Little Rabbit Who Wanted Red Wings, (circle story), 174–175

Millions of Cats, (circle story), 176

Mushroom in the Rain, (circle story), 177

A Plan Ride (narrative pantomime), 93–95

Staging Fights (control), 60–62

ESSENTIAL ELEMENTS

12. Information on dramatic structure and the conventions of television, film, and live theatre
13. Suggestions for adapting creative drama activities to share with an audience; emphasis should not be placed on the memorization of lines and the staging of formal theatre production
14. Suggestions for evaluating a student's progress and achievement in the theatre arts curriculum
15. Annotated bibliography of quality literature appropriate for the designated grade levels (Grades 1–3 or Grades 4–6)
16. Annotated bibliography of professional and student supplementary material

CORRELATION

Where the Wild Things Are (circle story), 178
Winter (extended lesson), 204–208
7–8; 15–17; 33; 42; 60–62; 90–92; 140–144; 246–247; 249

73–82; 111–112; 131–135; 155–184; 185–201

11–13; 21–23; 32–33; 52; 68; 100–102; 111–112; 133–134. See also "Evaluation in a Theatre Arts Curriculum."
36–37; 38–40; 47–48; 52–53; 69–71; 72–73; 77–82; 84–90; 115–117; 119–122; 124–125; 136–137; 163–184; 187–201; 204–218; 218–226; 240–241; 244–245; 251–252; 253–258
10; 29–31; 40; 241; 245; 251–252

Scope and Sequence of Student Learning Objectives for Theatre Arts: Kindergarten through Grade 6

Since drama is a new subject area for many readers, the materials in this text have been arranged to help you learn in a step-by-step fashion. As you move through the book, teaching the activities, the children will also be acquiring skills in a sequence. At the same time, each chapter follows a sequence. This feature allows you to begin with particular topics chapters that appeal to you or ones you feel more comfortable with. For example, you might choose to begin with verbal activities in Chapter 9, story dramatization in Chapter 10, or even puppetry in Chapter 13. You should still be able to follow the sequence within each chapter with the help of the cross references to other chapters.

Thus, the arrangement of the text should allow you some flexibility in your teaching. With the help of the activities and the *general* scope and sequence presented, you should be able to develop the methods and procedures that work best for you and that you feel comfortable with. (Just as we allow latitude for children's individual differences and needs, so too should we allow teacher's individual styles.)

BEFORE YOU LOOK AT THE SCOPE AND SEQUENCE CHART

In the opening of Chapter 2, three major goals have been identified for drama. These include drama goals, personal development goals, and additional curricular goals.

Drama goals are outlined specifically in the Scope and Sequence Chart presented below. **Personal development goals** generally refer to interpersonal relationship skills that are required for drama and for social awareness. These would include such objectives as: developing confidence and trust in self and others; showing respect for the feelings and attitudes of others developing imagination and creativity; and working productively in groups. Many of these goals and objectives are already part of your teaching concerns, so it should not be necessary to enumerate these in detail.

Additional curricular goals will be derived from the content material you choose to add to a drama activity. A pantomime of various kinds of transportation, for example, would incorporate the drama goals of developing pantomime skills and the social studies goal of identifying various forms of transportation. Thus, the curricular objectives will be determined by you as you become aware of the various ways to use drama as an educational medium.

In some drama activities, you may emphasize one, two, or perhaps all three of these major goals. And, as already indicated, some of the goals can overlap. For example, "nurturing of creative thinking" could be considered a drama goal, a personal development goal, as well as a goal in any area of the curriculum.

DRAMA VARIABLES

Also in Chapter 2 there are **eight drama activity variables** identified on a continuum chart. Some drama activities, for example, are played at the desk; some are played in pairs and groups; some are closely directed by the teacher; and so forth. It is important to keep in mind that these variables can affect the difficulty of an activity and hence the success the children have with it. For example, a solo narrative pantomime activity in which all the children play the same character at their desks simultaneously is usually easier to do than a narrative pantomime played in small groups utilizing a larger area of space. The more complex the variables, the more complex the activity is for the children to master and the more difficult the activity will be for you to direct.

Although the variables are quite logical and obvious as you undertake drama activities, they are included here so that you can keep them in mind as you consider the Scope and Sequence Chart in the next section.

Drama Activity Variables*

Easier	**to more**	**Advanced**
1. Desk area		Larger areas of space
2. Teacher direction		Creative or independent thinking
3. Pantomime		Verbal activities
4. Solo playing		Pair and group playing
5. Run-through playing		In-depth playing for greater involvement
6. Humorous or "light" material		Highly dramatic or "serious" material

*This listing is repeated in Chapter 2.

Easier	to more	Advanced
7. Minimal informational content (curricular)		High data content
8. Unison playing for one's own satisfaction		Playing to share/communicate with observers

SCOPE AND SEQUENCE OF DRAMA GOALS AND OBJECTIVES*

KINDERGARTEN

1. Develop expressive use of body and voice
  1.1 Develop body awareness and spatial perception using: rhythmic and imitative movement
    move rhythmically and in unison with others through participation in action songs and games
    develop coordination through simple activities for self-control
    imitate people and animals (characters)
    explore posture, gesture, and facial expression in simple pantomimes for guessing
  1.2 Imitate sounds
    imitate familiar environment and speech sounds in sound effects activities

2. Creative Drama
  2.1 Dramatize limited-action stories and poems using simple pantomime
    dramatize simple narrative pantomime stories and poems
    imitate actions and characteristics of people and animals (characters)
    participate in simple circle story dramatizations

GRADE ONE

1. Develop expressive use of body and voice
  1.1 Develop body awareness and spatial perception using: rhythmic and imitative movement
    move rhythmically and in unison with others through participation in action songs and games
    develop coordination through simple activities for self-control
    imitate people and animals (characters)
    explore posture, gesture, and facial expression in simple pantomimes for guessing **and sensory awareness**
    develop awareness of senses through sensory games
    sharpen ability to use senses through simple sensory pantomimes
  1.2 Imitate sounds
    imitate familiar environment and speech sounds in sound effects activities

2. Creative Drama
  2.1 Dramatize limited-action stories and poems using simple pantomime
    dramatize simple narrative pantomime stories and poems
    imitate actions and characteristics of people and animals (characters)
    create imaginary environments in dramatizing stories
    participate in circle story dramatizations

*Note: drama goals in bold type are the essential drama elements required by the state of Texas. Additional learning objectives appear in regular type.

end puppetry
explore body movement through puppetry
use puppets in narrative pantomime stories and poems

GRADE TWO

1. **Develop expressive use of body and voice**
   1.1 **Develop body awareness and spatial perception using:**
   rhythmic and imitative movement
   move rhythmically and in unison with others through participation in action songs
      and games
   develop coordination and control through activities for self-control
   imitate people and animals (characters)
   explore posture, gesture, and facial expression in pantomime for guessing
   sensory awareness
   develop awareness of senses through sensory games
   sharpen ability to use senses through simple sensory pantomimes
   and pantomime
   enact movements of others (animals, people, objects) through pantomime
   create imaginary environments
   explore posture, gesture, and facial expression as a means of communication
   communicate ideas through actions and nonverbal expression
   decode pantomimed actions of stories
   1.2 **Imitate sounds and dialogue**
   imitate environment and speech sounds through sound effects activities
   explore simple dialogue through puppetry
   participate in simple verbal activities and games
2. **Creative Drama**
   2.2 **Dramatize literary selections using:**
   shadow play
   experience nonverbal and verbal language through medium of shadow
      play/puppetry
   interpret narrative pantomime and circle stories through medium of shadow
      play/puppetry
   coordinate shadow play/puppetry materials (e.g., puppets, lights, stage, scenery,
      shadow screen) to produce simple dramatic presentation
   pantomime
   enact movements of others (animals, people, objects) through pantomime
   create imaginary environments suggested by stories
   explore posture, gesture, and facial expression as a means of communication
   communicate ideas through actions and nonverbal expression
   decode pantomimed actions of others
   and imitative dialogue
   recreate dialogue of familiar stories (circle and segmented stories)
   explore simple dialogue through puppets in story dramatization

GRADE THREE

1. **Develop expressive use of body and voice**
   1.1 **Develop body awareness and spatial perception using**
   rhythmic and imitative movement

move rhythmically and in unison with others through participation in action songs and games

develop coordination and control through activities for self-control

imitate people and animals (characters)

explore posture, gesture, and facial expression in pantomimes for guessing

sensory awareness

develop awareness of senses through sensory games

sharpen ability to use senses through simple sensory pantomimes

and pantomime

enact movements of others (animals, people, objects) through pantomime

create imaginary environments

explore posture, gesture, and facial expression as a means of communication

communicate ideas through actions and nonverbal expression

decode pantomimed actions of others

participate in developing simple skits from familiar material

1.2 Imitate sounds and dialogue

imitate environment and speech sounds through sound effects activities

explore simple dialogue through puppetry

participate in simple verbal activities and games

sensory and emotional experiences

pantomime believeable actions by remembering past sensory and emotional experiences and imagining new ones

2. Creative Drama

2.2 Dramatize literary selections using shadow play

imitate people and animals (characters)

explore posture, gesture, and facial expression in pantomimes for guessing

sensory awareness

develop awareness of senses through sensory games

sharpen ability to use senses through simple sensory pantomimes

and pantomime

enact movements of others (animals, people, objects) through pantomime

create imaginary environments

explore posture, gesture, and facial expression as a means of communication

communicate ideas through actions and nonverbal expression

decode pantomimed actions of others

participate in developing simple skits from familiar material

1.2 express concepts using interpretive movement

express abstract ideas and concepts in narrative pantomime literature and in pantomimes for guessing

1.3 create original dialogue

participate in verbal activities and games

participate in creating and sharing verbal skits

1.4 recall sensory and emotional experiences

pantomime believable actions by remembering past sensory and emotional experiences and imagining new ones

2. Creative Drama

2.1 Dramatize literary selections using shadow play

experience nonverbal and verbal language through medium of shadow play/puppetry interpret narrative pentomime and circle stories through medium of shadow play/puppetry

coordinate shadow play/puppetry materials (e.g. puppets, lights, stage, scenery, shadow screen) to produce simple dramatic presentation

experience nonverbal and verbal language through medium of shadow play/puppetry

interpret narrative pantomime and circle stories through medium of shadow play/puppetry

coordinate shadow play/puppetry materials (e.g. puppets, lights, stage, scenery, shadow screen) to produce simple dramatic presentation

pantomime

enact movements of others (animals, people, objects) through pantomime

create imaginary environments suggested by stories

explore posture, gesture, and facial expression as a means of communication

communicate ideas through actions and nonverbal expression

decode pantomimed actions of others

and imitative dialogue

recreate dialogue of familiar stories (circle and segmented stories)

explore simple dialogue through puppets in story dramatization

3. **Aesthetic growth through appreciation of theatrical events**
   3.1 **view theatrical events emphasizing**
   player-audience relationship
   understand basic theatrical conventions (e.g. use of curtain, lights, etc.)
   audience etiquette
   understand etiquette rules that make theatrical attendance enjoyable for all
   understand audience rules that are needed to aid the actors in performing

GRADE FOUR

1. **Develop expressive use of body and voice**
   1.1 **Develop body awareness and spatial perception using**
   rhythmic and imitative movement
   move rhythmically and in unison with others through participation in action songs and games
   develop coordination and control through activities for self-control
   pantomime
   enact movements of others (animals, people, objects) through pantomime
   create imaginary environments suggested by stories
   explore posture, gesture, and facial expression as a means of communication
   communicate ideas through actions and nonverbal expression
   decode pantomimed actions of others
   and imitative dialogue
   recreate dialogue of familiar stories (circle and segmented stories)
   explore simple dialogue through puppets in story dramatization

3. **Aesthetic growth through appreciation of theatrical events**
   3.1 **view theatrical events emphasizing**
   player-audience relationship
   understand basic theatrical conventions (e.g. use of curtain, lights, etc.)
   audience etiquette

understand etiquette rules that make theatrical attendance enjoyable for all

understand audience rules that are needed to aid the actors in performing

and recognition of similarities and differences between television, film, and live theatre

understand basics of how films are made as compared with theatre

understand basics of how television shows are made as compared with theatre

3.2 **participate in group planning for story dramatization incorporating analysis of character behavior**

identify story characters' feelings

identify a story character's motivations behind actions

recognition of dramatic conflicts

identify the conflicts or problems in the story that make the plot dramatic

and prediction of plot resolutions

understand the plot structure of beginning, middle, and end

anticipate story endings

GRADE FIVE

1. **Develop expressive use of body and voice**
   1.1 **Develop body awareness and spatial perception using rhythmic and imitative movement**

   move rhythmically and in unison with others through participation in action songs and games

   develop coordination and control through activities for self-control

   imitate people and animals (characters)

   explore posture, gesture, and facial expression in pantomimes for guessing

   sensory awareness

   develop awareness of senses through sensory games

   sharpen ability to use senses through simple sensory pantomimes

   and pantomime

   enact movements of others (animals, people, objects) through pantomime

   create imaginary environments

   explore posture, gesture, and facial expression as a means of communication

   communicate ideas through actions and nonverbal expression

   decode pantomimed actions of others

   participate in developing simple skits from familiar material

   1.2 **express concepts using interpretive movement**

   express abstract ideas and concepts in narrative pantomime literature and in pantomimes for guessing

   1.3 **create original dialogue**

   participate in verbal activities and games

   participate in creating and sharing verbal skits

   1.4 **utilize sensory and emotional recall in characterizations**

   pantomime believeable actions by remembering past sensory and emotional experiences and imagining new ones playing a character

2. **Creative Drama**
   2.1 **Dramatize literary selections and original stories using shadow play**

experience nonverbval and verbal language through medium of shadow
   play/puppetry
interpret narrative pantomime and circle stories through medium of shadow
   play/puppetry
coordinate shadow play/puppetry materials (e.g. puppets, lights, stage, scenery,
   shadow screen) to produce simple dramatic presentation
create original stories and skits using shadow play
pantomime
enact movements of others (animals, people, objects) through pantomime
create imaginary environments suggested by stories
explore posture, gesture, and facial expression as a means of communication
communicate ideas through actions and nonverbal expression
decode pantomimed actions of others
imitative dialogue
recreate dialogue of familiar stories (circle and segmented stories)
explore simple dialogue through puppets in story dramatization
improvisation
participate in verbal improvisation games
participate in creating dialogue in scenes, skits, and in segmented story dramatization
characterization
interpret people, animals, or objects, through pantomime and speech, in story
   dramatization
and puppetry
dramatize narrative pantomime stories, circle stories, and segmented stories with
   puppets
3. **Aesthetic growth through appreciation of theatrical events**
   3.1 **view theatrical events and emphasizing**
       player-audience relationship
       understand basic theatrical conventions (e.g. use of curtain, lights, etc.)
       audience etiquette
       understand etiquette rules that make theatrical attendance enjoyable for audience
       understand audience rules that are needed to aid the actors in performing
       and recognition of similarities and differences between television, film, and live
          theatre
       understand basics of how films are made as compared with theatre
       understand basics of how television shows are made as compared with theatre
       and evaluation and aesthetic judgments
       evaluate one's own and classmates' drama work
       evaluate a theatrical performance applying basic aesthetic criteria
   3.2 **participate in group planning for story dramatization incorporating analysis of**
       character behavior
       identify a story characters' feelings
       identify a story character's motivations behind actions
       recognition of dramatic conflicts
       identify the conflicts or problems in the story that make the plot dramatic
       progress the playing and heighten the tension in building toward the plot climax
       and prediction of plot resolutions
       anticipate story endings

GRADE SIX

1. **Develop expressive use of body and voice**
   1.1 Develop body awareness and spatial perception using rhythmic and imitative movement
   move rhythmically and in unison with others through participation in action songs and games
   develop coordination and control through activities for self-control
   imitate people and animals (characters)
   explore posture, gesture, and facial expression in pantomimes for guessing
   sensory awareness
   develop awareness of senses through sensory games
   sharpen ability to use senses through simple sensory pantomimes
   and pantomime
   enact movements of others (animals, people, objects) through pantomime
   create imaginary environments
   explore posture, gesture, and facial expression as a means of communication
   communicate ideas through actions and nonverbal expression
   decode pantomimed actions of others
   participate in developing simple skits from familiar material
   1.2 express concepts using interpretive movement
   express abstract ideas and concepts in narrative pantomime literature and in pantomimes for guessing
   1.3 create original dialogue
   participate in verbal activities and games
   participate in creating and sharing verbal skits
   1.4 utilize sensory and emotional recall in characterizations
   pantomime believeable actions by remembering past sensory and emotional experiences and imagining new ones playing a character

2. **Creative Drama**
   2.1 Dramatize literary selections and original stories using shadow play
   experience nonverbal and verbal language through medium of shadow play/puppetry
   interpret narrative pantomime and circle stories through medium of shadow play/puppetry
   coorindate shadow play/puppetry materials (e.g. puppets, lights, stage, scenery, shadow screen) to produce simple dramatic presentation
   create original stories and skits using shadow play
   pantomime
   enact movements of others (animals, people, objects) through pantomime
   create imaginary environments suggested by stories
   explore posture, gesture, and facial expression as a means of communication
   communicate ideas through actions and nonverbal expression
   decode pantomimed actions of others
   imitative dialogue
   recreate dialogue of familiar stories (circle and segmented stories)
   explore simple dialogue through puppets in story dramatization
   improvisation
   participate in verbal improvisation games

participate in creating dialogue in scenes, skits, and in segmented story dramatization
characterization
interpret people, animals, or objects, through pantomime and speech, in story
dramatization
and puppetry
dramatize narrative pantomime stories, circle stories, and segmented stories with
puppets
and situation role-playing
create character roles in skits, scenes, stories and specified situations

3. **Aesthetic growth through appreciation of theatrical events**
   3.1 **view theatrical events emphasizing**
   player-audience relationship
   understand basic theatrical conventions (e.g. use of curtain, lights, etc.)
   audience etiquette
   understand etiquette rules that make theatrical attendance enjoyable for audience
   understand audience rules that are needed to aid the actors in performing
   **and recognition of similarities and differences between television, film, and live
   theatre**
   understand basics of how films are made as compared with theatre
   understand basics of how television shows are made as compared with theatre
   and evaluation and aesthetic judgments
   evaluate one's own and classmates' drama work
   evaluate a theatrical performance applying basic aesthetic criteria
   3.2 **participate in group planning for story dramatization incorporating analysis of
   character behavior**
   identify a story characters' feelings
   identify a story character's motivations behind actions
   recognition of dramatic conflicts
   identify the conflicts or problems in the story that make the plot dramatic
   progress the playing and heighten the tension in building toward the plot climax
   and prediction of plot resolutions
   anticipate story endings
   and suggestions for alternative courses of action
   demonstrate ability to create new characters, situations, and varieties of plot development and resolution in dramatizing stories

Subject Index

Title Index of Books, Stories, and Poems

Note: An asterisk (*) next to page numbers indicates that a lesson plan of that title can be found on those pages.